MODERN PORCELAIN

Alberta C. Trimble

MODERN PORCELAIN

Today's Treasures

Tomorrow's Traditions

BONANZA BOOKS • NEW YORK

LIBRARY OF CONGRESS CATALOG CARD NUMBER: 62-8618

This edition published by Bonanza Books,
a division of Crown Publishers, Inc.,
by arrangement with Harper & Row, Publishers, Inc.
A B C D E F

To
Mary and Ken

Contents

List of Photographs

Royal Doulton's *Old Colony*
Royal Doulton's *Burgundy*
Royal Crown Derby's *Bali*
Royal Crown Derby's *Rougemont*
The Derby Dwarfs
Green Derby Panel
Royal Crown Derby's *Cobalt Heraldic*
Rörstrand's *Linnea*
Rörstrand's *Le Select*
Rörstrand's *Tweed*
Hertha Bengtsson designs, Rörstrand
Royal Copenhagen's *Flora Danica*
Royal Copenhagen's *Blue Fluted*
Royal Copenhagen figurines
Stig Lindberg of Gustavsberg
Gustavsberg's *Farsta* by Wilhelm Kåge
Andersen figurine, Bing & Grøndahl
Bing & Grøndahl's *Jule Aften* plate for 1961
Bing & Grøndahl's *Hazelnut*
Arabia's *Delicasy* series, by Ulla Procopé
Arabia toned porcelain
Arabia's rice china designed by Friedl Kjellberg
Anne-Marie Ødegard, designer at Porsgrund
Porsgrund's *Myrtica Gale*
Original Haviland factory
Present Haviland factory
Haviland's *Torse White*
Haviland's *Bergère*
Dinnerware from H-B, Quimper
Breton figures, Jules Henriot & Fils, Quimper
Raymond Peynet with *The Little Lovers* series for Rosenthal
Rosenthal vase by Tapio Wirkkala
Rosenthal's "2000" shape created by Raymond Loewy
Rosenthal's *Fortuna*
Decorating Lenox's *Rutledge*
Lenox's *Westport*
Lenox's *Meredith*

MODERN PORCELAIN

Chapter 1

The Trail for Treasure

IT is not always possible to put one's finger on an instant in time and say, "Here my life changed its course." Certainly when fellow guests in a Palma de Mallorca hotel suggested that I break my trip home to Winnipeg and spend a fortnight on their Staffordshire farm, I had no premonition that by accepting the invitation I should switch my writing life from the path of fiction to fact, especially to the factual dealing with pottery and porcelain.

In our family, having a few old pieces, we had always been interested in china but in a taking-it-for-granted way. (One exception occurred in my teens when, chancing upon a thumbnail sketch of Josiah Wedgwood, I made a nuisance of myself by inflicting the story upon anyone I could buttonhole.) If in the friendly little Parque Hotel my future host and hostess had hinted that I should find pottery and porcelain, in particular the lives of the potters, more romantic and more dramatic than any flights of imaginative writing, I should have become really alliterative.

"Potters and pottery! Pooh! Plain prosaic!"

At Hill Top Farm itself it did not occur to me that the unexpectedly beautiful countryside around Tamworth, crowned by its medieval castle on the swan-dotted River Tam, was anywhere near the potteries, *and the bottlenecks*, of the despised Black Country. Yet only a few miles away were the Six Towns: Burslem, Hanley, Longton, Tunstall, Fenton, and Stoke. Arnold Bennett made them immortal in *Anna of the Five Towns*. (He "forgot" Longton.) His "Bursley" is a thinly disguised Burslem, birthplace and heart of the industry.

The *deus ex machina* of my literary transmigration was Ken, my host at Hill Top Farm. Acting dutifully in that capacity, he arranged a visit to one of the potteries. As a dutiful guest I acquiesced—went along for the ride as it were, with my hostess. Mary, at the wheel of her Daimler.

Out of the blue the thing hit me. The way a lump of drab clay became an

1

elegant figurine was completely captivating. Each process was a separate en-thrallment and a separate mystery. I wanted to know more. I wanted to write about it. *If I am as interested as all this, other women will be too.* I discussed the project with the neighboring housewives whom I met over coffee at elevenses, afternoon tea, and pre-dinner cocktails in the idyllic English farm environment. They enthusiastically offered suggestions and invited me to look at their family china,—whole books could be written about the collections I was shown. A niece of the Archbishop of Canterbury, no less, offered me a letter of introduction to Wedgwood's deputy managing director and chief of publicity, Major John Hamilton Wedgwood—Sir John since the death of his father who was created a baronet for his work in reorganizing the British railways. Much as I appreciated the gesture, I decided to go on my own. It would reflect on her if I muffed the job. After all, starting at scratch, what did I know about the potting industry?

My fortnight at Hill Top Farm at an end, Mary drove me to Stoke-on-Trent, the city which is the fusion of the Six Towns. Taking up residence in the North Staffordshire Hotel, I began the rewarding round. Notebook in hand and cameras over shoulder, I visited not only the members of the Fine China Association but others in which I had a special interest. Before long the pageantry of porcelain had taken over to the exclusion of practically everything else.

In the next few years I sailed from New York in vessels ranging from a Portuguese cargo boat to the super-luxurious *Gripsholm* of the Swedish-American Line. I crisscrossed Europe from Lisbon to Istanbul, and from the Mediterranean littoral to the capital of Finnish Lapland on the Arctic Circle. One whole summer—too short, alas!—and part of another were spent in the four hospitable, individualistic Scandinavian countries. Two spring-to-autumn seasons were spent on the Continent proper.

Unfortunately the sun has set on the three greatest European fabriques of royal inception—Capo di Monte, Sèvres and Meissen.

Capo di Monte you may be offered anywhere. But beware. Genuine Capo di Monte is about as common as mermaids. In the Chicago Art Institute the curator showed me a gold-lined basin and ewer made by the founder of the pottery, Charles III of Naples and the Two Sicilies, who became the first Bourbon king of Spain and moved his plant to Madrid and renamed his porcelain "Buen Retiro." I believe the two pieces were insured for the same amount as the Rospigliosi Cup of Benvenuto Cellini in the Metropolitan Museum, and if someone tells you the policy is for a million dollars, do not look askance. I did look askance—when told of a woman who had a barrelful of Capo di Monte. Not that I doubted the veracity of my informant, for it was beyond question, but I had to doubt the information. The pieces in the barrel may have borne the Capo di Monte Mark, a crowned N, but they had probably been manufactured in Naples by the old firm of Ginori, reputed to have copied them by the thousands. The Ginori people are still producing them. At least I was recently shown a pair of Capo di Monte candlesticks, crowned N and all, brought back from Bermuda by a honeymoon couple. However, as befits the leading Italian china manufacturer with a large establishment in Milan, they now bring out these articles of virtu under official license.

Sèvres, still halfheartedly producing, is, according to the authoritative Gordon Forsyth, "artistically mute." It is ostensibly under Communist control. An Iron Curtain is drawn except for once a month, a day for which you must obtain a visitor's permit from the Government well in advance unless you are satisfied with a visit to their museum. There, strangely, you will see quantities of Meissen ware. But modern France has proceeded to porcelain of extremely fine quality, that of Haviland of Limoges. In their streamlined factory in that city of potteries you will be greeted by a large WELCOME on the doormat.

As for Meissen, founded by Augustus the Strong who sired 359 children, if its porcelain bears the hammer-and-sickle now instead of the crossed swords, western Germany can point with pride to the empire of Rosenthal in northern Bavaria, almost on the Soviet-garrisioned border of Czechoslovakia.

Portgual, the country being discovered by more and more tourists all the time,—it vies with Norway for beauty—has a pottery, Vista Alegre, at Aveira northward on the Atlantic coast. Its output is small but exquisite, in particular its black porcelain. Again the trouble is the red tape which must be cut in Lisbon before one can visit the plant, and even then cameras are barred.

Spain offsets this with a warm greeting at Talavera de la Reina, about 40 kilometers from Madrid. (I should have liked to visit the pottery in August when it holds its annual fair.) In the sixteenth century, Talavera was the center for all earthenware products decorated with tin glaze, progenitor of maiolica, faïence, delft, English earthenware and Scandinavian flintware, the names being synonymous. This small town on the Tagus, at a point spanned by a bridge with thirty-five arches, has a special place for us on this continent, seeing that Talavera potters came to Mexico, taught the Indian craftsmen, and founded an active industry. Except for the native scented red pottery, *boccaro,* long in demand for the infusing of tea, the Spanish influence on the Mexican ware is still apparent.

Ireland's famous Belleek plant was on the agenda, a dream for another

3

trip. I even toyed with the idea of a voyage to Japan, vigorously competitive, and still have it in mind.

"Searching for romance?" my friends teased.

"Yes. The romance of porcelain."

It was not possible to visit all the potteries in person—there are 181 in Staffordshire alone—and, sad to relate, I let many opportunities pass. Though I spent four months in Turkey, I went only to Eyup, producing mediocre ware, and failed to go to Kutahya, a busy ceramic center, manufacturing, I am told, "thinly potted china painted with small patterns such as scale and leaf diapers in lively colors with a predominant Mohammedan blue."

Years ago, I spent six months in Switzerland. Whether or not porcelain is manufactured there, I cannot say. It probably is. Contrary to the popular opinion that the Helvetian republic is devoted wholly to the tourist trade, it is actually one of the most highly industrialized countries in Europe—only Great Britain and Belgium have a relatively higher industrial population—and that in spite of the fact that all raw material must be imported. The only thing Switzerland does not have to import is scenery.

In Lugano I picked up several charming bonbonnières in a slightly glazed biscuit, almost as white as the snow on the picturesque mountain peaks, and with the same refreshing clean lines and little more decoration. The proprietor of the gift shop assured me that they had been made right in the Ticino, but he did not know where, and there was no mark. One day I shall return and find out.

The next time I go to England I plan to visit Adams, Addersley, Aynsley, Royal Albert, Moorcroft—the name is legion—but especially Coalport, from which came my collection of superlative cups and saucers, many used as wedding gifts during the war. This plant, founded by John Rose who did away with silicosis, the potters' bane, was forced to close down several times since his day, and was closed in 1959 when I attempted to visit it. Fortunately, as I was informed recently at Tiffany's, it has reopened and is producing excellent new patterns yet with the character of their former ware. As a matter of fact, I saw two new ones, exclusive with Eaton's of Canada in the College Street store in Toronto, *Grey Hazelton* and *White Hazelton,* elegant with a heavy gold grape border.

Also to be visited are the Egernsund earthenware plant in Norway, the historic Swedish *fabrique* at Uppsala, and Portugal's Vista Alegre in more favorable circumstances if only for another look at what started out to be *rouge flambée* and came out of the kiln a gorgeous exotic deep rose. Bear these in mind when a trip takes you to these countries.

In the United States, the Vitrified China Association has seventeen members, providing employment for many persons and producing exceptionally pleasing designs. (If at one time their ware was classed as "hotel" china, that is far from the case now.) A few of the factories allow visitors so you can see the various processes, but it is advisable to write first. A number of Canadian firms are getting into the game, too, although more in cooperation with British firms than in competition.

These potters, both north and south of the forty-second parallel, have the advantage of being on the ground. They know what the Americans want at the moment, can actually sense it ahead at times and thus create a demand for the new and novel to satisfy the urge for continual change. The casual standard of living—picnics, barbecues and television—has given some of them the inspiration for ware of the harlequin and fiesta types. Good strong colors and bold designs—one writer uses the word "audacious"—have made these transitory dishes popular for this mode of living. Or should I say, for this transitory mode?

For many reasons—finances, children, other ties—it is not possible for every china-loving woman to visit the potteries abroad. In her local china emporiums or departments in the larger stores, she can make substitute tours, and, browsing, compare porcelains, patterns, and prices. Whether she buys or not, the salespeople are eager to supply information.

If a certain make of porcelain fires your imagination, write to the firm for its brochures. Most of them explain potting processes in detail, and many are quite attractive.

Another gold mine of information is your public library. While you may find little about current productions, you will get an over-all picture of porcelain practically from the pat-a-cake stage. It is an engrossing subject. To quote from a fan mail letter, "Reading one book on china is like eating one salted peanut. You cannot stop there."

Porcelain history in a nutshell, and visually—the easy way!—can be gleaned in museums. I realize that the word "museum" is anathema to many, usually because they have tried to absorb too much in too little time, and have ended up with mental indigestion. If only one could follow the advice given in the *Atlantic Monthly* years ago when that periodical wore its old buff cover! To see a museum properly, it said, engage a wheelchair at the front door, have an attendant blindfold you and trundle you to a designated spot. In that way you could concentrate on the exhibits in the porcelain galleries, for instance, with your mind uncluttered by antique armor and Gobelin tapestries passed en route.

5

Pursuing the progression of porcelain through the centuries, from primitive to medieval to modern, you will soon find yourself wondering and speculating about the persons who made these things—*what manner of man was the potter to have put the handle on just that way?*

It was not the potteries and their "pots," regardless of the unfailing enjoyment I derived from them, which led me from place to place. No! As was inevitable with one whose field was fiction, to whom people and what makes them tick are infinitely more important than places and things, it was the potters. In fact, while I admitted the beauty of Rosenthal's superb porcelain, it struck me as cold and austere until I met Philip Rosenthal himself and came to understand the motivating force behind every piece produced in his many plants.

The biggest question to confront me was: What individuality and personality go into the wares of the potters in different countries, into the wares of one potter to make them unlike those of a potter on an adjoining site—for instance, between Spode and Minton's, almost across the road from each other for nearly two centuries, or between Bing & Grøndahl and Royal Copenhagen, twin trees sprung from the same roots?

I consulted books on the subject, everything I could lay hands on. The kindly librarians in Winnipeg made straight for the "pottery" shelves whenever I entered the reference department. And not only did I borrow, I bought. I acquired a five-foot shelf of porcelain literature, beginning with a paperback by George Savage, a dealer in Surrey, England, which I picked up while looking for a whodunit to read on a plane. Unexpectedly this *Pottery Through the Ages* proved to be a whodunit, but with a difference. For a time it was my only work of reference, except for the Encyclopedia Britannica, and an invaluable one. Later I splurged on handsome, incidentally expensive, volumes, with illustrations worthy of being framed. The prize of these was *Pottery and Porcelain* by the outstanding authority, Warren E. Cox of the Boston Museum. Running it a close second was Mankowitz and Haggar's Concise Encyclopedia of English Pottery and Porcelain.

Outside of reading interest, these books were mostly for collectors. Many of the writers could see value in nothing more recent than Sèvres, while some drew their double line at the end of Ming and Sung. If they deigned to mention present-day production at all, they painted a gloomy picture.

For example, take *English Pottery and Porcelain* by an authority both moderate and conservative, the late W. B. Honey of the Department of Ceramics, Victoria and Albert Museum, London. One paragraph leaped from the page and hit me between the eyes.

The period of the Napoleonic Wars marks a definite break with the old traditions of craftsmanship. The financial and cultural impoverishment they caused left the industrializing process, already well begun by Wedgwood, irrevocably complete.

Cultural impoverishment! Was the statement true? About Wedgwood! Had the industrializing process brought an end to the old tradition of craftsmanship? What of the craftsmanship I had seen in the factories of the Six Towns and Derby? Were all the impressions I had gleaned false? Was there not a bright side to the picture? Were not Honey and the other authorities speaking only from the collectors' point of view?

Collectors, I argued, were in the minority. Meissen, Capo di Monte and the *pâte tendre* of Sèvres were for the very, very few—as were custom-built cars. The Ford, however, provided transportation and a change of scenery for people at many economic levels. Yet today Ford is producing cars which compete in color and line, and performance, with others in the luxury class.

In England the famous Bow and Chelsea works, to name only two, designed their celebrated soft paste porcelain for potentates and plutocrats. For *hoi polloi* pottery was manufactured only in a jogtrot way until Josiah Wedgwood replaced the old wooden, pewter, and horn vessels, and coarse clay "pots," with earthenware dishes of line and grace, and at prices which made them available to every housewife in the kingdom. Later his *Cream Colour* ware was by royal command of Queen Charlotte, wife of George III, renamed *Queensware*. Under that name it flooded the markets of Europe, and drove many of Josiah's continental rivals, including Sèvres, out of business.

What prompted me to write this book was not the questions the aforementioned volumes propounded, answers to which are still unformulated in my mind, nor was it the contentions of the experts, most of them still unrebutted. It was the interest in the subject, the desire for specific information, shown by women. From my first published article, which was naturally on Wedgwood as it was the first pottery I visited with intent, I was besieged. By letter. By telephone. In person. What amazed me was that to many of the readers Wedgwood meant only Jasper ware, like their grandmother's blue pitcher with the classic white frieze.

"Wedgwood doesn't make dinnerware!" they expostulated in the tolerant, not quite patronizing tone one would use to a fiction writer who had strayed into the foreign field of fact. The china departments in the three big Winnipeg stores—Eaton's of Canada, the Hudson's Bay Store, and Birks-Dingwall, jewelers—were bombarded. "Show me!" customers demanded. They were shown—in window displays.

7

That almost every woman is interested in china is taken for granted, but the interest of men, especially men of a certain cultured type, is keener—it was practically a youthful passion with my son. And, whether Sigmund Freud is right or wrong, which sex produced the great collectors? Into the bargain, the male mind is inclined to delve more deeply into the subject of basic material and production. I found this out at first hand.

In Viano do Castelo in the north of Portugal—*there* is a place for a vacation!—a group of English physicians and their wives had been kind enough to include me in their evening parties. Having no way to repay their hospitality, I suggested that *pour passez le temps,* they accompany me in a huge, hearselike rented limousine to visit a native pottery, Fabrica de Meadala, about 14 kilometers away. The women spent most of the time in the shop, buying the pottery of gay color and peasant design, but the men followed each step of the primitive production with scientific awareness, and it was not only because of the pretty girls carrying baskets of clay on their heads as their ancestresses had done five centuries ago.

Occasionally a man will ask me about a particular process, such as glazing or how they get those elliptical transparencies in rice china. One wanted to read my chapter on gilding, if I had one, as the gilt on his wife's otherwise quite good pieces was tawdry. He read it and she switched, with considerable success, from cheap liquid gold to paste.

Not that this book proposes to be a how-to. Nor is it, let me warn you straight off, by any stretch of the imagination a study in antiques or collectors' items. Such matters can be dealt with only by the authorities on the subject.

Deciphering the hieroglyphics stamped on the bottom of a piece of an early date is impossible unless one is familiar with the lore of significant marks. (You will find a fairly comprehensive tabulation of them in Cox's *Pottery and Porcelain.*) Even then, if you are a prospective collector but a novitiate, it is a hazardous game, the way marks are falsified and forged. Your safest course is to put yourself in the hands of a reputable dealer.

Dealers have a hundred ways of telling the phony from the genuine, the really old from the artificially aged. Often they can recognize a forgery by the clay. For example, Belleek is manufactured of a brilliant white feldspathic clay peculiar to the district of Castle Caldwell in County Fermanagh, Ireland. The piece must show that clay or be pronounced a fake. In this respect a bit of good advice comes from the Surrey dealer, George Savage, who has three books on my shelf, *18th Century English Porcelain* and *Ceramics for the Collector,* as well as the one mentioned before, *Porcelain Through the Ages.* Arm yourself by reading in the first a chapter entitled, "Forgeries,

8

Frauds and Reproductions." As to the date of production of pieces from the late eighteenth century on, most of the potters will supply on request a chart from which you can tell within a decade the year of manufacture.

Neither have I made an attempt to write a learned treatise on the science which enables the expert to differentiate at a glance between, say, Rörstrand and Rosenthal. Unless we are familiar with the pattern, most of us still have to turn the piece over for the manufacturer's name. Luckily, with few exceptions, modern markings are straightforward and reliable. Let us consider one of these exceptions so that this book may serve another purpose and prevent your being bilked as does happen now and then. A little vital knowledge may save you many dollars, subsequent discomfiture, and, what is most important, your prestige.

An interior decorator had fobbed off on a couple in the Cadillac class half of an "imported" dinner service. The ware had a greenish tinge. Immediately above the well of the plates the rim showed an unprepossessing brassy gold band which suggested that it had been repeatedly widened in order to conceal defects. The most impressive thing about it was the price.

"But it's Limoges! Look! Stamped right on the bottom! Limoges!"

There it was, beyond a doubt. *Limoges.* But, to croak with Poe's raven, "Merely this and nothing more."

In fiction, one dare not employ the "long arm of coincidence," yet how else explain my strolling down an unfamiliar New York side street and chancing upon a table setting of this same ware in the window of a little gift shop? My curiosity was piqued. When the effusive proprietress found that I was not a customer, she about-faced and admitted that she had bought a "pig in a poke" —at least had accepted half of a dinner set to sell on a fifty-fifty commission. She had cut the price twice, she had glamorized a place setting with a lace mat, gilt flatware and a charming centerpiece of Portuguese gold *filigrano.* Still it would not sell. It was not Haviland or one of the good Limoges firms.

"Even on their gold bricks these days," she laughed bitterly, "they demand the stamp of the U.S. mint."

Since then I have found to my amazement that to many persons "Limoges" is a generic term, a synonym for all the porcelain made in France. Whenever I mentioned my visit there, it was usually taken for granted that I meant the porcelain factory. The only one. Probably founded by a M. Limoges.

My grandmother gave my aunt her set of china from Limoges when she was married, but it was always referred to as "Auntie's Haviland," or "Aunt Emily's Haviland from Limoges." Thus, at an early age, I painlessly imbibed the fact that Limoges was not the name of a porcelain fabrique such as Minton's or Royal Copenhagen, but a place name. Later, being an Encyclopedia Britannica addict, I learned that the thriving city was the delightfully picturesque capital of the French province of Limousin, "center of an original culture and cradle of the troubadours," that there in 1199 Richard Coeur de Lion had been killed in battle, and in 1841 Renoir was born to the wife of a tailor.

Instead of a single pottery, "Limoges," there are thirty-three, twenty-four making porcelain. Indeed, if the French used the word "china" and not "*porcelaine*" the city could be called "Chinatown." Some of the twenty-four, having ambition greater than ability, hope to get by—in the above case they did—on the abracadabra of an indefinite designation, *Limoges*. Fortunately, the few potters making really fine porcelain and decorating it in their own establishments always sign their names, and are proud to do so. Haviland, the outstanding firm, never allows a piece of its pure white ware to leave the premises unless inscribed on the bottom, THEODORE HAVILAND—LIMOGES, FRANCE. They would no more sign a bare "Limoges" than would Minton's sign one of its superlative products, "Stoke-on-Trent."

All the well-known porcelain manufacturers have their own showrooms, mostly for the wholesale trade, though in some of them you may look around. To the general public they retail through reputable merchants, if possible those with "snob" appeal such as Tiffany's, Georg Jensen, Altman's and Bonnier's of Madison Avenue, to name four in New York. Reputable potters do not have to offer their wares at catch-as-catch-can markdowns through glib interior decorators or little gift shoppe owners who count on high pressure salesmanship to unload at a hundred per cent profit a white elephant and saddle it on an unwary buyer. I use "saddle" advisedly. No one invests in an expensive dinner service, or even half of one, every week.

In so many words I have told you what this book is not. Perhaps the above incident will suggest what it proposes to be, the evidence of my own eyes and experience set down in black and white, occasionally threaded with a few bright beads of historical fact winnowed from the works of those who have made porcelain through the ages their specialty. If you are prepared to go on from this point, you will have to be content with a sort of layman's version, an amateur's handbook, sounding like nothing more than a series of chats over a cup of tea. Actually, the chapters dealing with the potteries I visited were just that, but in print, a series which, as the flattering editors said, aroused an unprecedented reader reaction, proof of the interest taken in china by the smart young and young-in-entertaining chatelaines across the country. Some chapters, quoted in part or whole, were published in English magazines as well as in other publications here and abroad. In each case the editors were kind enough to give me permission to use the material, either verbatim or according to my needs.

Porcelain stands for more than beauty and functionalism. It is a way of life. The setting of a table constitutes a barometer of the household culture. The higher the standard of living rises, the more exacting does the modern housewife become about day-by-day details such as dishes, and the more aware of the impact upon her family of these details, far from trivial.

Spiritually, the fastidious chatelaine demands a plus value. And she gets it in the aura of great potting traditions. Consequently, for her a rounded knowledge of materials and processes, of designers and artists, and the histories of the outstanding potteries and potting families, is vital. It is with these that this factual effort will deal.

This means that its most obvious function will be that of guide to the best in current porcelain productions, not only for brides, many of whom consult me, but for the maturer woman who has tired of an outsize dinner service perhaps hastily bought, now ravaged by time or rendered incomplete by the discontinuance of her pattern. Instead of charging into a china shop with a blind eye, as one of my correspondents described her own experience, she may enter knowing what she is looking for, and what she can expect to find in a field today unlimited. Such a plenitude of patterns, the letter writer went on plaintively, that in her bewilderment she almost turned around three times with her eyes shut and pointed. If, I thought, she had known the traditions behind the patterns, it might have made her choice easier. For example, the rose is a favorite garniture for china. Had she been told that the plate in her hand was Spode's *Billingsley Rose,* and had she known the tragic story of the itinerant artist who, because of bigamy, had to travel under an alias, would that plate not have made a greater appeal to her than another which had a pretty rose but was nameless?

If this book then can assist you to choose with confidence, and to love and cherish what you have chosen because of your knowledge of the craftsmanship and tradition your choice embodies, I shall be repaid for what, in an unfamiliar metier, threatened to involve hard work.

Perhaps even more important, we shall have added a new dimension to our thinking. With our new knowledge we can appraise the potters of today and see what they have made of their inheritance. For none stands alone. None is an isolated unit. Each is a branch of the tree with roots in the remote past— of the Chinese, the Moslems, and of the Gabri, those pre-Islamic fire-worshiping people after whom some of the most decorative and unexcelled Persian tiles have, though mistakenly, been named. We shall see which potteries put out roots of their own, which withered on the vine, which spelled romance and which tragedy.

We shall see also how highly individualized is the art of pottery; how each manufacturer of merit, copyist at times or not, has his own ingenerate touch; how each country has its own *genre*.

Only Spain could have bequeathed to the world the lustrous Hispano-Moresque. Only Italy could have produced the della Robbias. Only English humor could have converted the dour German bellarmine into the jovial Toby jug. And only Josiah Wedgwood could have timed the moment to bring out his *Cream Colour*, and so leave his mark indelibly on the world-wide standard of living—yours and mine.

So. *Happy browsing! Happier choosing!*

Chapter 2

Pottery Terms and Processes

BEFORE we set out for Barlaston, it may be well to acquaint ourselves with some of the vernacular and processes. In this way you will know what we are talking about without having the main thread of the story interrupted.

Potting has a distinct nomenclature, all its own. For example, a plate is made on a *jigger*, while a *jolley* performs the same function for a cup. The worker who tosses the clay upon the potter's wheel is a *thrower*, the one who shaves away the surplus clay a *turner*, he or she who attaches handles is a *stonker*, and the nimble-fingered craftsman who assembles the various parts of a figurine is a *repairer*.

Most of these colorful terms we shall acquire as we proceed through the plants. What we cannot get in the hour or two of these conducted tours is the picture of the progress made through the ages, from the beginning when a pair of hands patted out a clay plate and dried it in the sun to the present when probably a hundred pairs of hands have contributed to a single piece of the elegant porcelain on your dinner table.

Shall we take a look, then, at the potter's wheel?

It is claimed that no single step did more for the advance of civilization and the betterment of mankind than the invention of the wheel. Similarly, no single device did more for womankind, by raising the standards of living in the home, both in regard to the amenities and to sanitation, than did another inspired piece of machinery, the potter's wheel.

Fittingly, I saw my first one in Turkey, in Anatolia or Asiatic Turkey—to give it its Biblical name, Asia Minor—for from there, brought by the Crusaders, came the western world's first pottery of merit. En route from Trabzon on the Black Sea to Erzurum within the Taurus, our bus made its noon break in the small town of Ashkale on the banks of the Western Euphrates. A young

Turkish lieutenant, between whom and the driver I sat, suggested lunch in a nearby *lokanta*. I did not get that far. To quote the Persian poet:

> For I remember stopping by the way
> To watch the Potter thumping his wet clay.

The potter's wheel, responsive to the least whim of the potter squatting on the dirt floor of his open-front shop, held me spellbound. The way he threw the soggy lump upon the wheel, the swiftness with which it assumed the graceful curves of a vase beneath his deft fingers, were sheer magic. The Turks are *cordon bleu* cooks—they ought to be if there is any foundation for their boast that they have practiced the art of cuisine for seven thousand years. Instead of lunch, I satisfied my physical hunger with a glass of tea brought to me by the solicitous lieutenant, and spent the hour watching one inanimate lump of clay after another become a thing of beauty. If it had been *pâte dure*—hard paste—with which the potter was working, I might have finished the line of Keats from his "Ode to a Grecian Urn" and added "a joy forever." Nor would the adverb have been an exaggeration, for of all materials known to man, porcelain comes nearest to being indestructible. Even when shattered to fragments, the shards are still porcelain. No temperature, no acid, no half-century exposure to the salt depths of the ocean, can make of these potsherds anything but porcelain.

Some of the pieces on the shelves of the shop, or strewn on the dirt floor beside him, were not only fine evidence of his own innate ability but also of the artistry he had inherited down the long ages—specimens of pottery unearthed in the Middle East are believed to be eight thousand years old.

Watching the Asia Minor potter in that oldest inhabited region on earth, little imagination was required to conjure up behind him his naked nomad ancestor "throwing" his phantasmal clay on the flat top of a boulder, and his frown each time he had to take up the tenuous material. *If the stone were not so heavy, it could be rotated, and the clay shaped without lifting it up.*

Necessity is the mother of invention. Behind that frown, was the potter's wheel conceived?

The significance of that invention goes beyond the material aspect. The ancient Egyptians, who were already using the potter's wheel 4000 years before Christ, believed that man himself had been fashioned on a wheel by a divine potter called Num. Omar Khayyam makes many references to pottery in his *Rubaiyat*. For example, about an ill-formed man he demanded, "Did the Hand of the Potter shake?" The ancient Jews, mastermakers of articles in precious metals and gems, although they never expended their talents in pottery manufacture yet realized that it was a basic art. We gather that from the frequent mention of the potter in the Bible. The great prophet Isaiah is made to say, "We are the clay and Thou the potter, and we are the work of Thy Hand."

Carrying the metaphor still further, to describe a pot or pitcher the potter used words from the human anatomy: the neck, the shoulder, the belly, the waist, the foot, the mouth, the lip.

The potter's wheel was part and parcel of the very stuff of life.

Of course, as goods were carried in packs or drawn on crude sleds and moved from place to place long before the wheel was invented, so, long before the potter's wheel was invented, pottery was made.

The art of potting seems to have been instinctive with all primitive people, including the Eskimos. It was attended by an infinite number of superstitions and taboos—to this day no Ashanti woman may construct a pot of human or animal design for fear she be rendered sterile. Except in the case of the potter's wheel, which only a man might operate, the craft was usually confined to the female of the species. In certain localities a man was not allowed to come near a woman who was potting, his presence being regarded as inimical.

Among primitive people even yet, vases and similar hollow objects are formed by coiling snakelike lengths of plastic clay in a spiral and pressing them together. The first mugs and pitchers in all countries were made in that manner, or by piling rolls of damp clay one above the other until the required height was reached. Then the vessel was smoothed inside and out. Sometimes the inside smoothing was effected by winding the clay rolls around a cylinder of polished log.

Cooking pots were also made with these rolls, but, being larger, required reinforcing. This was done by incorporating fibers into the clay, or lining the vessel with a piece of straw or basketwork.

The first plates of all people were made as a child would make them, by kneading a lump of clay in the hands. You may see the same procedure today if you happen to be in Arizona or Mexico where a group of native women have assembled for the social making of *tortillas*. Squatted around a large circular sheet iron plate above a fire, they take a ball of cornmeal dough, slap it flat with a swift rotary motion of their palms until it is paper-thin and six or eight inches in diameter, when they toss it onto the baking sheet.

The next plates were made by throwing a lump of wet clay onto a flat boulder where it was kneaded or pounded, either by foot or by hand, until the required thickness was obtained. To make it circular, *sun-shape,* it was lifted

15

from the boulder and turned round and round. Then someone—who, we shall never find out, for the potter's wheel was arrived at separately in various countries—realized that the process would be less arduous, and result in fewer marred pieces, known in modern parlance as *wasters,* if the boulder could be turned instead.

The original wheel, which after all was not really a wheel, was a heavy stone pivoted on a sharp spindle and rotated by hand. During the early Christian era, the Egyptians introduced one rotated by foot. This was a tremendous stride forward as it left both hands free for working the clay, thus making for greater symmetry and a greater variety of forms.

The seventeenth century saw another forward stride: a potter's wheel—actually a lathe—spun by means of a cord working over a pulley. Then in England, where the Romans are said to have introduced the potter's wheel around 55 B.C., came the revolutionary invention of Henry Doulton, son of the founder of the Royal Doulton Works at Burslem—the *steam* power-driven wheel. In the plants of today, needless to say, the power is electricity.

Unlike the maize *tortillas,* for many centuries pottery owed such firing as it got to the rays of Old Sol, and was sun-baked, as the adobe of primitive folk the world over still is. But in all countries, in diverse ways, it was found that kiln-firing gave the piece greater strength. Incidentally, the "n" in "kiln" is silent.

Needless to say, no one knows exactly how the firing of pottery was brought about. Schoolchildren are all familiar with the story of Alfred the Great, who, when told to watch the cakes in a neatherd's hut-hearth, allowed them to burn. Perhaps another preoccupied cook may have allowed the dinner in a clay pot to burn, which would mean that the straw or basketwork used in the construction of the vessel would be consumed. From such a mishap would be reaped true benefit, as the burned pot would prove stronger and more durable than its fellow pipkins.

Perhaps fire worshipers were responsible, and achieved the same end as a result of observing their religious ritual. Might it not have been the "Gabri," the pre-Islamic fire worshiping people in Persia whose name was given to tiles unearthed at Rhages? (Now it is known that they were of eighth to tenth century manufacture.) Still, it *could* be that they offered up to their fire-gods the choicest of their crude tiles, sun-baked, which when retrieved were not only undamaged but better than before. It *could* be that they attributed the boon to the beneficence of their gods, and went on to make "bigger and better" tiles, until in the fourteenth century other Persians produced their rare lustered *mihrabs* or altar pieces of indescribable loveliness, three of which

16

I saw a few years ago in the Metropolitan Museum but alas! cannot see now as they have been boxed up for safety during a rebuilding program.

Neither is it known who made the first kiln. The early people, as do many present-day tribes, built their first firing ovens underground. In the beginning they were merely covered-over holes in the earth, like those found in England at Nottingham, at Cheam in Surrey and Rye in Sussex, with their crude painted ware lying about. Crude, indeed! According to Bernard Rackham, as regards perfection of workmanship the medieval pottery of England was much inferior to the wares made on the island by the Roman conquerors.

From these holes in the ground, the pieces came out lopsided and reduced to half their size. What rectified this? Was a potter interrupted at his task? Did he leave the modeled clay lying in the sun for a day or two? Did he thus learn that if the water were dried out to a point where no steam could form, uneven warping and shrinking were avoided? The first lesson in ceramics. . . .

It was the Greeks who gave us our word "ceramics" or "keramics"—take your choice of spelling and pronunciation, too, although it comes from *keramos* which means "burned stuff" or "fired." The first European pottery was Greek. It was made, although not invented, in Crete, the "cradle of civilization," between 3000 B.C. and 1200 B.C.

That the ancient Egyptians, as well as the Greeks, possessed kilns is evident from paintings on walls and on their pottery itself. The ancient city of Babylon, in Mesopotamia, had kilns in the middle of the sixth century B.C. They must have been both effective in accomplishment and of great magnitude, for Nebuchadnezzar used fired bricks in the reconstruction of his city razed by the Assyrians under Sennacherib.

It was to the Chinese, who had such superstitions as never doing any firing during the wane of the moon for fear the pieces would lack brightness, that was left the discovery of the effect of firing at high temperatures. According to Warren E. Cox, they reached 1350 to 1450 Centigrade—2430 to 2610 Fahrenheit—for their glazed ware. (This is what the French potters call the *grand feu*. The kiln temperatures for their *pâte tendre*, or soft paste, was only 1100 C. for bisque and 1000 C. for glost.) Modern potters can do no better, although I seem to have been told that Haviland of Limoges can obtain a heat of 2800 F. for their hard white porcelain. Royal Copenhagen can reach 2740 F. but it is seldom necessary. Royal Crown Derby claims a peak heat of 2550 F. but "to the detriment of their wares." Rosenthal's in Bavaria are satisfied with 2500 F. in their modern kilns for their ultra-hard porcelain, while Spode's bottlenecks achieve perfection around 2200 F. Bing & Grøndahl casually mention a modest 2700 F. and 2800 F. for their underglaze, but then their glaze is a profound secret. I have no figures for Minton's. When they undertook the making of the Queen's Vase, gift of the 181 English potteries for the coronation of Elizabeth II, their first or biscuit firings were failures. The potters enlisted the aid of Wedgwood at Barlaston. Their great electric tunnel kilns, capable of a safe 2600 F., succeeded, thereby justifying for the sixth generation of Josiah Wedgwood's descendants the immortal sobriquet, "Prince of Potters."

To quote the Royal Copenhagen Porcelain Manufactory on the difficult problem of firing:

The fire is the great magician that transfigures all this lifeless material. It is the fundamental factor in the whole process of manufacture and is, therefore, also the one that strikes the spectator most. . . . In the ceramic industry there is an added tension during the actual firing, which creates a special atmosphere fraught with excitement. In the glost oven, as it is called, the ultimate result will be determined and the question is, will all the preceding efforts be rewarded, or will the work be irrevocably wasted?

When the ware is being "placed" in, or "drawn" from the kiln, there is always a tremendous bustle. In some mysterious way the rumor of what is going on spreads all over the factory; you will see artists and technicians, the kiln men, and the young apprentices rushing up to ask the news, to peer at the kiln, and to return satisfied to their various posts if everything seems to be progressing favorably. It is the sum of their common interests that is at stake.

Nowhere did the art of porcelain making attain such glory and perfection as in China, though even the staunchest Sinophile admits that the Chinese may have owed much to the Sumerians, the non-Semitic peoples of Mesopotamia, as well as to the Greeks—for the direct caravan routes between the eastern and the western empires were through Persia.

In China, jade was held in the same veneration as precious metals. It was in an attempt to make a ware known as "artificial jade" in the Kiangsi province where vast deposits of china clay had been discovered that porcelain—Honey calls it the stepchild of jade—got its start. One variety of it was celadon—*ch'ing tz'u*—or green porcelain, cherished by those in high position because it was thought to render harmless any poison which might be poured into it. There are many explanations for its name but generally it is agreed to have been derived from that of Saladin. Wedgwood's do this ware particularly well.

Porcelain was given its name by Marco Polo when, in 1275, he traveled to the court of that beneficent ruler, Kubla Khan. The Venetian adventurer and author arrived there four years before the end of the Sung dynasty, 960–

1279 A.D., just when the peak, the Golden Age of ceramics, had been reached. Shown the amazing treasures created by the potters, he exclaimed in awe, "*Porcellano! Porcellano!*"

To him the fine glaze resembled the lustrous white sheen of the carapace—non-biologists like me would use the word "shell" for the hard case found on such creatures as the lobster and turtle—of a small crab, the *porcellano*, common to the Mediterranean littoral. The claim that the word is derived from the Italian for "little pig" cannot be substantiated, nor that the *porcellano* was the Venus sea urchin, a pretty fantasy supported more by poetry than prose.

Two hundred years after Marco Polo's visit to Kubla Khan another Italian navigator made his voyage westward. It is doubtful that Christopher Columbus was ever aware of his role as a promoter of porcelain, yet he was indirectly involved. After his so-called discovery of America, plus the world-shaking and epic discoveries of other daring navigators, especially the Portuguese in the fifteenth and sixteenth centuries, Chinese "china" along with tea and spices began to arrive in Europe, where it set up an insatiable demand.

As this demand could not be satisfied, the solution seemed to be the manufacture of porcelain in Europe. Venice, the great glassmaking center as well as the hub of trade with the Far East, made experiments with milk-white glass in about 1470. (You who have been in Venice have probably seen the old pieces in the museum of the glass factory at Murano, the town built on several small islands in the lagoon.) But alas! it was not porcelain.

The first attempt to make that ware was staged at Florence for Cosimo de Medici, 1389–1464, and was called *porcellano contrafacto*. As Cox points out, the name showed that they recognized its being only an imitation. In 1527 the manufacture of Medici porcelain ceased.

The genuine porcelain proved to be beyond the skill of the masters. And the secret baffled them for two centuries. Finally their questions boiled down to one: Was it the clay?

In every country, naturally, local clay was used. For example, in Egypt it was the soft silt of the Nile from which pebbles and other impurities were picked out with the fingers.

The Chinese drew out impurities with the magnet, already in their possession. Other countries followed suit. Gradually a series of magnets, arranged in steps, came to be used. The clay, mixed with water to form a thin *slip* of creamy consistency, was poured over the steps to form a cascade. In the process all the metallic impurities were extracted. Nowadays an electric magnet performs the function.

But neither this purifying, nor the fine grinding the Chinese stressed, was enough. The greatest Western craftsmen were in despair. The excellence of T'ang, Sung, Ming, and all the other supernal porcelains must, they eventually concluded, be due to something else. What about the story circulated to the effect that babies' blood was necessary to obtain a certain quality? In China, where it was routine to dispose of girl babies, that might be all very well. In Europe, no!

Finally, having eliminated everything else, they agreed that it must be a peculiar kind of china clay, whose existence the Orientals carefully guarded. If the secret could be ferreted out, a great new age of porcelain could be inaugurated in Europe.

Research showed that the essential ingredient of Ming and Sung *was* an unknown clay. Early in the eighteenth century a French Jesuit missionary, Père d'Entrecolles, smuggled home some samples of this *kaolin,* its name a corruption of Kao-ling—"High Ridge"—a hill west of King-techen. Upon analysis the clay was found to be decomposed granite, its constituents silicon and alumina, the latter the most abundant of all earths, thus the basis of many rocks and soils. Mixed with water, it was so plastic that it was often referred to as "plastic stone." Its absolute whiteness, before and after firing, made it indispensable to porcelain manufacturers.

In no time, the search was on. Great quantities were found in Limoges, France, and in Saxony, Germany. The high point for England was reached when immense resources were brought to light in Cornwall and Devon.

The English potters' good fortune did not end there. At the same time that they found kaolin or china clay, they also found china stone, known locally as "growan stone" or "moor stone," produced by the weathering of silicate of aluminum, commonly called feldspar.

The Chinese weathered their feldspar for twenty or thirty years. The English reduced this to seven or eight months in a damp cellar. In its purified state it is transparent and colorless. Being a diluting element, as well as a cement or flux in firing, feldspar is an important ingredient of porcelain.

Body is the name given to the composite material of which potter's clay is made—for example, earthenware body or stoneware body. When the reference is to porcelain or china, the word *paste* is used almost exclusively. The ingredients are kaolin, ball clay, china stone, and flint, and, in case of bone china, calcined bone.

Kaolin, as we have seen, is granite rock which has undergone decomposition for a long period of time. It is the whitest clay known. Its discovery in Devon and Cornwall by a chemist named William Cookworthy made possible the fine English china we enjoy today.

20

Ball clay is a fairly dark-colored clay quarried mainly at Poole, Dorset. It gives plasticity and strength to the pottery body, and becomes lighter during firing.

China stone, also known as Cornish stone, is similar to china clay, but at an earlier stage of decomposition. At high temperature it vitrifies—fuses into a hard opaque glass.

Flint is a form of silica found on the shores of Britain. Calcined in kilns and ground to a fine white powder, it imparts strength and solidity, and also prevents warping.

Calcined bone, of course, is the fine ash of bones, usually beef bones from the Argentine.

The different ingredients are ground in mills in the slip house to the required degree of fineness. Each is separately mixed with water in the *blunger* —there's a nice English word!—a machine fitted with rotating blades which churn the liquid to the necessary consistency. The next step is transferring each to a separate *storage ark* where it is kept in agitation to maintain its consistency until needed for blending.

From the storage arks, the correct proportion of each ingredient is pumped into a measuring tank. A gauge on the outside of each tank indicates the volume of the liquid. The scales show the weight. The specific gravity of each material is calculated before it is run into the *blending ark*. In this vast ark, the liquid clay body, known as slip, is thoroughly blended, forming a liquid of creamy consistency. Samples are tested at regular intervals.

Next the liquid is forced by powerful pumps through a series of fine-mesh screens, at least three, after which it flows over electromagnets to remove every minute particle of ferrous matter or iron which would discolor the ware when fired. Then it flows into the storage tanks where it is kept constantly in motion.

From the storage tanks, the slip is pumped under heavy pressure into a large filter press, an apparatus which is formed of compartments lined with filter cloths. The surplus water is forced through the fine mesh of the cloth, leaving behind a thin square slab of plastic clay. Each slab weighs about a hundred pounds.

Now comes the processing in a machine known as the *pug mill*, a giant mincing machine which produces a consolidated homogeneous mixture of just the right consistency and texture for the potter to use. (The filter press has rendered the clay solid, but not sufficiently plastic. Also, to achieve the correct texture, the air bubbles have to be driven out and the clay thoroughly kneaded.) From the pug mill, the clay is extruded in an endless snakelike roll which is cut off in suitable lengths for use by the potter. For *casting* purposes, however, the clay is used in the form of liquid slip, and pumped through pipes to the *making-shops*.

It is clay until it is fired, when it becomes *bisque* or biscuit, and ready for the next processes.

Five centuries before the Minoan pottery achievements on Crete, as early as 3500 B.C., Egypt, borrowing from Turkey and Persia, had evolved the glazing process, one of the most important in pottery manufacture.

Glazing, which is simply enclosing in glass, began, as most other processes, as a strictly utilitarian measure. It made vessels, formerly porous, watertight and easier to clean, and increased their usefulness in the storing of foodstuffs and liquids. Eskimo tribes had attained the same result by rubbing their pots over with grease. Primitive Mexicans coated their utensils with a solution of boiled maize, though this was not readily washable. In Fiji and Borneo the clay while still hot from the kiln was rubbed over with pine resin, and in southern Nigeria it was boiled in palm oil. Among the Pueblo of North America the juice of a green cactus was applied externally, and the inside smeared with piñon juice or pitch, after which the pot was fired again.

Unglazed pottery, as was stated before, is called *biscuit*. In Turkey, because of its refrigerating properties a food vessel of biscuit holds as important a place in household management as does the *torra* or water jar of Mexico.

In addition to the above-mentioned advantages, glazing played a vital part in sanitation, a word derived from the Latin *sanitas,* or health. The practical Romans of two thousand years ago had systems of sanitation and central heating which would make the technological experts of the twentieth century look to their laurels. The ancient Roman baths, social clubs where citizens met for discussion and wine, were marvels of engineering. But you have probably seen some of them in England,—at Bath, for example, or at Cheltenham in the Cotswolds.

Tin provided the best glazing medium. Tin glaze does not become excessively fluid in the firing. As a result the colors painted on it do not run or smear. Unfortunately, that metal was not easy to come by. The Phoenician voyages to far-off Britain were due to the trade in Cornwall-mined tin. It was costly, as costly as gold. Substitutes had to be found. Over the centuries four general types of glaze came into use:

1. The alkaline glazes of the Egyptians, Syrians, and Persians.

2. Lead, or non-feldspathic, compounded of lead and glass. This was the commonest and best for everyday use, and was employed in England before the Norman Conquest in 1066. Though the lead in this glaze was a killer—

the casualties among the potters were colossal—it was not discarded until 1820 when John Rose of Coalport perfected a leadless feldspathic glaze.

3. Feldspathic, suited only to porcelain. Meissen was the first factory to appreciate its importance.

4. Salt glaze, the special glaze of stoneware, made by throwing common salt into the kiln after a temperature of 2200 F. had been reached, when the sodium in the salt combined with the silica and alumina in the clay to form the thin transparent salt glaze.

Two variations are the *chicken's skin* of Chinese porcelain with its bubbles and pits, and *craquelé,* or crackle, brought to perfection in the Royal Copenhagen Porcelain Manufactory.

Glaze was applied by various methods. Some potters dipped. Some brushed. Some sprayed. But all had the same difficulty with the final process, the firing. While the biscuit firing was the hottest one, the glaze or *glost* firing was barely a hundred degrees lower. The slightest error of judgment might mean the loss of the whole contents of the kiln.

Glazing also limited the range of colors. With the high temperature demanded by glost firing, the only reliable ones were green from copper oxides, blue from cobalt, purple from manganese, yellow from antimony, and orange from iron, as well as a little brick-red from Armenian bole, a special clay from that Middle East region. In the second firing, if color were to be applied on the glaze, the range was increased to include vermilion, red, crimson, pink, and leaf gilding.

But long before that, glazing itself—glazing for the sake of the glaze—became pre-eminent, and passed the point of mere utility to reach the highest point of porcelain manufacture, the art of decoration.

In the early stages of pottery, all was functional, utilitarian. Such ornamentation, decoration, or color taken on by a piece was purely incidental. The shape of a vessel depended upon its use. Any appurtenances—handles, spouts, feet, legs, knobs—were only for convenience.

Handles and spouts came first, though which preceded the other is a pottery chicken-or-egg riddle.

Probably handles began as stirrups, set in the middle of the top. Again, they may have begun as an imitation of a stout broad leather strap, or several narrow clay straps braided or twisted into a *ribbon* and made strong and large, in many cases large enough to be carried on the arm. Pilgrim's bottles, a common medieval traveling accessory, had, if of any size, two handles so that they could be slung by a rope over the pilgrim's shoulder or around his neck.

Stirrup handles were superseded by handles on the side. They had to have perfect balance, be easy to grasp, and instill confidence.

As time went on, the peasant potter began to consider ways of making the handles ornamental as well as useful. He decorated them with thumbprints, or added small garnitures in places where they would not interfere with the grasp. For example, he transformed a plain jug into a thing of beauty by a handle with a gadroon, or godroon edge—an olive or ruffle form. Little by little he proceeded to handles such as those pictured in the Hughes' Encyclopedia—*crabstock,* resembling a short curved branch of a crab apple tree, *foliated scroll,* the same ornamented with leaves, and *double interlaced,* two strings of clay entwined.

The first spouts were formed by pressing a portion of the damp clay rim between thumb and forefinger, but it was not long until they, too, developed into deliberate ornaments—birds' beaks, animals' mouths, the tricorn hats of Toby jugs.

Gradually spouts began to be made and attached separately as handles had been. Long spouts and short spouts. Round ones and square ones. On chocolate pots and pots for *café au lait* it was found easier to pour if the spout was inset at right angles to the handle.

Knobs ranged from plain unadorned round protuberances to the most elaborate creations of the ingenious designer's art. The acorn was popular, especially in England and Norway, as was the cedar cone, symbol of longevity. The crown, too. (A crown tops the highly prized New Hall teapot which I was fortunate enough to see on exhibition in the Tea Centre in Lower Regent Street, London—there is a place to go for the "cup that cheers," and the exhibit is changed every week.) Towers and turrets were used. Curled leaves and flowers, in particular the rose, embellished many covers and lids. Birds and butterflies perched there, as well as small animals, dogs being the most numerous. Nor was the human figure overlooked. A teapot, probably made by Thomas Turner of Caughley in Shropshire—the *Willow* pattern originated in his factory—has four groups of children in relief on the white body, and a seated girl on the lid. And, of course, the knobs on rococo were replicas of every kind of shell in the conchologist's glossary.

Bases, feet, and legs reached about the same heights, or depths. No effort was spared in the search for novelty.

At first, the potter pinched the clay at the bottom into crude feet, or he put his hand inside the vessel and pushed out *bosses* on the base. The whole lower edge could be molded to form a base. Sometimes, before firing a bowl, the potter added a roll of clay to the bottom. Another base was formed by attaching a small inverted plate, a general practice in the Far East. A potter could make actual feet by affixing balls of clay to the bottom and pressing them on firmly or even *luting*—cementing—them with slip. Short lengths of iron rod set in the base before firing became actual feet, longer lengths became legs.

The roll of clay added to the bottom increased to two, or three, the same size or successively larger. Perhaps the top and bottom ones were the same size, the middle one larger or smaller. Later the rolls were smoothed out into a single-surface base. Dots began to be applied, or studs, or the clay was incised in a pattern inspired by the potter's whim. Bases made by pressing out a rim might be crimped. Crimping led to scalloping or a series of overlapping crinkles. From all of these it was but a step to the pedestal base, which became elaborate and of intricate design. In many cases the bowl or vase remained severely plain, while the base was given over to lavish decoration.

In England the *gobs* or balls of clay progressed from those crude forms to the feet beloved of Chippendale—the claws of birds and paws of animals. Claw feet were often set in metal, notably ormolu.

If you have ever watched an imaginative child making mud pies, pricking the edges and top, or sprinkling the whole thing with white sand to simulate sugar, you will readily appreciate that even the crudest pottery would almost at once take on some form of ornamentation more deliberate than the basic handles, spouts, and such, we have just discussed.

Perhaps it was only the crimping of the rim of a plate as a woman crimps a piecrust. Early in the making of pottery, scalloped edges began to appear, the cutting done in the damp clay with a sharp knife. Another early form of ornamentation is *repoussé*. It was done by inserting a hand inside the damp clay vessel and, as the name indicates, with a finger pushing out bosses or bubbles.

Another early decoration for hollow vessels was a strip or strips of clay pressed on with the potter's thumb. The band of wet clay could be affixed horizontally in a girdle about the belly of the piece, or, in numbers, attached vertically at spaced intervals. These ribbons not only proved ornamental but strengthened the pot.

An edging was made by pressing a twisted rope into the wet clay. The result was the cable pattern popular in knitted goods. It was called *guilloche*, and was done by the Etruscans with engraved wheels. This instrument gradually became the *roulette* or runner now used to impress networks, bands, or trellises running vertically up the sides. Frequently *studs*, resembling nailheads, were applied between.

Apparently *guilloche* was followed by *barbotine*, small foliate or floral motifs to be found on the rims of bowls on Rhenish pottery made early in the second century. *Barbotine* was generally done by piping on with a quill a thin slip of clay in a contrasting color. The decor of Wedgwood's jasperware with its molded flowers, leaves, and even classical figures such as those of John Flaxman's *The Dancing Hours,* was a form of this method of ornamentation. So was the *pâte sur pâte* introduced at Minton's by the great Sèvres artist, Louis Marc Solon.

Sgraffiato—sometimes *graffiato* or *graviata*—was a type of "scratched" decoration in which slipware, the name for a coarse reddish-burning clay dipped in slip, displayed a design in two slightly contrasting colors. The procedure, roughly, was as follows. To the slip-coated vessel a lead glaze, often mixed with manganese oxide, was applied. This when fired, gave the pottery a rich yellow transparency. With a sharp pointed tool, such as a graver or burin, the design was incised through the glaze and the slip, thus disclosing the basic ground in the desired pattern. It was then reglazed and refired.

In England, Ralph Wood, of the prolific family of potters, made what was known as *slipware* by dipping colored ware into white slip and scratching the latter so that the result was a dark design on a white ground.

Fluting and ribbing early came into their own. Celebrated silversmiths such as Hester Bateman and her brothers were partial to "ribs" and *flutes*, and anything the silversmiths fancied, the potters were never slow to imitate.

In an effort to produce a more ingenious and elaborate design, sometimes the damp clay was *pierced* and the interstices filled with glaze. Fired, it yielded an airy-fairy effect. The Chinese name for the ware is *ling lung*—Devil's work—but we know it better as rice china. One story goes that the name came not from the shape of the holes but from the holes actually having been made in the first place by grains of rice pressed into the damp clay. In the firing, the grains were consumed. The same principle applied to the lacework skirts of Dresden figurines. They were made of actual lace dipped in the slip, the threads disappearing in the kiln. A ware in which the openings were not filled with glaze was reticulated or netted ware, a favorite of many potters. A Leeds potter named Hartley was a master at this, but not from love of the pattern. His aim was to outdo Josiah Wedgwood's continental trade. Duty was charged by weight. Hartley, having achieved a very light porcelain, pierced wherever possible. Thus, although he failed in his financial aspirations, he created some pieces of surpassing loveliness.

From primitive times to the present, decoration often took the form of inscriptions such as are found in the "love-names" of Attic red figure drawing. For example, "Panaitos is handsome"—his good looks, alas! his only claim to immortality.

The Germans also were addicted to inscriptions. In the Hamburg Museum is a chocolate cup of Vienna manufacture inscribed: *Gott' allein die Ehr' und sonst Keinem mehr.* (To God alone and to none other be the honor.)

The English were not without their devout moments. On a simple jug of red clay we find in white slip: "Be not hy minded but fear God, 1638." Most of the time they seem to have gone in for more homely sentiments, such as "Happy Birthday," and "From Tom to Ann," not to overlook the ubiquitous "Souvenir of Blackpool."

Besides their inscriptions, on their peasant pottery the English had *combing* and *feathering*. Though these were fairly common to many countries, the English made them their own by accenting them with white dots to simulate stones.

On a higher social plane was a heraldic device, or shield, borrowed from silver. From the same source was borrowed a similar decoration, the crest or coat-of-arms, still popular, especially on dinnerware for the embassies. At Minton's I watched a paintress decorating a plate of a service for Turkey with the star and crescent. The crescent, I was told in Istanbul, was originally a Byzantine symbol, adopted because one dark night a sudden gleam of moonlight disclosed an approaching enemy, and gave the citizens time to arm. The Turks liked the idea, and adopted it themselves, with the addition of the star.

For color, early pottery depended upon the kind of clay used. As an example, Böttger's red stoneware first made at Meissen near Dresden owed its distinction to the red earth of Nymphenburg. But not always could the clay be depended upon. So varied were the clays in their composition that they fired all the way from white to a bronze which was almost black. In fact, John Dwight, "Father of English Pottery," made some clay figures which, when fired, were mistaken for bronze.

The clays could provide ornamentation as well, as in the ribbon and checkerboard pottery made as ribbon and checkerboard cakes and sandwiches are made today. Marbling, and even the famous agateware and tortoise-shell pottery of Thomas Whieldon when he was Wedgwood's partner, resulted from combining and manipulating with a comb or the fingers a number of clays in a hand-molded piece. The only limits to his multicolored effects were imposed by the permutations and combinations of the clays themselves.

At first the tin glazes of Turkey and Persia, which were transmitted through Greece to Spain to become maiolica, then to Faenza ware and faïence, and so to delft and English earthenware, constituted sufficient color for the delighted potters. One authority claims that the rich green, yellow, and brown glazes of the medieval European potteries were their only contribution to the ceramic art.

However, human nature being what it is, it was not long until separate color was applied. In no time, it was playing a leading role.

All primitive people love colors, the gaudier the better. It is sophisticates such as the Parisiennes who give the palm to black.

If that is a criterion, the Etruscans were evidently the sophisticates of their era, for their decor began with black, with striking effect, as you know if you have ever visited an exhibition of Etruscan pottery. Soon white was added, then other pigments. But it was a long time, even as time is measured on a ceramics calendar, before the range grew to embrace the entire spectrum.

Firing was the obstacle, and the culprit. When the colors did not turn out as expected, the Chinese potter said a devil had sneaked into his kiln. In the circus of color, firing was the ringmaster who cracked the whip.

Axiomatically, painting could be done in only one of three ways:

1. *Under* a translucent glaze
2. *In* a translucent glaze
3. *Over* either a translucent or opaque glaze

As glaze requires almost as hot a fire as that for biscuit, underglaze colors had to be able to withstand temperatures too great at first for any but cobalt blue and a rarely used manganese purple. Spode claims that these were the only two successfully fired under glaze until 1800 when Josiah Spode announced that he had employed eleven—orange, pink, two tones of green, two tones of brown, and four or five tones of blue. The formula for the green has been lost.

Inglaze colors, as in the tin glaze of majolica or delft ware, were naturally subject to the same restrictions.

Overglaze colors changed the picture. When the painting was done over the glaze, it could be refired at a comparatively low temperature in a muffle kiln, one which did not expose the pottery to the direct action of the fire. (William Billingsley's son-in-law, Walker, invented such a muffle kiln and sold it to the original Worcester factory, with the result that they achieved superb tones, and fame.) In overglaze painting, the *enamels*, as they were known, attained an almost unlimited range.

Copper oxides provided the most useful pigments. They resulted in blues and greens, brilliant turquoise, and, if carbon monoxide replaced the oxygen of the kiln, in *rouge flambée* or *sang de boeuf*, the "sacrificial" red of Ming, with us commonly called oxblood or pigeon-blood. The Ming reds, especially the dark chestnut tones towards the end of the dynasty—1369–1644—are in a class by themselves.

Turkish porcelain made at Isnik in the sixteenth century was unequaled for its lustrous turquoise, aubergine purple and tomato red. (The last was approximated by the Japanese sealing-wax red of Imari.) Some of the distinctive, bold Turkish designs were outlined in black, à la Rouault, but with a more delicate and subtle touch.

The greatest difficulty with overglaze pottery was that the enamel scratched or wore away. Under the glaze the hues were permanent. As cobalt was at first the only known substance which could take the heat of the glost fire, the underglaze blue of cobalt was the most beloved color on the palette.

The first blue used by the China potters was Mohammedan blue, or ultramarine, made from the azure stone *lapis lazuli* and imported from Persia. Blue from cobalt was not used until the Ming period. As the final pulverizing of the cobalt might occupy more than a year of continuous hand labor with pestle and mortar, only the most skilled artists of the realm were permitted to paint the underglaze blue—once applied to the absorbent body of the ware, no corrections were possible—and they used only the finest of brushes, made from the whiskers of a mouse.

Cobalt, the "goblin of the mines," occurs as an ore in rocks in columnar strata such as the Giant's Causeway. It was first found in Saxony, a district rich in minerals. In 1540, a glassmaker of Neudeck discovered that cobalt oxide, produced by roasting cobalt at great heat, resulted in an attractive transparent blue. He named the product "zaffre" or "smalt." *Sèvres bleu, mazarin bleu* and *bleu de roi* were all smalt under a different name.

Augustus the Strong of Saxony, founder of the Meissen factory, was dismayed because the local zaffre did not produce a blue as rich as that of the Chinese. He offered a prize of 1000 thalers to anyone, of any nationality, who could provide him with a blue to rival it. He also imposed severe penalties for anyone caught smuggling out zaffre, although in 1733 he allowed a medium quality to be exported to England at £11 an ounce. When Frederick the Great seized the Royal Smalt Works during the Seven Years' War, a quantity of supersmalt arrived in Plymouth, and was sold at 15 shillings an ounce. Used at the Worcester Porcelain Factory under Dr. Wall, this smalt got a shade nearer the K'ang-hai blue than that of Meissen. In the late 1820's, Spode reproduced it on blue-and-white bone china, the only time the color was ever equaled.

The Saxon zaffre was costly, but the Dutch smalt, stored in white leather bags and called Dutch ultramarine, cost ten times as much. In 1755, the English Society for the Encouragement of the Arts offered a prize of £30 for the discovery of cobalt in quantities large enough to warrant development. Francis Beauchamp of Longreed claimed the prize when he found large deposits near

Truro in Cornwall. Later, rich deposits were discovered on the Duke of Ancaster's estate in North Wales, and in the lead areas of Derbyshire, Yorkshire, and Cumberland.

Thomas Turner at Caughley, in Shropshire, used smalt for his *Brosely Dragon* and *Blue Willow* patterns, the latter a best-seller from his day to ours. Contrary to widespread belief, it bears no relation to any Chinese design nor is the immortal-lovers story anything but romantic fiction. The two patterns were the invention of a young designer who made his name, Thomas Minton, one of the great names in the eighteenth century and subsequent potting history. These two chinoiserie patterns were done *en camieu,* or monochrome —painting in several tones of one color. In their *Pink Tower* service, popular since its introduction several years ago, Spode-Copeland has been very successful with *en camieu.* Employing a similar medium, *en grisaille,* a monochrome in grays, they recently made a hit with *Colonel in Grey.*

By the end of the eighteenth century, colors had been given names. An intense yellow was *jaune jonquille.* Pinks were *famille rose* and *Pompadour rose,* in England perversely called *rose du Barry.* A deep ruby was known as *Chelsea claret.* Sèvres' green was *claire de lune,* but at Worcester less poetically *apple green* and *pea green.*

Naturally the blues came in for the greatest distinction. *Bleu soufflé,* of course, was just what the name suggests, blue powder blown on through a bamboo tube screened by a piece of silk. *Bleu de roi* was Sèvres royal blue, and *bleu turquin* their brilliant turquoise. *Gros bleu* or *mazarin bleu* was their dark blue. Cobalt became *Mediterranean blue,* or, in the terminology of the ecclesiastical palette, *Madonna blue,* than which name could go no higher.

Color had definitely come into its own.

With color *un fait accompli,* its pigments readily available and their idiosyncrasies understood, applied decoration began to be introduced in its more elegant relationships, and took on an even greater importance than form. In most cases, it was the decoration which caught the eye, as Louis XIV was shrewd enough to recognize. When, at Madame de Pompadour's instigation, he took over Sèvres and reorganized it, his first step was to hire a host of artists. They included painters and etchers, sculptors and modelers, goldsmiths and silversmiths. Probably the outstanding ones were the illustrious three: Boucher the painter, Falconet the sculptor, and Cotteau the enameler who invented the acclaimed "jewelled Sèvres," enameled dots over gold foil.

The most eminent artists of the period contributed their genius to the art of ceramics in England, too. The list of decorators who have illumined the rolls of English pottery design is infinite. Unfortunately, few of them inscribed their signatures for posterity. Wedgwood did not encourage—indeed, he forbade—his artists to sign their work. At Minton's, some of Marc Louis Solon's pieces bore the monogram MS, but no matter for which potter the itinerant and bigamous Billingsley wielded his fine brush, his only signature was his immortal roses. An artist who probably got more renown than she merited was the Swiss historical and portrait painter, Angelica Kaufman. (Twice she had her own portrait painted by Reynolds.) The Derby factory under the indefatigable Duesbury, himself an enameler, had a whole stable of outstanding painters, not the least of them being the great landscape artist, Zachariah Boreman.

Unfortunately for English original and individual painting on ceramics, Robert Hancock, an engraver employed at Worcester, brought to perfection a new process known as transfer printing. Soon it and its running-mate, bat printing, had replaced free designs. On the whole it resulted in what the artists called "the stereotyped monotony of mechanized decoration." Its merit lay in the fact that it meant accelerated porcelain and earthenware production at less cost. That, even before he accepted the controversial process at Etruria, had been Josiah Wedgwood's aim from the first.

How he succeeded, we shall now find out at Barlaston.

Chapter 3

Wedgwood

WHEN you emerge from the railway station at Stoke-on-Trent, you are confronted by a statue etched starkly in grime against the sky. The upraised hand of this man of granite holds a vase, symbol of the prosperity he brought to this part of England. The statue bears the dates 1730–1795, and the name JOSIAH WEDGWOOD.

To me it was a magic name. Having fallen heir to two pieces of priceless old Wedgwood in my teens, I had delved into the story of the "Prince of Potters" and had found it more romantic than any fiction.

Josiah had potting in his blood. His great-great-grandfather had come in 1612 to Burslem, heart of Staffordshire's Black Country, had married the daughter of the Squire, and through her had inherited a pot-bank. Josiah's father owned the Churchyard Pottery beside Burslem Church. He died when Josiah, the thirteenth child, was nine, and to each of his surviving seven children left the sum of £20. Josiah he apprenticed to his oldest son, but, once the terms of the indenture were fulfilled, the brother refused to employ the youth. Josiah worked in several potteries, but at twenty was master of his own at Ivy House. Five years later he leased the commodious Brick House, sometimes called the Bell House because the workmen were summoned by bell rather than by a whistle as elsewhere in Stoke.

Another ten years, prosperous to an unprecedented degree, he had built halfway between Hanley and the quasi-aristocratic Newcastle-under-Lyme, a spacious and grand mansion known as Etruria Hall. To celebrate the opening of the new plant, he gave a supper for 120 workmen in the Town Hall, Burslem.

He had also providently married his cousin, Sarah, a woman of some education, means, and sound common sense. Sarah provided Josiah with three sons and three daughters. Sukey, the eldest, became the mother of the renowned biologist, Charles Darwin, F.R.S. The third son achieved posthumous

32

fame as one of the inventors of photography. Another direct descendant was the celebrated composer, the late Dr. Ralph Vaughan Williams, O.M.

From 1754 until 1759 Josiah had as partner Thomas Whieldon of Fenton Low, a potter of distinction and taste who had built up a good business of his own, although during that interval only one notable contribution was made, the famous cauliflower ware of *famille verte,* a glaze which was the result of many experiments.

In 1762, while convalescing from an accident to a knee already weakened by an early attack of smallpox, Wedgwood was introduced by his surgeon to a Liverpool merchant, Thomas Bentley, who later became his partner. Bentley had traveled on the continent, spoke French and Italian, and had a considerable knowledge of classical and Renaissance art. The friendship lasted until Bentley died in 1780. His death was probably the greatest misfortune in Wedgwood's life.

Bentley introduced Wedgwood to the antique. The day the new works at Etruria were opened, the two men made six vases to commemorate the event. Wedgwood threw them and Bentley turned the wheel. These "First Day's Vases" are in the Wedgwood Museum.

It was in the manufacture of "useful" ware that Wedgwood first made his name. The Act of 1751, placing a high tax on spirits and forbidding their sale by distillers and shopkeepers, helped to make tea the national beverage, and aroused a clamorous demand for tea sets.

Salt glaze pieces, then in use, were called *scratch blue* on account of the scratches the ware made on silver spoons. Salt glaze sets went out when, in an effort to combat the defect, Wedgwood perfected his new ware, *Cream Colour.*

It was not long until it brought him to royal notice. In 1756 he received an order from Queen Charlotte, wife of George III, for a tea service "with a gold ground and raised flowers upon it in green." Her next commission was a complete service and two toy tea sets of the *Cream Colour* ware. It pleased her so greatly that she commanded it henceforth be known as *Queen's Ware,* the name which it bears today. Josiah was also appointed Potter to Her Majesty, the first of a long line of royal warrants and other honors for the firm including the Certificate of Merit in 1957 awarded by Prince Philip for the pattern *Strawberry Hill.*

Queensware, soon being sold all over Europe, was proved typically English by the names it was given abroad—*faïence anglaise* in France, *englische Steingut* in Germany, and *terraglia inglese* in Italy. Wedgwood's own name was a household word on the continent.

Another feather in his cap was an order in 1773 from Catherine, Empress of Russia, for a 952-piece dinner service. Each piece was to be decorated with freehand paintings of 1244 English landscapes, castles, and country houses. For this, he scoured the country to procure artists. As it was to be placed in the Palace of la Grenouille near St. Petersburg, and had the device of a green frog in a shield on the border of each piece, it was known as the *Frog Service*. The price agreed upon was only £3000, barely enough to cover the actual cost, but to offset that, the service was on view in London for two months, and gave Wedgwood enormous publicity.

If Josiah mounted to success on the ladder of ware in daily use, he had the soul of an artist, and dreamed of raising pottery from a craft to an art. His first ornamental ware was Black Basalt, about which he had a prophetic vision. In 1773 he wrote:

The Agate, the Green and other coloured glazes have had their day, and done pretty well, and are certain of resurrection soon. . . . The Cream Colour is of superior class, and I trust has not yet run its course by many degrees. The Black is sterling, and will last forever.

He was right. *Queensware* is still the company's largest product, and the *Black Basalt* remains popular throughout the world.

It was followed in two years by the famous Jasper ware, whose popularity seems never to wane. Of all his products, Josiah prized Jasper most, probably because of the difficulty of manufacture—he made over ten thousand pieces before he was satisfied. This ware, a hard vitreous porcelain body, is stained by the addition of metallic oxides to a variety of colors, the favorites being black, dark blue, Wedgwood blue, lavender and sage green. Thinly potted, it is translucent.

The decoration of Jasper, doubtless suggested to Wedgwood by antique cameos, is usually in the form of a frieze in white relief, the black and white being particularly suited to the Adam rooms at that date bourgeoning into popularity. One of the best known is *The Dancing Hours* by John Flaxman, then only twenty but a great sculptor. The ruling at Etruria was that all figures should be roughed out in the nude in order to achieve anatomical accuracy, and then draped. The young artist stopped short of the draperies. Wedgwood, prudish in spite of being a freethinker, asked his right-hand man in the modeling shop to provide the "Hours" with flowing robes. It was at Flaxman's instigation, by the way, that in 1816 the famous and controversial Elgin marbles were bought for the British Museum.

The single piece for which Josiah Wedgwood is most famous is his reproduction of the Portland, or Barberini, Vase. The original, probably made about 50 B.C., belonged to the Barberini family of Rome. They sold it to a Scot, James Byrne, who sold it to a friend of Josiah, Sir William Hamilton, husband of Nelson's Emma. In 1785, he sold it to the Duchess of Portland for 1800 guineas.

When the Duchess died and Wedgwood heard it was being put up for auction, he attended the sale, bidding against the son of the late owner. He rose in his bids until the Duke strode across the room and asked him why he wanted it. Wedgwood said he wished to copy it. The Duke said he would lend it to him if Wedgwood would stop bidding. The Duke paid the equivalent of $5000 for it, and Wedgwood carried it home. It is now in the British Museum but in a restored condition as a few years ago it was smashed to pieces by a madman.

It took Josiah four years to achieve a "correct and faithful imitation," as Sir Joshua Reynolds declared it to be when he was called in to pronounce judgment. It was the great potter's last achievement for he died in 1795.

At his father's death, Josiah had inherited £20. At his own death he was worth half a million pounds sterling, and was held in high repute by the landed gentry, for, while amassing a fortune for himself, he had not been unmindful of his country's good. He had pushed the building of roads and a canal which cut freight rates to one-tenth. He had been instrumental in changing England from a rural to an industrial country, and had brought it an international market which still persists. He had housed his workmen in model villages.

As a freethinker, he was bound to be suspect by certain of the hidebound church and chapel folk. As a sympathizer with the American colonies' desire for independence, he was suspect with the chauvinists. But he went his way with courage and resolution, and keenly supported the Slave Emancipation Society, even making a jasper medallion of a slave with the inscription, "Am I not a man and a brother?"

Essentially a just man, he could be generous, too. Whatever the motive, conviction or shrewdness, he paid his artists liberally, and in full measure was repaid. In 1788 one of them was ruined by a bad debt. Wedgwood took him into his employ, and arranged that at his retirement five years later he had a pension settled on him for life.

One authority calls Wedgwood the most celebrated English ceramist and one of the most outstanding potters of all ages, and also credits him with being a business man, an engineer, and an artist, qualities rarely found in one person. Opening the Wedgwood Memorial Institute at Burslem in 1863, the Prime Minister, Gladstone, said of him, "He was the greatest man who ever, in any age or in any country, applied himself to the important work of uniting art with industry."

We housewives consider his greatest achievement the sweeping changes he made in English eating habits. Previously, only the nobility and the wealthy had anything resembling a dinner service. The people had wood, horn, and pewter, "pots" of coarse clay, and communal bowls and trenchers. By stepping up production, the Prince of Potters made useful dishes of his *Cream Colour* ware at prices within reach of all, as if he had taken for his motto, "The greatest good for the greatest number."

A fitting epitaph. . . .

When I set out to visit the potteries of the six members of the Fine China Association, it was my introduction to the romance of china manufacture. Naturally, I went to Wedgwood's first. To Barlaston.

The pottery at Etruria had to be abandoned because of the sinking of coal mines underneath, although the Hall and Etruria Village, a model village in Josiah's time, were shown to me that evening when Major John Wedgwood drove me by a roundabout way to my hotel in Stoke.

The new plant was at Barlaston, halfway between Stone and Stoke. There, in 1937, a country estate of 382 acres had been bought, the site chosen because one branch of the family had already lived there for several generations. Barlaston Park is a pleasant wooded country with open meadows and streams. It is only a few miles from Burslem, heart of the Black Country, where the skyline is broken by hundreds of "bottlenecks" belching out smoke and soot. Yet it might be leagues away, for not a single bottleneck cuts the horizon. Everything has been electrified. Windows and lighting are the last word in modern construction. The attractiveness of the bright, airy building is increased by the attendants' costumes of the familiar Wedgwood blue.

Mr. John, as everyone then called the tenth generation Wedgwood who, in his forties, was deputy managing director and chief of publicity, said that he would see me later—I had no idea that he meant at lunch in the directors' dining room—then consigned me to the care of Miss Nellie White.

"Miss Nellie is an old and valued employee. Her sole duty now is to show distinguished visitors around, especially in departments not open to the general public. If there is anything at all you wish to see, don't hesitate to ask."

What impresses one immediately throughout the plant in Barlaston is the friendly atmosphere. In its entire two centuries there has never been a strike in the Wedgwood works. An excellent pension scheme for staff and workers, now numbering 1700, helps in that respect, added to which profit-sharing has been in force for twenty-five years. Needless to say, with such a volume of business, these bonuses are never negligible. Continuous employment prevails—mother and daughter, father and son, uncle and nephew. Sometimes a whole family is on the payroll. Many employees spend all their lives in the company's employ. The master ornamenter has been with the firm well over fifty years, as has the master medallion and cameo maker. One son of the latter is in the Canadian office in Toronto, the other in the New York office on East 54th Street. Miss Nellie could barely remember the time when she had not "been Wedgwood."

My tour would not have been half so interesting had she not initiated me into the pottery vernacular, for example, *jigger* and *jolley*.

The jigger is the machine on which plates are made. First a ball of clay is flattened on a revolving disc by the lowering of an automatic *spreader*. The circular *bat* thus formed is *thrown* by the platemaker onto a plaster mold which shapes the front of the plate. The mold is then mechanically rotated at high speed on the jigger. The back of the plate is shaped by a horizontal metal *profile* which the maker pulls down with his left hand, leaving his right hand free to work the clay.

The jolley is the cup-making machine. A ball of clay cut by wire to ensure the right size is thrown by the jolleyer into the plaster of paris mold which forms the outside of the cup. The mold is then placed on the rotating head of the jolley, and the cupmaker skillfully draws up the clay inside it. She then pulls the lever to which is attached a profile, correctly shaped to form the inside of the cup. The *setting* of the profile regulates the thickness of the finished piece.

The clay pieces are removed from the molds and dried to the consistency known as *cheese-hard*. Before firing, flatware, mainly plates and similar dishes, must have the edges and surfaces *towed* or *smoothed* with tow or fine sandpaper. (Steel wool would leave slivers and discolor the ware.) Then they are *fettled*—that is, the edges are rounded off with a wet sponge.

Cups, vases, and other hollow pieces go to the *turner*. He works at a lathe similar to the type used for turning wood or metal. With great precision he turns or shaves off the surplus to the correct line and dimensions. He can also add beads or fillets by impressing a special tool called a *runner* on the revolving piece. To finish the job, he reverses the motion of the lathe and burnishes the surface with a smooth steel tool.

The turner invited me to operate the electric device. It looked simple enough for a baby. Alas, it was a case of the quickness of the hand deceiving the eye. In no time I reduced the embryo vase to a pile of clay shavings.

"Don't feel badly," Miss Nellie said tactfully. "It takes years for the turner to master that one operation. Pottery-making is a highly skilled art, with specialists for each process."

At affixing the raised blue "grapevine" ornamentation on a cream ashtray, I was less clumsy. These embossed bas reliefs, such as flowers and leaves, are simply the old *barbotine* of medieval potters. The figures, pressed by the figure maker into fired pottery molds called *pitcher* molds, are extracted by a special process, and applied by the ornamenter after the surface of the clay has been moistened with water. A skillful pressure of the craftsman's finger fixes the ornament. A sensitive touch is necessary. Otherwise the fine details of the ornaments would be spoiled.

The same process is used for the more complex white classical figures in bas relief on the familiar Jasper ware. This method of ornamenting by hand has not altered since the day of Josiah Wedgwood.

What fascinated me were the Barlaston kilns. Six electric tunnel ovens, the first of their kind to be installed in England, fire biscuit and glost—glazed ware. Without interruption, trains of fifty trucks are propelled in opposite directions through contiguous tunnels each 273 feet long. The maximum temperature in the firing zone, according to one informant, is 2600° F. for biscuit and 2500° F. for glost.

Figures when they approach the astronomical mean little to me, but I was impressed when told that four million units of electricity a year are required for *each* tunnel oven. (Thermonuclear energy should be useful at Barlaston.) After three days of firing, the clay has been transformed into the hard, durable but porous substance known from its texture as *bisque* or biscuit ware. Glost firing is similar to biscuit firing, but with one important difference. In the glost oven, the pieces must not be allowed to touch one another as they would be fused into a solid mass by the glaze which vitrifies at that high temperature. The various articles are kept apart by three specially manufactured clay supports known as *stilts*.

The perils of firing are many. For example, all articles shrink one-eighth, or even as much as one-sixth. They must shrink in the same ratio. Some explode, some warp. But at Barlaston, with thermally the most nearly perfect kilns in the world, the incidence of wasters has been reduced to practically nil. Of course, the controls are read every hour. As Miss Nellie said, "If the elements fail, it's the same as if your baking oven shut off—you've had it!"

Wedgwood puts out a multitude of patterns in both earthenware and bone china, although they did not enter the latter field until 1812 when they found that Minton's, Spode, and Davenport were taking away their trade. Between 1879 and 1919, an interval of forty years, 9999 bone china dinnerware patterns were produced.

The favorite older ones were not dropped, however. In 1815 the Prince Regent ordered from Josiah II a dinner service for the use of the ex-emperor Napoleon at St. Helena. *Napoleon Ivy* is still in current production and still going strong.

Coronation, with its three white plumes outlined in platinum on a crimson ground, is a twentieth century interpretation of the royal motto, *Ich dien.* It was designed in 1937 for the coronation of George VI and Queen Elizabeth, the present Queen Mother, by Star Wedgwood, granddaughter several times removed of Josiah. Her husband, F. Maitland Wright, is one of the managing directors.

Victor Skellern, an artist of boundless imagination combined with a hard realism, is the art director at Barlaston, but the founder's namesake, Josiah Wedgwood, who has been head of the company since 1930, has the final word in choosing a design. In this he follows the maxim of the Prince of Potters, "A pattern must be as good two hundred years from now as it is today."

One of what Sir John calls "persistent patterns" is *Florentine,* a Renaissance style carried out in four colors. *Turquoise Florentine* and *Dark Blue Florentine* have been favorites for years. The elegant *Black Florentine* is rapidly becoming one. Service plates in that pattern were used with dramatic effect by Tiffany's in a table setting of *Colonnade,* a gold-rimmed black-and-white service made at Barlaston in 1904 for Theodore Roosevelt and revived a year ago to great acclaim. The row of columns circling the rim suggests the moonlit beauty of the ancient Parthenon.

The last of the quartette, *Gold Florentine,* was, in spite of its price, Wedgwood's best seller for 1960 when sales rose by 95 per cent. With its quiet splendor and antique motif as lacy as a bridal veil, it is as timeless as a wedding ring, and actually belongs to their Wedding Ring Group which comprises such white-and-gold patterns as the ivy bordered *Whitehall, Golden Fleece* with its simple wreath edging the well of the plate, and *Gloucester,* a true double wedding band on the traditional rim of bone white ware. In the same group, ringed with platinum, for wedding rings are made of that costlier metal too, is *Doric,* on the shape Savoy, a coupe or rimless and shoulderless plate of fairly recent popularity.

Among the Modern Classics are *Wedgwood White* in either the traditional shape or the contemporary coupe, a copy of Josiah Wedgwood's first cake plate, and *Asia,* a Greek key design in black flanked by gold. Its companion pattern is *Asia on Highland Green*. Either assures a hostess of a stunning table.

Getting into floral decor, one finds *Strawberry Hill,* named after the small Gothic castle, a showplace of England in the eighteenth century, which Horace Walpole, fourth Earl of Orford, built at Twickenham, Surrey. There he entertained the Berry sisters, Mary and Agnes, who shared the famous bachelor's affections. *Lichfield,* bordered lavishly by "everlastings," recalls the everlasting fame of Samuel Johnson, the great lexicographer, who was born in that cathedral city but transferred his bulk to London and, when the mood was on him, sent little notes around to his lady love, Stella, inviting her for coffee. Another immortal, Shakespeare (at least his wife's house in Stratford-on-Avon) is called to mind by *Hathaway Rose,* that favorite of English flowers, a delicate pink with foliage of muted green. *Ice Rose,* strongly appealing to current brides, shows two even more delicate roses, but in blue, and yellow-green leaves on a coupe-shaped—shoulderless—plate.

Beaconsfield suggests Disraeli, who became Earl of Beaconsfield merely so that his beloved and elderly Mary Anne might bear the title of countess. In dealing with Queen Victoria, he found that it paid to lay flattery on with a trowel, but on the plate named after him, the flattery is subtle, a tribute to the selectiveness of the chatelaine. Last but by no means least in this category is *Charnwood.* Its fresh crisp rose and yellow flowers accented with green foliage is an interpretation of an authentic blue Chinese print from the private collection of Josiah Wedgwood, and was engraved from it in 1799 by Richard Morton. *Charnwood* has a heartwarming brilliance which makes it a host, or hostess, in itself. Having been named for the English baron who wrote an outstanding biography of that greatest of Americans, Abraham Lincoln, has possibly helped to boost its sales over here.

A pattern which spells sheer elegance for my standard of living is *Halford,* a two-color slipware, the plates white with a platinum wreath inside a platinum edged celadon rim, the hollow ware celadon with white inside and white handles. The color, being right in the clay, is as durable as the clay itself. Wedgwood, celadon specialists, brought it to a peak in this successful pattern which enjoys wide distribution, especially in Canada. As it has the full merit of a Wedgwood traditional design with a contemporary feeling, it is scheduled for a long future.

When it comes to Wedgwood's earthenware or Queensware, one can only skim the surface. Of late the capacity of the plant has been taxed to fill the orders for the original Cream Colour, slightly modernized and given new names: *Edinburgh* and *Mountbatten* for the blue with white barbotine, and

Princess Anne and *Margaret* for the white with that applied decoration in blue. *Cornwall* is the hand-embossed cream with a shell edge, while *Prince Charles* is white in the same traditional shape.

In the Catherine shape, created for Catherine the Great, are three patterns which run neck-and-neck: *Richmond,* its rim explosively gay with flowers; *Drury Lane,* a cheerful arrangement of a lemon, an apple, and a cherry or two; and the twins, *Blue Avocado,* centered by that fruit in blue and rimmed by a blue lattice, and *Yellow Avocado,* a charming blend of yellow and a clear brown-beige.

The floral names, such as *Wildbrier, Purple Old Vine, Crimson Bramble,* speak for themselves, and give unexpected competition to two immensely popular numbers, *Wildflowers* and *Potpourri.* The former has a simple morning glory centered on a plate with the shell edge perfected by the founder in 1770, while the latter is a block-print design in tapestry blues and reds on the Catherine shape. These two are reproductions of Queensware used by the American colonists, and were unearthed during the restoration of Colonial Williamsburg. The Williamsburg Restoration, Inc. especially appointed Wedgwood to produce this ware. The shapes and designs were copied from excavated shards, from drawings in old Wedgwood pattern books, from Williamsburg documentary prints, and from eighteenth century molds still in possession of the Wedgwood company.

For unadulterated luxury is the glowing *Ruby Tonquin* of regal air. High price? Rather, but despite that it gets a top sales rating.

With apologies to a London couple who are very old friends, let me tell you how *Ruby Tonquin*—the tonquin bean of South America is a source of perfume—transformed a depressing drawing-room into an inspiring salon. Theirs, as I recall shudderingly, was as dull a room as one could find "from Maidenkirk to John o' Groats." When I was ushered into it a few months ago, I blinked. Same old heirloom furniture and family portraits, but given a lift by being set against soft gray walls and plain gray carpet, plus semi-brilliant drapes.

"Before and after," my host gestured jubilantly. "Before and after *Ruby Tonquin.*"

In a burst of unwonted extravagance, and possibly a desire for improved morale, he had bought his wife a tea service of *Ruby Tonquin* as an anniversary gift. In that grim room, it had stood out like the proverbial white bandage on a black thumb. Either it had to go back to the shop in South Audley Street, or an adequate setting had to be provided for the jewel. His wife absolutely refused to let it go back.

"It was not the initial cost," he laughed ruefully. "It was the upkeep. But it has been worth every penny we spent on refurnishing. Even the conversation of our friends seems to have taken on a new luster."

A group of eight plates, destined to become a collector's item especially for nautical folk, portrays famous Canadian sailing ships. They will make excellent gifts for anyone interested in Canadiana. I have a special and proud interest in them as they were designed by my cousin, Rowley Murphy, A.R.C.A., O.S.A., Toronto, who first came to notice with his outstanding stained glass windows in the Swedenborgian cathedral in Bryn Athyn outside of Philadelphia. Rowley is the official artist for the Royal Canadian Navy. During the war he had to be lashed to the ship's rail so that he could paint his celebrated pictures of convoys in a gale.

The first four plates, brown on white bone china, are of sea-going vessels: the *Mathew,* 1497, of John Cabot fame; the *Griffon,* 1679, built for Sieur de la Salle; H.M.S. *Discovery,* in which Captain George Vancouver explored and charted the west coast; and the *Bluenose,* a Nova Scotian salt banker which won every international series in which she sailed, and was one of the world's greatest sailing vessels, especially to windward.

The second four, on gray-green, are famous Great Lake ships: a later *Griffon;* the U.S. brig *Niagara;* the H.M.S. *Nancy;* and the *Eureka,* which stepped out of the freshwater class for a period by sailing around the Horn.

A United States series, the profits from it going to bombed-out victims, was shown to me in Wedgwood's New York showrooms.

Almost from the first Josiah Wedgwood marked his wares. A letter addressed to any Wedgwood center will bring you the details. For instance, WEDGWOOD alone in red, blue or gold is a genuine Wedgwood mark, but in black it is ware from the mid-nineteenth century factory of W. Smith at Stockton-on-Tees. WEDGWOOD & CO. is the mark of Ralph Wedgwood, a cousin of Josiah, of Ferrybridge, Yorkshire.

Forgeries abound, both at home and abroad, but most of the time they are promptly detected, although not in the case of a china enthusiast who bought an apparently old piece in an out-of-the-way village in Nova Scotia. It was marked WEDGEWOOD. Only when he read this chapter in manuscript did he learn that his treasure was quite unrelated to the products of Josiah and his successors. During one of my visits to Stoke, the firm was actually prosecuting a potter who persisted, after two warnings, in stamping his wares WEDGEWOOD.

Eighteenth century Wedgwood is marked only with the name, in either upper or lower case, sometimes accompanied by a letter or symbol, except between 1769 and 1780 when ornamental pieces were marked WEDGWOOD & BENTLEY. On cameos or small pins sometimes only W&B was used.

Another exception was made for a short time in 1790 when a very rare mark, WEDGWOOD & SONS, was used on some pieces. Otherwise the WEDGWOOD impressed stamp remained the mark.

Between 1795 and 1840 there was little change. On their first bone china, produced between 1812 and 1816, WEDGWOOD appeared in red, blue or gold. About 1841, Etruria was added.

(The British Registry Mark, employed by the British Government between 1842 and 1883 was a diamond-shaped backstamp.)

Wedgwood marks: The mark at left, in sepia and other colors, has been used for bone china from 1878 to the present. At right is the mark for *Queensware, Jasper, Black Basalt,* etc., used since 1769. The word "Barlaston" has been used in addition since 1940.

After 1860, code date marks were placed on Queensware in addition to the impressed WEDGWOOD stamp. They consisted of three capital letters, the first indicating the month, the second being the potter's mark, and the third the year in which the piece was made. Since 1930 the actual date has been used.

When bone china was reintroduced in 1878, the mark was an interesting backstamp of the Portland Vase.

After 1891, the word ENGLAND or MADE IN ENGLAND was added to comply with the American regulation known as the McKinley Tariff Act.

Wedgwood ware has always been marked, except for some of the earliest pieces made prior to 1759. These are so rare that they are mostly in museums or fine collections. For a time only the larger pieces of Queensware dinner services bore their stamp, which means that cups and saucers of that era as well as small butter plates may be unmarked. But in general, it is quite safe to say that unless a piece has WEDGWOOD on it, it was definitely not made by Josiah Wedgwood and Sons.

Wedgwood outdoes all other porcelain or bone china coming into the United States or Canada. It is outstanding wherever china is shown. The great department store of Stockholm, NK—Nordiska Kompaniet—devotes a showroom to Wedgwood. That, in Scandinavia, a stronghold of the ceramic industry!

I have seen Wedgwood on display along the Mediterranean from Portugal to Turkey, and points north. It is for sale in the United Nations Gift Shop, and on ships plying the Seven Seas. You will find great collections in most of the old mansions and palaces open to the public in England. Tamworth Castle, fortress of the Marmions in the Middle Ages, boasts several early examples, one a shoe to hold hot water to keep the feet warm in bed, or spirits to warm the inner man. At Blenheim Castle, where Sir Winston Churchill was born, whole cabinets are devoted to Josiah's early ware, some of it presented in 1752 to the then duke by the King of Poland, one of the 359 offspring of Augustus the Strong.

Old pieces are to be found in the homes of workers. One ancient crone had in the front window of her Burslem almshouse two teapots of "cauliflower" ware. She grumbled toothlessly about lucky Americans with money to travel, and the high cost of little luxuries for her.

"Why don't you sell your teapots?" I suggested. "The money would provide you with *big* luxuries for the rest of your life."

She was shocked. "Sell my teapots? Never! Them be willed to The Family for Wedgwood Museum. Them—them be *Family Affairs*."

Family. That is the secret. Wedgwood's has been a family firm from first to last, and promises to remain so. The eldest of Sir John's sons, after finishing his military training, was educated in America so that he could take over on our side of the Atlantic when the time came.

It is a family which has forged steadily and brilliantly ahead. *Who's Who* devotes more pages to the Wedgwoods than to any other single family. Old Josiah's character was so powerful that it has persisted in most of his descendants. For instance, in Sir John. So long as he lives, his intimates claim, the "Prince of Potters" lives too.

Family. . . . your guarantee of quality, the Wedgwood mark.

Chapter 4

Spode-Copeland

Driving to The Old Ride, his fine boys' school in Buckinghamshire, my host stopped his Lea-Francis in a small village and suggested that we go into the sixteenth century inn and have a morning coffee. Inside the pleasant room we immediately gravitated towards a cabinet on which was a single object, a teapot.

"Spode!" we exclaimed together. "An heirloom."

The proprietress was standing behind us.

"Every piece of Spode," she said with confidence, "is an heirloom."

Spode is quality. You immediately think of gracious living, that phrase which has become a nauseating cliché from being mouthed by persons who have little idea of what gracious living means. You think of *Cranford,* genteel ladies in fingertipless gloves carrying shallow baskets to gather their roses. You think of—well, gracious living.

It is one of the reasons you give Spode to a bride—it embodies the wish that in her new life she may live graciously. So you choose from the old, time-hallowed favorites, perhaps with a Cranford-type rose in the name. *Maritime Rose* with its broad bands of soft blue embellished with white flowers of a singular delicacy. *Dresden Rose,* strewn with dainty sprigs. *Savoy Rose,* a technical triumph when Spode-Copeland perfected the deep and intricate embossing of the sixteenth century French potters who used the curled and crinkled leaves of the Savoy cabbage as models for decorating their crude faïence bowls and jugs. And, needless to say, *Billingsley Rose.*

You may choose *Sylvan,* the dishes molded in the shape made famous by late Georgian silver. *Geisha* with its prunus blossoms, symbol of spring. *Colonel in Grey* from a motif used widely during the Renaissance by the monks illustrating manuscripts in their cells. *Pink Tower,* a favorite since 1780, its scene *en camieu* in the manner of chinoiserie but its border English

45

with a gadroon edge. *Jacinth,* airy bells on a Flemish green body. *Wicker Lane* out of molds from the Chelsea factory when it was dismantled. *Blue Camilla,* lustrous white earthenware with border of rich flower-sprayed azure. *Gainsborough, Reynolds,* and *Rembrandt,* all using the old Marlborough shape, a Dutch one, with apple-knob handles for the pieces with handles.

Let us take a look at the dates of some of Spode's patterns, and see how they have flourished for two centuries—well, a century and three-fourths. For example, *Blue Italian,* underglaze on the Cottage form, went on display in 1786, and went out of the shops as fast as the plant could fill the orders. Four years later their designers created a rival, *Camilla,* underglaze pink and blue on form Hamburg, and another, *Rhine,* in blue, pink and brown. Spode *Tower*—it comes in light blue, dark blue, and pink on the Gadroon shape— has been on the market since 1795 and is still a favorite. 1800 saw *Lady Anne,* hand-painted on the Mansard form, lead the sales, but almost immediately it was rivaled by *Billingsley Rose* of the same date, with a popularity which never wanes. Four years later another excellent rose pattern, *Maritime Rose* on Flower Embossed, was given to the public. Within a year in 1805, they picked another winner, still a runner-up, *Indian Tree,* hand-painted on the fluted surface of form Chelsea. A current favorite in brown, of fairly recent date, 1818, is *Fleur de Lys,* the "fleurs" diapered on the same form. A third on that shape is at present ahead in the running, *Colonel in Grey*—also in *Blue, Brown, Green, Pink,* and *Red.* Of course the "Colonels" have yet to stand the test of time, being rank newcomers, *anno* 1887. Recently the old *Verdun* in both leathery green and crimson was revived. Tiffany's featured it not long ago, the 10-inch plate bearing a price tag of $33.50.

You can see for yourself that what a Spode-Copeland executive said was true—they could get by if they never brought out another pattern. But they are not content to rest on their oars. They *want* to move with the times. And do, as anyone will see by looking at their latest designs. For instance, *Florence,* whose delicate colors in black outline make it ideal for use with wrought iron furniture; *Madeira,* brown, rust, and yellow berries and leaves on embossed wicker; and *Provence,* brought out in 1958, an opulent blending of gold bands and jadelike gray-green.

Still newer are *Elizabethan* and *Apollo,* both designed by the Royal College of Art. The former has classic gold bands on the ultra modern white shape. The lines of the latter are its own adornment.

This Royal College shape in white was awarded the Duke of Edinburgh's Prize for Elegant Design in 1960. Critics from many countries consider that it is one of the finest modern English designs they have seen. The man in the street may tend to classify it as Scandinavian, but the Europeans who have a true understanding of design as a whole are, in spite of its lack of resemblance to, say, *Wicker Lane* or *Buttercup,* impressed by its unmistakable Englishness. It is selling all over the world.

Apollo was selected by Swedish experts from amongst the Design Award winners from 1957 to 1961 and was displayed in the "Svensk Form" Exhibition held during October and November of '61. Spode-Copeland regards this as a feather in its cap in view of the high regard paid by the Swedes to good industrial design.

But the list could go on forever. As Spode bone china will. . . .

Josiah Spode, 1733–1797, came of a long line of Staffordshire potters. At an early age he was apprenticed to Thomas Whieldon of Fenton Low who agreed to pay him 2s.3d. a week, or, if he deserved it, 2s.6d. His apprenticeship over, he continued to work with Whieldon, for, to his mind, that potter surpassed in range of form and color any other he knew.

In 1762, Josiah met John Turner of Turner & Banks, whose works were on the nine-acre site of the Spode-Copeland factory today. Turner greatly admired the young potter, was confident of his future, and, being anxious to retire, prevailed upon him to take over the management of his plant. Eight years later Banks retired also, and sold his share to Spode on mortgage. By continuing to manufacture inexpensive domestic earthenware and sporting jugs with decorations in relief, within six years he had cleared off the mortgage and was sole owner.

An innovation which had much to do with Spode's early prosperity was transfer printing. (Of that process, more anon.) It rendered his earthenware low in price. From Thomas Turner of Caughley, heavily in his debt, he had procured the secret of engraving on plates and the tremendous advancement of printing the ware in blue underglaze. Still, he never sacrificed quality to quantity. Even at that early date, Spode's blue with the gadroon edge belonged in the highest category.

He was fortunate in having as chief engraver the renowned William Greatbach, and for executing the designs, Thomas Minton. Production went rapidly ahead. Both at home and in his overseas markets he reaped rich rewards. In 1785 he established a London office in Cripplegate, under the management of a tea merchant, William Copeland. This venture was an immediate success.

In 1795, two years before his death, Spode took over the warehouse of Thomas Turner, the "Salopian China Warehouse." The new premises were at #5 Portugal Street, Lincoln's Inn Fields, formerly the Theatre Royal where Gay's *Beggar's Opera* was produced in 1727.

It was at the Spode-Copeland plant in Stoke that one matter was clarified for me: the difference between the various wares. Perhaps it might be clarified for some of you. If not, here is a place you can skip.

Earthenware is opaque and still porous after the first, or biscuit firing. It is made of plastic clay freed as much as possible from iron, and burns white. Mixed with the clay are quartz, feldspar, and occasionally kaolin. Put more simply, it is a compound of ball clay, china stone, china clay, and flint, the last added to prevent warping.

Porcelain is a vitreous, semi-translucent body made from a mixture of kaolin and petuntse. The former, produced by the decay of feldspar, is a refractory, or non-cohesive, material. The latter, or less feldspathic china stone, acting as a cement to bind together the particles of the refractory kaolin, fuses only at a high temperature.

Porcelain is made of two kinds of paste, soft and hard.

Soft paste, or *pâte tendre,* is an imitation of true porcelain, and is actually called false porcelain. It is made of ground-up glass mixed with white clay and other substances. It is exceedingly plastic, though according to Savage sometimes soft soap has to be worked into it before it can be molded. It fuses at a low temperature, and is easily glazed with fusible lead glazes.

Hard paste, or *pâte dure,* was given its name because it takes a hard fire— a high temperature in the kiln—to fuse it, though generally the name is supposed to refer to its hardness when given the "file" test. It is white and translucent. If broken, a drop of red ink put on the fracture can be easily washed off. In earthenware it would be absorbed.

Now, with Spode, we come to another ware, English bone china, a hybrid porcelain. It may be as opaque as earthenware, or as translucent as the finest piece of Cho Keng Lu. Translucency depends upon thickness. Because you cannot see your fingers through it when you hold it to the light does not mean, as many think, that it is not bone china. Translucency, a fact which was stressed, depends upon thickness.

Josiah Spode was still in his twenties when he began to dream dreams. Since the Stuart Restoration in 1660, translucent porcelain had been coming into England from China. His great dream was of making a practical yet artistic porcelain to compete with it. For centuries the white ash of calcined bone had been used in the manufacture of glass. For a short time it was a characteristic ingredient of the soft pastes of Bow and Chelsea. Was bone ash the answer?

Spode was barely thirty when he began experimenting with it, and his experiments, hundreds and hundreds of them, he carried on for twenty-five years. At the end of that quarter-century he found that this white ash, mixed with kaolin and flint, could be made to produce a ware combining strength and durability with the exquisite translucence of the porcelain from the East. To his new product he gave the name "bone china."

Spode-Copeland and their adherents claim that all the credit for its invention must go to Josiah Spode. On that point the ensuing controversy has been intense. His rivals insist that he share the honor with the West England potter, Enoch Wood. But no one can contest Spode's claim to the credit for perfecting the formula, now used by all English china manufacturers * and with such success that it has exalted English bone china to the position it holds in the world.

By 1796 Spode was issuing bone china in quantity. That year the profits exceeded £15,000. Copeland received £1000 as a gift and was made a partner.

The Honorable East India Company with its factory in Canton in China unknowingly contributed an idea in the teaboxes and tea-papers which came west in those days. Spode realized the potentialities of the designs. He copied them and improved upon them, though the two famous ones, the *Blue Willow* and the *Brosely Dragon,* were, you recall, the creation of his designer, Thomas Minton, perhaps influenced by the spirit of chinoiserie.) Of them, Hayden said in his book *Spode and his Successors:*

> While Wedgwood was winning acclaim for his classic triumphs, Spode was tapping the East. . . . those designs which Spode snatched from fugitive teaboxes, now gone forever, are of value as indicating, in a poor translation maybe, what the little delicate bouquets of the Chinese merchants may have been as a gesture of artistry and grace in sending forth their fragrant tea to that great outer world of which then the Chinese knew nothing.

Josiah Spode must be given credit for the complicated Chinese patterns in blue and white and red and white. He based designs, too, on the Japanese Imari patterns with their strong reds, royal blues, and gold. Still, if Spode can be accused of copying, others greedily copied him. Those old designs which became so popular are perhaps less familiar to us on old Spode than on old Derby and old Worcester, and on the products of other factories which made them their own. The one thing to be hoped, Hayden stresses, is that Spode, who died in 1797, realized his great indebtedness to his partner, William Copeland, who had shown him the path to the East.

Josiah the First was followed by Josiah the Second. A pioneer like his father, in 1805 he developed a feldspathic earthenware known as stone china,

---

* Except at Gustavsberg, Stockholm, it is still not used on the continent where the principal factories prefer the true hard paste.

the "aristocrat of earthenware." It was opaque but of a far finer texture than earthenware, and extremely hard. When lightly tapped, it gave off a clear ring. Perhaps it was not the porcelain for which potters everywhere were in search, but it was the missing link between that and earthenware. Moreover, the delicate blue-gray of its body was an ideal background for the old Chinese designs executed in brilliant enamels. In no time it swept the country.

The second Spode had developed this stone china in response to requests from noblemen and wealthy citizens who already had Chinese dinner services in their possession, but wished to increase the number of pieces. In 1945, a lady whose grandfather had been a solicitor in Bideford, on the coast of Devon, told an interesting story in this respect to a member of the Copeland family. Her father, who died in 1920, had bequeathed a large dinner service to be divided among his ten children. In it had been a number of genuine Chinese plates acquired by their grandfather in barter with a sea captain. (Like most seafaring men of the eighteenth century who came to Bideford and Appledore Quay, the captain paid his bills with merchandise brought from the East.) The Chinese plates were later sent to Spode-Copeland who manufactured enough additional pieces to form a gigantic dinner service. This is now in the possession of a member of the Copeland family.

Two other achievements must be chalked up to Josiah the Second's credit. He installed a Watt steam engine "with the power of ten horses,"—later 30 horsepower—to turn the grinding pans for flint, stone, and pigments. It increased the output so rapidly that the difficulty was to get enough raw materials. He also copied early Worcester, with the result that the *gros bleu* of his salmon-scale productions was livelier than that of the famous Dr. Wall period.

William Copeland died in 1826. He was followed by his son, William Taylor Copeland, for many years Alderman of Bishopsgate, London, then Lord Mayor of London, and later M.P. for Stoke. In 1827, Josiah II died, leaving great wealth and so many bequests that his will was twenty-eight pages long. Two years later, Josiah III died. William Taylor Copeland became sole proprietor.

In 1833, exactly a century after the birth of the first Spode, a Stoke man named Spencer Garrett was taken into the firm. The following years saw a renewed demand for sculpture in simulated white marble for interior decoration in the style started at Meissen. The two rival firms, Copeland & Garrett and Minton's tried to produce a *bisque* of this type, but were unsuccessful. One of Copeland's technicians in 1845 invented a highly translucent frit porcelain suitable for statuary ware and not at all costly. Spencer Garrett was also given credit for the invention. Within five years numerous firms were making this *Parian* ware named after an island in the Aegean. Wedgwood's called theirs *Carrara*, but the trade name was *Statuary Pottery*. From 1833 to 1846, the mark on Spode-Copeland ware was an impressed COPELAND & GARRETT. If you are in Portugal and want to see a really old Spode dinner service of this period, go to the British Consulate and request them to get you an invitation to Factory House, Oporto. (This meeting place of the "factors" of the wine industry is interesting, if only for the foyer, its pillars so spaced that sedan chairs could be parked behind them, while along the rear wall are benches on which the bearers could sleep while waiting.) Garrett died in 1847. Since that date, no one but Copelands have been in the firm.

William Taylor Copeland was a keen sportsman. He kept a stud of race-horses. A steel engraving in the Spode Museum preserves the tradition of his appearing at the works mounted on a horse, on his head an old-fashioned beaver hat. He died at Russell Farm, Hertfordshire, on April 12, 1862, in his seventy-second year.

Several years before his death, he had taken his four sons into partnership. Eventually the business became the property of the youngest of the quartet, Richard P. Copeland. He left the business to his two sons, under whose control tremendous strides were made. In 1932 a private limited company was formed with the name of W. T. Copeland & Sons, Ltd.

In 1948, three members of the next generation became directors. These three—R. Spencer C. Copeland, Gordon Hewitt, and T. Robert Copeland,—are presently at the helm.

Spencer Copeland was the director whom, through the kindness of Major John Wedgwood, I was permitted to contact personally. He invited me to be the board's luncheon guest in the directors' dining room when we would have plenty of time to chat. At the moment he regretted that he had to run off to a conference of their designers, but his cousin Robert would actually do much better by me, as he was extremely knowledgeable.

Robert, as he signs himself informally in his letters, is the youngest director and abrim with enthusiasm. An ardent photographer, and an expert, he envied me the late model Leica M3 I had picked up as I passed through Frankfort. He arranged the lights so that it could capture Josiah II's first stone china plate with its border of Oriental flowers but its center motif of posies from an English garden, the colors as brilliant as the day they had been applied.

He drew my attention to the pierced or reticulated rosette dessert set presented by Josiah I to William Taylor Copeland on the occasion of his marriage. He also pointed out the punch bowl and two goblets made from the bones of the "joint" at a dinner given to the firm at the old Wheat Sheaf Arms. They had been found at Llandudno, Wales, and brought back.

The Copelands have scouts out all the time looking for old pieces of this sort. Occasionally they turn up duds, but often the genuine article. For instance, in an antique shop in New York, the dealer casually mentioned a cup he had just taken in—"It had belonged to a Mr. Spode." It turned out to be the cup presented in October, 1803, to Josiah I by the Stoke-on-Trent branch of the Staffordshire Yeomanry, a cavalry unit. For pieces such as this, the Copelands are willing to pay any price.

"Now," said Robert, "I'm going to give you into the charge of the man who knows more about Spode than any man alive. Sydney Smith."

"Spelled with a 'y,' " Sydney said in his pleasant Staffordshire accent. "I was named after the famous wit."

And not for nothing! With great glee he introduced a thrower named Potts and a slip-worker named Clay. The latter showed me a powdery substance known as alumina, a boon to the potters, as it had replaced flint, the cause of so much silicosis.

Sydney's wit was not in evidence when he told me about the late Queen Mary's visit to the plant in 1912, and her chatting to him in her dignified way.

"Ah, she was a regal lady, every inch a queen! And she recognized quality in china, as well as in other things."

Yes, at the Cluny Museum in Paris she had been looked up to as an authority.

When she lay in state in St. George's Hall, Sydney had been chosen to give the Spode broadcast in tribute to her.

"Mine," his voice trembled, "was the first tribute of that night."

For fifty-six years, man and boy—Sydney Smith had started at the age of thirteen—he had worked there, and loved the plant.

"Every grain of bone dust," he grinned.

"Even the soot from your bottlenecks?" I could not resist asking.

Even it. He was emphatic on that point. Smoke abatement was all very well, but Spode had reasons of their own for not converting to electricity *in toto*. They had found out that certain processes turned out better with coal, and Spode products must not turn out only better, but best—100 per cent best!— all the time.

"They should start filling a bottleneck any minute now. Let's go!"

After the pieces have dried to cheese-hardness and are ready for biscuit-firing, they are packed in *saggers,* fire-resistant containers made of a particular kind of marl. (Saggers are not necessary in electric kilns.) On the inside bottom of each is a layer of alumina upon which the clay articles rest. The saggers are then built into pillars or *bungs* inside the ovens. Each is capped by a ring of *wad* clay to prevent smoke getting in, the sealing effected by the next sagger in the bung. Thousands of saggers go into each pot oven. When the ovens are filled, the doors are sealed, fires are lighted in the various fireplaces of the bottleneck, and the contents are left at a temperature of 1200 C. for three days and three nights. Before being emptied, the ovens are allowed to cool for thirty-six hours.

I climbed into one of the bottlenecks—before the fires had been lighted, needless to say. In half a minute, and with one sharp twinge of claustrophobia, I sagged, and was glad to be helped down. It was much more comfortable standing outside and taking a picture of the men moving about inside, like gnomes working in a deep, dim cavern.

Gnomes? Or alchemists? For it is the fire which brings the dull clay to life, turns it to gold for the exchequers. That you hear over and over, in each pottery you visit. The important process, the vital one, is the firing.

Sydney was a fount of stories. One was about the familiar Spode china known as *jewel embossed.* It was modeled by an early Spode artist from the halo of a saint in a sixteenth century painting. *Jewel embossed* is used for several patterns, including *Billingsley Rose,* at least one piece of which is to be found among the gifts of almost every bride.

"Another fellow and I discovered an old unused chamber beside the canal which Josiah Wedgwood and Josiah Spode had constructed in order to bring materials cheaply from the Liverpool docks. I was a bold young chap then, and got a key and barged in. On hands and knees we found a lot of discarded stuff. There was the master mold of a plate, also of an oval and a round dessert dish. They looked too good to be left rotting away. I took them to the boss.

"He agreed with me, so a new master mold was made, though master molds take many days. Then a case was made. Then a potter's mold. Then the plates themselves. Was I ever pleased?

"At first there was just a ring for decoration, but not long after it became a rose. The queen of English flowers in that particular manner was the concept of an itinerant artist named William Billingsley, a painter who enjoyed precious few of the good things of life, mostly poverty, humiliation, and remorse. For twenty years, having committed bigamy, he was forced to live under various assumed names, though all the time his roses were making his own name immortal. When he died, an artist whose roses are strewn over the whole world of gracious living, he was buried in the potter's field."

"Have you any idea," I asked at last, "how many *Billingsley Rose* plates have been made from the duplicate of the resurrected master mold?"

"Ah, Madam! One would have to be an astronomer to know numbers big enough for that!"

An operation I watched with interest was the burnishing of the gold. The gold used on Spode ware is never the unstable liquid variety but pure gold in the form of a brown paste made of gold dust mixed with mercury and rubbed up with fat oil. Some of the gilding on pieces a hundred and fifty years old is exactly as when it came from the hand of the gilder. One detail may interest you: The cloths which are used in wiping off the burnished gold portion are burned and the gold collected from the ash.

Girls do the burnishing with a bloodstone pencil. In former days, bloodstones, or hematites, were washed up in the rivers of Derbyshire, collected by old men, and sold. Recently they have been difficult to obtain. The shortage at Spode-Copeland became so acute that an appeal was made to retired employees to relinquish the pencils—their own property—which they had taken home. So generous was the response that enough were handed in to last the company for five years.

In exchange for his stories, I told Sydney one.

Halfway between Los Angeles and San Diego is the famous monastery of San Juan de Capistrano—where the swallows return on the same date each spring. Nearby is a wayside market where they sell "Spode" manufactured by a local pottery. Oh, they are candid about it! They frankly admit that it is an imitation of the genuine English earthenware. But it is a clever imitation. In a row of a dozen plates in the *Rembrandt* pattern is one right from Stoke-on-Trent. *If you can pick it out, madam, it is yours.* When I was there, the only person who had picked the right plate was a little girl, and she did it by an eeny-meeny-miny-mo elimination.

Anyone who buys the imitation soon finds out how different it is from the English ware. Because it lacks the constituents and workmanship to make it durable, at the second or third washing it begins to crock, crack, and chip. Bad advertising for the real Spode? By no means. A salesman in an exclusive Pasadena shop told me that it had immeasurably boosted sales. Women bought at the wayside market, loved the dishes on their tables at home, were horrified by their failure to stand up, but had fallen so deeply in love with the pattern that they marched downtown and bought genuine Spode printed or impressed on the bottom with the mark which guaranteed quality. Spode has been marked since 1770. Some recent marks are shown.

From 1920

Spode's "Royal Jasmine" England

From 1932

From 1910

Some Spode marks.

With great pride, Sydney told me of a piece which had a unique mark. In fact, he introduced the employee who is the heroine of the tale, a liner, Mrs. Patty Chell, at her hand-operated turntable on which she accurately centers the piece before applying the lines and bands.

We watched while she worked on a pattern brought out in great quantities each year for the Christmas trade, and actually called *Christmas Tree*. In an effort to speed up the export drive to Canada and the U.S.A., it was designed during the last war.

"Some of it was lost as a result of enemy action, but only one complete consignment went down. And," Sydney added, "I'll warrant that if it is ever salvaged, it will be as good as the day it was made."

It was while this project was in full swing that, as a compliment to Spode and *one which they paid no other pottery*, George VI and Queen Elizabeth visited the works. The royal visitors were quite taken by the way Mrs. Chell was painting the gold border with a pencil on the revolving disc.

"Very clever!" said His Majesty. "Very clever, indeed!"

He picked the plate up. The royal thumb left its print. It was fired in.

"That," my guide leaned towards me confidentially, satisfaction in his voice, "is a souvenir which not even Scotland Yard can boast." I was shown the plate in the directors' dining room at lunch.

No Spodes now in name, but Spode-Copelands in deed. Carrying on through thick and thin—sometimes it was pretty thin—but never lowering their standards. Not even during the depression, not even when two wars struck almost a death blow. Maintaining Spode quality, as if from all over the world they heard the voices of women saying, *"Every* piece of Spode is an heirloom."

55

Chapter 5

Minton's

WHEN you enter the elegant foyer of Minton's remodeled china factory in London Road, Stoke-on-Trent, the first object to strike your eye is a ceramic peacock of life-size proportions—it is 5'2" tall—standing beside the grand stairway, its exquisite blue, emerald, and browns glowing against the English mottled chestnut. The imperious crest is a separate piece fitted into a slot in the head. In the magnificent tail, even furled, fifty "eyes" may be counted.

One of three, it was modeled in 1874 by the celebrated Italian artist, Paul Comolera, for the Minton exhibit in the Melbourne Exhibition of 1880. It was despatched to Australia in the sailing ship, *Lock Ard*, which was wrecked off Sydney in 1878. Fifty years later, it floated ashore in a cask at the caves fourteen miles from Moonlight Heads, Victoria, in perfect condition.

The peacock is carelessly regarded as a symbol of vanity. Classically it symbolizes resurrection and survival. When this old-established firm advertises, "MINTON—the world's most beautiful china," the claim springs not from vanity but from confident pride. When they add that their average price per finished piece is higher than that of any other manufacturer, that is pride too. A five-piece place setting of their *Cobalt Blue*, of which I own a candy dish, costs $168.

If the peacock is a symbol of survival, it serves Minton's in this respect as well. On two occasions they had a struggle to remain afloat.

One crisis came before World War I in 1911. Times were bad in England. All the potteries suffered. Being exclusively in the luxury class, Mintons' probably suffered more than their competitors. Their financial situation was precarious. They tottered on the brink.

Judge Gary, the multimillionaire chairman of the board of directors of the United States Steel Corporation, heard about it.

"Can't let a firm like that go under," he said.

He immediately went to Tiffany's of New York and placed an order for three services, one with Rose du Barry background, one with green, and one with turquoise, each piece to be marked with an ornamental *G* adroitly worked into the pattern.

No other set made by Minton's, the gold experts, had as much encrusted gold as those sets. (You may still see the odd piece in their showroom.) The dinner service cost £1000, in the days when a pound was nearly $5. A single plate cost £35. The craftsmen who made the plates were paid 75s. each, and for other pieces were paid in proportion.

The day was saved.

The great crisis came during the depression. For lack of orders the factory was practically closed. The office lent the workmen as much as £400 to keep their homes going—each man, regardless of his salary bracket, was paid £3-10-0 a week. (Every penny was paid back.) Eighty gallons of milk were distributed every day.

This time it was James of Kansas City who came to the rescue. (The firm has been taken over by Hall Brothers, the largest greeting card manufacturers in the U.S.A.) They placed an order for several patterns in flower painting and raised gold. As the china had to pass through many departments, the whole factory benefited.

Now Minton's were out of the red for good.

The founder of the firm was Thomas Minton, a handsome Shropshire lad born at Wyle Cop, Shrewsbury, in 1765. Having served his apprenticeship as designer-engraver, he migrated to London and there did some fine work. But his ambition was to be a potter. With his wife, Sarah Webb, he moved from London to Stoke where he engraved patterns for Spode, Wedgwood, and others. Among them, as was said before, was the original *Blue Willow* pattern.

Becoming acquainted with two brothers, Joseph and Samuel Poulson, of the same mind as himself, he joined forces with them. In 1793 the trio set up their own pottery. From the beginning they prospered, largely as a result of their foresight in acquiring land in Cornwall with deposits of kaolin, Cornish stone, and even tin, enough to furnish them with raw materials for over twenty years.

Thomas Minton, whose portrait looks down upon the chaste foyer, was, one might think, much too good-looking to be anything but a Beau Brummel, —one rarely sees such a beautiful man—yet when he died in 1836, his firm was the largest producer of bone china in the Six Towns.

He left two sons. The elder, Thomas Webb, became a parson. The younger, Herbert, at sixteen joined the firm as traveling salesman. At his father's death he took over, holding the position of general manager until his own death at Torquay in 1858. Herbert proved to be the real brains of the business. Under his guidance the firm made the world-wide reputation it has enjoyed ever since, earning it the present name, "Rolls-Royce of the Potteries."

A man of vision, in 1853 he went to the Exhibition in New York where his firm had a display. Then, laying the foundation for the extensive business still prevailing in the United States, he made a complete tour of the country. Two years later Minton's won the Grand Medal of Honour at the Paris Exhibition, the first of a long line of such coveted awards.

In addition to native shrewdness, Herbert Minton had great luck. In 1848 he met Leon Arnoux, son of a Toulouse porcelain maker. Arnoux had come to England to study English methods of manufacturing bone china. Immediately Minton took him into his employ. When the Germans occupied Paris during the Franco-Prussian War of 1870, Arnoux managed to get a staff of artists from Sèvres. These included the famous Louis Marc Emmanuel Solon who ultimately became *the* authority on English china, and before his death in 1913—he died in England—wrote a book on the subject which is now a classic.

Solon was a great pottery designer and decorator. He developed his own special line, *pâte sur pâte*. It is an application of clay diluted with water to the consistency of a batter, and laid on by thin washes with a paint brush, one wash being followed by another until the required thickness is obtained, after which it is fired and decorated. The lumpy surface is then scraped, smoothed, carved, and incised by sharp steel tools in the same manner in which a sculptor proceeds in dealing with other materials. Therefore *pâte sur pâte* is an art which combines the skill of a painter with the technique of a sculptor.

One of Solon's vases, dated 1871, recently sold for 385 guineas. Another, with historical scenes all around it, was presented to Queen Victoria in 1887. A third vase, which had to be kept damp for seven months while being made, sold for 600 guineas. Unfortunately, no one knows where it is.

The firm suffered an irreparable loss when a unique and priceless Solon vase—it cost £250 in the making in 1899—was broken while being taken to Edinburgh to form part of an exhibition in connection with British Pottery Week in Scotland in 1961. Over two feet high, it had a Parian body decorated in the *pâte sur pâte* style. The ground was peacock blue, the ornate handles heavily gilt, the decoration male and female figures with cupids.

A London connoisseur who owns many splendid examples of Solon's work was told by a friend that he would get a lot of money for it if he sold it across the Atlantic.

"I don't sell," he replied curtly. "I buy."

So does Mr. John E. Hartill, managing director of Minton's. He saw the collection when he was in London for the young Queen's coronation. If that connoisseur ever changes his mind, he told me at lunch, he hoped that he would be on the ground with his check book, for the collection would make an invaluable addition to the treasures already in the Minton museum.

"Solon," Mr. Hartill added, "stands alone in the world of ceramics."

In 1849, nine years before his death, Herbert Minton took into partnership his nephew, Colin Minton Campbell, grandfather of the company's present chairman. He devoted himself to the pottery, yet, without sacrificing its interests, became Member of Parliament for Stoke. The three present directors— Mr. Colin H. Campbell, Mr. John E. Hartill, and Mr. George Campbell—are all lineal descendants of Thomas Minton.

Both the board room and the office of Mr. Hartill are paneled in natural Elizabethan oak. It is interesting to record that this wood is said to have sprung from an oak tree planted by Queen Elizabeth I. From that tree, runs the legend, seedlings have been planted, and the wood from now mature trees is highly regarded. Some are said to have been planted in Canada. One of the Minton patterns made for the Dominion market is called *Elizabethan Oak*.

Spencer Copeland had been kind enough to contact Mr. F. A. Timmins, Minton's export sales manager, who sent a car to the North Staffordshire for me the next morning and himself volunteered to show me over the plant. As I hesitated to engage the time of a busy executive when so many of the processes were becoming familiar, he decided to turn me over at once, rather than later, to their archivist, Mr. J. Steel, a mine of stories and information.

Mr. Steel started in the office sixty-five years ago, a lad of fifteen. He was not only devoted to Minton's, he was an integral part of it.

"Do you wonder? At twenty I had T.B. Minton's sent me to the Isle of Wight and kept me there until I had made a complete recovery. I'm writing a history of the firm." He pulled out a box of letters from dead-and-gone employees recounting unusual experiences at Minton's. "Trouble is, I have so much material I'm afraid I'll never get the job done."

He produced an assortment of early knife handles which he had found under a floor when the building was being altered. Now that a process for holding the blade in the ceramic handle had been perfected, they were coming back into favor. He also displayed an interesting collection of old buttons found in the same place. They were made of porcelain ground to powder and subjected to great pressure between steel discs. This was the principle which Arnoux applied to his famous encaustic tiles so much in demand for churches.

"Encaustic? Merely a fancy name for fired."

We watched the stonker, the worker who attaches spouts and handles. Handles can be made in three ways: by casting, by pressing in a mold, and by shaping with the hand a section of clay squeezed into long strips through a *dod* machine to come out like thick gray macaroni. With just a touch of clay mixed with water, and the right degree of pressure of the stonker's fingers, the handle is firmly fixed in the correct position. In order to secure a thoroughly strong joint, handles, spouts and ornaments must be of the same consistency as the ware to which applied. Formerly—due to an unequal moisture in the pastes, one writer claims—hard paste handles were bound to twist askew if attached straight. A deliberate twisting in the opposite direction was necessary to right them in firing.

As I had told Mr. Steel that the process I particularly wished to see was their gilding, he had some lithograph sheets of their borders in that medium run off for me in the printing shop.

Minton's specialize in gilding. There is no more prolific user of burnished gold. They do the best acid gold—others call it encrusted—in the industry. Their process was invented in 1863 by James Leigh Hughes. Minton's bought the right to use it, and from George IV got the letters patent for seven years, then renewed it. Now it is theirs for all time.

The gold used is an amalgam of mercury and gold, with a very little flux to fasten the precious metal to the glaze. The mercury volatilizes in the kiln and leaves the pure gold adhering to the ware. Afterward it is burnished with a red hematite stone called a burnisher.

In acid gold borders the pattern is etched in the glaze by hydrofluoric acid, and then gilt. When burnished, the burnisher brightens only the raised portion, leaving the background dull. Minton's were the originators of this type of decoration. So popular is it that they cannot at any time fill their orders.

" 'We'll put you on our waiting list,' we tell them," said Mr. Steel. "Most people are willing to wait, too. The only person who ever objected vehemently," he chuckled, "was an American army officer, General Van Vliet."

A party of American officers stationed at Stone, ten miles from Stoke, were being shown over the pottery by an ordinary workman when the archivist happened along and overheard the undistinguished talk the guide was giving the guests. Mr. Steel went to the directors.

"It's not good enough. We should show them the courtesy of appointing someone in the know."

"How about taking the next lot yourself?"

"Me? With all my work!—Very well! I'll do it."

The next lot, to his great delight, included General Van Vliet.

"We got along like a house on fire. When I showed him the blue-and-gold dinner service which President Eisenhower, when he was a junior officer in Panama, bought for his Mamie, the General ordered a service of the same pattern for his wife. 'Deliver it to my quarters in—well, a month will do, I shan't be leaving before then.' My mouth flew open so wide that it threatened to stay that way permanently—I must have looked as if I had lockjaw. 'A month!' I stuttered. 'Impossible! Our orders are four years in arrears now.' They were actually five, but I thought fit to soft-pedal that. 'Look, Mr. Steel,' he said. 'We fought over here, but let's not fight over this.' Then he grinned. 'Who can tell where an old soldier'll be four years from now? I might not be needing dishes then.' Well, the next day he was back, burning up those ten miles, tearing into the building in search of me. He handed me a bottle of whiskey which he had carried through the whole campaign. 'Now,' he said, folding his arms, 'how soon do I get my dishes?' "

Mr. Steel did not say how soon, but the General got them. The set cost £400 and included forty dinner plates at 60s. each.

"I hope," my guide said, "that Mrs. Van Vliet's servants appreciate Minton, too."

Minton's have created bone china ware for rulers of empires and emperors of finance. Among their famous productions were dessert services made for two such dissimilar royalties as George V and Emperor Maximilian of Mexico. They have made services for royal tours, and they make the china supplied to the British embassies and legations—plain white and gold with a crown. For the Turkish diplomatic missions, the ware is white with a gold crescent and star, an insignia of especial appeal to me who spent long enough in Turkey to love that glamorous country. One large order upon which they were engaged while I was in Stoke was for the Leofric Hotel in Coventry. Leofric, in case you do not know—I did not—was the husband of Lady Godiva.

What is their most popular pattern? There is not one. *Symphony,* pale blue and silver leaves on a delicate blue background, is one of the most popular—Minton's gave the then Queen a dinner service of that pattern when she opened the University of North Staffordshire at Keele in 1951. *Ancestral,* with its lively yet restrained rose and blue star-blossoms, is in unceasing demand and promises to remain that way for years to come. *Dainty Sprays* too.

In Canada, naturally, with Birks' elegant jewelry stores in cities all the way from Halifax to Victoria, the orders are heavy for the crimson and gold *Birks* pattern.

Their pre-eminent dinnerware is their encrusted gold. Its sales have a permanence amazing to anyone but themselves. A recent one, exclusive with the College Street store of Eaton's of Canada, is known only by number, K 160, and has made a great hit. Lately, however, women who formerly would have settled for nothing less imposing and conventional are succumbing to the discreet sumptuousness of *French Green* and its two companion patterns identified only by numbers, H 5031 and H 5042. Some of the still more flexible members of this perceptive group of hostesses have opted for *Athena,* black and white touched with gold.

Autre temps, autres moeurs.

During World War II Tiffany's made their fifth move uptown, this time to the corner of Fifth Avenue and Fifty-seventh Street where Cross and Cross designed for them the first fully air-conditioned building in New York City. For they had seen the handwriting on the wall and realized that the day of the *grande dame* with her chauffeured Rolls-Royce town car was finished, whereas the day of the matron driving her own Cadillac or Mercedes-Benz, or midget sports car, was at high noon. Now these matrons flocked in ever-increasing numbers to their inviting second floor which in its entirety had been given over to select chinaware.

Quick to observe the same trend, Minton's had taken steps to go along with it. Outstanding artists who could work with their traditional artists were engaged, with the result that their productions maintained their innate dignity yet were up to the minute. It paid dividends.

Cameo in Grey on the Latona shape overnight became a favorite of current brides. On the same plain shape is *Carlisle* with a gold wreath, and *Corinthian* with one in pale blue and gold. An appealing pattern is *Tapestry* with 18 beflowered panels on the rim. *Ancient Lights* arrests the eye with its unusual arrangement of bright blue motifs on a pale blue ground, while *Adam* —but an Adam pattern needs no description. Another is the delicate *Pandora—* in spite of the name, "delicate" is the right adjective.

On Fife, a swirl shape, are *Greenwich* exquisitely limned in seductively soft green leaves and pale yellow blossoms; *Marlow* sprayed with winsome roses, pansies and forget-me-nots; *Gold Cheviot,* its plain center bordered by leaves of gold against a rich cream rim; *Downing,* an inspiration of stylized blue leaves; and another on which I plan one day to serve dessert, *Ermine,* with no color except gray and the rose tint of a tiny flower at the end of each stem of the plumes in the wreath. For me—this may be partly the connotation of the name—it conjures up royal pageants and spectacular ceremonials.

Minton's are still three years behind in their orders, Mr. Steel * said. They could turn out their wares faster by employing extra help and taking short cuts, but it would not be the same ware. Their customers all appreciate that and are willing to wait.

"May we make you one of our 'ladies in waiting,' too?" he chuckled. "Ladies in waiting all over the world!"

"But now," he added with a glance at his watch, "we are keeping a gentleman waiting."

The gentleman was Mr. Hartill who asked if he might have the honor of being my host at lunch. The honor was mine, for he was an informed conversationalist, and made shrewd comments on the various sections of the United States and Canada which he had recently toured. He disliked the cliché "gracious living," especially since a shipping firm had incorporated it into their advertisements, and deplored "casual living," in his eyes but a euphemism for sloppy living. He preferred the newer phrase, "elegant living," probably because it had the Minton flavor.

We lunched at the Potters' Club, the only club in England devoted to the members of a single guild. I had dined there a couple of nights previously with Major John Wedgwood but had not paid particular attention to the famous Queen's Vase which my host pointed out. Minton's had the lion's share in its production.

The vase occupies a lighted niche in one clear wall of the lounge. By pressing a button, it can be made to revolve slowly and allow one to study at will all the façades of this exquisite jewel in porcelain, the peak of the potter's art, and an *objet d'art* with significance.

When a ruler is to be crowned, all his subjects strive to do him honor and shower him with precious gifts. When the ruler is a young and lovely queen, a happy wife and mother, a fairy-tale princess whom they have watched growing from childhood, what gift can be precious enough?

This was the problem which faced the British Pottery Manufacturers' Federation, composed of 181 firms, when the time approached for the coronation of Her Majesty, Elizabeth II.

For a long time it looked as if no inspiration would be forthcoming. The Federation was at its wit's end. Then the president approached one of the members, Colonel G. A. Wade, who responded with the suggestion that it must be a "superb piece of pottery that would embody in beauty and craftsman-

---

* Mr. Steel has since died and is greatly missed at Minton's.

ship the best of which the industry was capable." By March, 1953, Colonel Wade had formed a committee which included Mr. J. E. Hartill of Minton's, Mr. J. K. Warrington, general manager of Doulton's, and other members of the Federation. The project was to manufacture twelve to fifteen pieces to be presented to: (1) Her Majesty the Queen; (2) the mother countries of the United Kingdom—England, Scotland, Northern Ireland, and Wales; (3) the realms of the Commonwealth—Canada, Australia, New Zealand, South Africa, Pakistan, and Ceylon.

Finally the decision was made. A *vase*. The committee chose a design submitted by Mr. John Wadsworth, the art director of Minton's. The vase was the "supreme achievement of Mr. Wadsworth's long and distinguished career" —Minton's suffered an irreparable loss when he died late in 1955.

Next came up a ticklish diplomatic question. Should India be included? India owed no allegiance to the Queen, but, with the agreement of all the other nations when she became a republic, had retained her membership in the Commonwealth. The question was put to the Indian High Commissioner. He was charmed with the proposal. Later his government gave its consent.

As it turned out, this was a fortunate move. The vase was ten-sided. In each alcove above the base was to be placed a model of one of the ten Queen's Beasts. Immediately below the shoulder of the vase would be reproduced the floral emblems of the four mother countries and the seven members of the Commonwealth—six, rather, for being a Moslem country, Pakistan has no floral emblem, instead the crescent and star. This circle of flowers would be broken at the top of the center panel by the Royal Coat of Arms. The problem became: How could they arrange ten floral and two heraldic emblems around a ten-sided vase?

After prolonged deliberation and an infinite drawing of plans, the solution resolved itself almost with simplicity. The Royal Coat of Arms would be put at the top of the center front panel, and flanked by the floral emblems of the four mother countries: the Tudor Rose, the Shamrock, the Thistle and the Leek. Three panels were filled. Seven were left for the emblems of the Commonwealth countries. The committee congratulated itself on having had the perspicacity to have India join them.

Outside the actual making of the vase, nothing remained now but the Queen's consent to the acceptance of it. Her Majesty expressed her pleasure at the proposed gift, and graciously approved of the scheme to present a replica to each of the four mother countries and the seven of the Commonwealth.

To Minton's were entrusted the initial stages of the manufacture, and never had they been faced with such an exacting commission. Working in close touch with Wedgwood's, they produced the "biscuit" vases. Their modeler spent five and a half months modeling the body of the base and helping with the necessary molds. They also glazed the vases, gave them their second, or glost, firing, and applied the ivory groundlay with which, except for the embossed white shields, the body of the vases is colored.

The other five members of the Fine China Association—Spode-Copeland, Royal Doulton, Royal Crown Derby, Royal Worcester Porcelain, and Wedgwood—were all called in to help with the Queen's Beasts. Only with this full cooperation were the vases possible. To Wedgwood was owed a great debt for the successful biscuit firing. To Spode-Copeland for the exquisite precision of modeling the crown on the cover of the vase and for casting with slip, as the liquid china body is known. A further debt was acknowledged to Royal Crown Derby who gilded the covers. The main gilding and burnishing was done by Minton's. Decorators from Spode-Copeland, Doulton, and Worcester helped on the finishing touches. As a result the vases were ready for presentation well before the dates set.

Each vase is 25½ inches high with an extreme width of 11½ inches, and stands on a wooden base of Australian black bean. The weight without the base is 20 pounds—29 pounds with it.

The Queen accepted the vase at a private audience at Buckingham Palace on July 14, 1954. It is housed at Windsor Castle.

The vase for England is now in the Tower of London, that for Scotland in Holyroodhouse, for Northern Ireland in the Parliament Buildings at Stormont, and for Wales in the National Museum of Wales. In any of these four places you may see it when you go to the United Kingdom—if you are not fortunate enough to be invited to the Potters' Club! The Canadian replica is in the archives of the Parliament Building at Ottawa. A copy, presented to President Eisenhower, is on view in the Smithsonian Institute.

The choosing of the ten beasts proved an arduous task. Her Majesty had inherited thirty of these royal beasts worn as armorial bearings, but it was finally decided to use the ten which, in plaster six feet high, were later chosen to stand in the place of honor in front of the great window of the Abbey Annex at the Coronation.

The ten are:

1. The Lion of England—a gold lion, wearing a royal crown, and bearing on its shield the present Royal Arms of the United Kingdom.

2. The Griffin of Edward III—a golden griffin bearing a shield of the present royal livery colors, red and gold, upon which is the Round Tower of Windsor Castle, the badge of the present House of Windsor.

3. The Falcon of the Plantagenets—a silver falcon with wings outspread, its legs and beak golden. It holds a shield of the livery colors of the House of York, blue and mulberry red, on which is the same falcon with a golden fetterlock partly open.

4. The Black Bull of Clarence—a black bull with hoofs and horns of gold, and a shield of the Royal Arms as borne by the sovereigns of England from 1405 to 1603.

5. The White Lion of Mortimer—a white lion holding a shield of the livery of the House of York, blue and mulberry red, and on it a white rose amidst rays of the sun.

6. The Yale of Beaufort—a silver yale with golden spots and mane, tufts, hoofs, horn, and tusks of gold. The shield is divided white and blue, the Beaufort colors. On it is a crowned portcullis.

7. The White Grayhound of Richmond—a grayhound with a red collar edged and studded with gold, and a ring of gold. It supports a shield of the Tudor livery, white and green, with a crowned Tudor rose upon it.

8. The Red Dragon of Wales—a dragon mostly red, though underneath yellow, bearing a shield associated with Wales, four counter-tinctured lions.

9. The Unicorn of Scotland—a milk-white unicorn with golden hoofs, mane and tufts; about its neck a royal coronet to which is attached a chain of gold. It supports a shield of the Royal Arms of former Scottish kings.

10. The White Horse of Hanover—a white horse bearing a shield of the Royal Arms of the United Kingdom as borne from 1714 to 1800.

With the Coronation some years in the past, a long time in this frenetic age, I had decided to give the story of the Queen's Vase a "by." I should have done so, indeed, had I not only recently seen the Queen's Beasts on display at Tiffany's and learned that, though there was no mad rush for them—the price precludes that—they sell steadily, either singly, or in sets, both as collectors' items and as conversation pieces. Many brides have allotted their entire breakfront or their mantelpiece to the set, while others give the place of honor to a single beast of their choice. One hostess uses hers, nine of them around the Yale of Beaufort, as a centerpiece when she entertains VIPs.

"It is one way," she laughs deprecatingly, "that I can call attention to the family claim to Beaufort blood."

Her dinnerware, by the way, is Minton's spirited *Downing* in blue and white, the Beaufort colors.

That, I must admit, was not my only reason for including the story. The Queen's Vase is a remarkable example of what can be achieved by cooperation. It symbolizes the unity which exists among the Staffordshire potters, especially among the members of the Fine China Association, keen competitors all—I was astounded at the total lack of jealousy or trade rivalry displayed.

There was a moral in this. Their attitude seemed to say, and I do not want to sound sentimental or sermonizing, that if all the people of the Commonwealth, all the peoples of the globe, could work together and each make use of his own special gifts and talents while submerging his selfish greed, the world could emerge into a life as beautiful as that precious treasure, translucent in its niche—the Queen's Vase.*

* Such information on the Queen's Vase as I did not get personally from Major John Wedgwood or Mr. Hartill, came from the handsome brochure, *The Queen's Vase*, by W. F. Wentworth-Shields, Director of the British Pottery Manufacturers' Federation. To him I tender my grateful thanks, and apologies if inadvertently I have quoted him.

Chapter 6

Crown Staffordshire

On May Day, in former times, children used to welcome the loveliest month of the year by hanging baskets of flowers on their friends' doorknobs. A charming custom!

Nowadays practically every young chatelaine numbers among her most cherished possessions a May basket or two, but in bone china. Received as wedding or shower gifts, these exquisite pieces have the same freshness and the same gay hues, but—this is a boon—their delicate blossoms do not wither and fade. With them, every day is May Day.

Nothing can vie with them for lighting up a dark spot in one's breakfront or for bringing into brilliance an obscure corner shelf. They are refreshingly welcome when reflected in a mirror as a centerpiece for the table if the telephone announces a last-minute guest and you have no time to send out for flowers or, even though you may have a gardenful, to arrange them with your own individual touch.

On such occasions, these small treasures really shine—or as conversation pieces, especially if you know the history of their manufacture, or, sharing my good fortune, have watched them being made.

What impressed me more than anything else in the Black Country was the *esprit de corps,* the lack of professional jealousy among the Stoke-on-Trent potters. Major John Wedgwood arranged my visit to Spode-Copeland. Spencer Copeland did the same for the Minton visit. Mr. Hartill put in a trunk call to Royal Doulton at Burslem, and offered to drive me over there, but when I begged off, for two plants in a day would prove a tax, he called back and canceled the appointment, making it for the next day.

Yet after all, I did "do" two plants that day. When I said that one pottery I was particularly anxious to visit was Crown Staffordshire, source of my May baskets at home, he drove me to Fenton, the one of the Six Towns which

Arnold Bennett "forgot," and introduced me to Samuel Sinclair Green, the tall, youngish managing director known as Sam on both sides of the Atlantic.

With Sam as guide, I saw the whole process of May basket manufacture, from pallid clay to colorful elegance. In fascination I watched the deft fingers of the green-smocked girls in the workroom as they fashioned the diminutive petals and leaves from the gray clay—the grayness is mostly olive oil to keep the clay from drying out—and assembled them into a composite whole, ready for their baskets.

Head of the flower-making department is Miss Barbara Linley-Adams, one of the leading sculptors in England. She has exhibited at the Royal Academy, has also visited America and done demonstration work for Crown Stafford-shire at exhibitions here, including the British Exhibition in New York, with special sessions in some of the leading department stores, as well as in Canada at the cross-Dominion stores of that venerable institution, the Hudson's Bay Company.

One thing which had puzzled me was how the latticed baskets were made. Now I know. The clay comes out of a machine in long strings like putty-drab spaghetti. On a mold turned upside down, the "spaghetti," cut into lengths, is applied first in one direction then the other. The latticed bottom is added, and the whole thing set aside to cheese-dry. After that a rim is put around the top, with or without a sprinkling of tiny flowers, and, if that model demands it, a handle. When it has been biscuit-fired, and cooled, the colors are applied. Next comes glazing, and the glost firing. The final step is the enamel firing.

"You must have green fingers," I told my guide, "to produce from mere clay such a wealth of dainty blossoms."

"If you were born with the name of Green," he chuckled, "wouldn't Green fingers be part of your heritage?"

The first of the Staffordshire Greens to become a potter was one Thomas, who could trace his ancestry back to the 1500's of the Virgin Queen, Elizabeth I. Since that time, the family has farmed the same estate near Stone.

Towards the end of the eighteenth century, a descendant of this Thomas had worked for Josiah Wedgwood in the Churchyard Pottery of Burslem, and later for both Minton's and Spode-Copeland. Under these master potters he acquired an invaluable training in the making of bone china. In May, 1833, he decided to forge ahead on his own, so rented the old Minerva works in Fenton. In spite of vicissitudes which would have downed a less stouthearted man, the plant remained firmly in the family's hands.

Thomas had brought four of his eight sons into the project, two as travelers, one as an artist, and one as production manager. For his partner he chose a brother-in-law who was not a potter but an architect. In that capacity he attended to the erection of substantial buildings on the old site. During the twenty-year tenure of this shrewd pair, the business, which specialized in toy tea and dinner sets and small ornaments, made considerable progress.

Thomas Green died in 1858. His widow and four sons carried on successfully. At their mother's death, two brothers severed their connection with the firm. The third became the London agent. The fourth, Spencer, carried on alone. An efficient executive, he laid the foundation for the extensive North American trade in the surge of prosperity which followed the Civil War.

Spencer Green was succeeded by his two sons, Alfred and Samuel. The ideas they entertained would have seemed revolutionary to their progressive yet conservative father. Spreading out, by 1876 their products included dinnerware, tea and coffee sets, as well as miniatures, vases, cutlery handles, and door accessories. The flowers that Billingsley painted at Derby and elsewhere were among their schemes of decoration.

It was these two brothers, Alfred and Samuel, who, to commemorate the 80th anniversary of the founding of the firm, introduced the woven china baskets decorated with realistic flowers and filled with eye-capturing bouquets. The slogan they adopted was, "A May basket for every bride."

In 1913, the firm suffered a crushing blow—Alfred's death at forty-one. The next year administered another—World War I. It brought restrictions to a firm producing heavily decorated china of the finest class. (If any branch of trade suffers in hard times it is the luxury branch of porcelain manufacture.) As if that were not misfortune enough, a serious fire gutted the lodge and part of the main warehouse.

Handicapped thus, the fourth generation of Greens at Fenton took over. These were Alfred's son, Richard, and two of Samuel's sons, Frank and Samuel Sinclair. The current Sam, having gained an Honours Chemistry degree at Manchester University, set out as a traveler to study the customer's needs. Finally, mastering the business step by step, he reached his present position, managing director of the firm which, since 1890, has functioned under the name of the Crown Staffordshire Porcelain Company.

Crown Staffordshire is responsible for many of the outstanding reproductions of eighteenth century porcelain in continual demand. The critic, J. F. Blacker, was enthusiastic in his praise of this achievement.

By long and careful experiment their chemists have discovered the exact shades of the marvelous enamels which the Chinese brought to perfection . . . the powder blue on the vases made by the Crown Staffordshire Porcelain Company is the result of some thousands of trials extending over ten years. Each piece is what it professes to be, a copy, which is marked with a crown over "Staffs" or "Stafford-shire" surmounted by two **G**'s, one reversed in monogram.

On ware of their own creation the mark is a crown above these two **G**'s, and the words "Fine bone china, Crown Staffordshire, England, Est'd 1801."

To keep in touch with our changing tastes and requirements, and in order to adapt popular American decoration to British quality bone china, the managing director, Sam, visits our shores every year. He has crossed from Halifax to Vancouver several times, for the firm's biggest customer is Birks, the elegant jewelry stores across Canada—magnets for women from south of the line. In fact, many Americans plan a Canadian vacation purposely to buy English bone china, seeing that the Dominion, as a member of the Commonwealth, does not have to pay the 25–45 per cent duty imposed by the U.S.A. Illogical as this may seem, these tourists are not performing an unpatriotic act. On the contrary. They are fostering good relations with the neighbor to the north, and also—this is important—helping to bridge the 9 to 3 trade gap with the United States' best customer.

Like all the Six Towns potters, Crown Staffordshire is always on the alert for new ideas and timesaving processes. They were the first to adopt a modern scalloping device, a precision-made steel cutter fitted to a lathe. Depressing a pedal brings the cutter to bear on a cup or other clay piece. A plate by this method takes about two seconds compared with the twenty seconds of a fully experienced hand scalloper. Scallops done this way are absolutely regular.

Watching a plate scalloped brought me up short. I was in the same league as some who read my first article on china and wrote to expostulate with me—was I sure that Wedgwood made anything except Jasper? I had not known that Crown Staffordshire made anything except May baskets and florals. Sam was amused. Profitable as the luxury part of their output was, it would not support a firm with so many Greens, and so many employees.

That got us into an involved argument about what was a luxury and what a necessity, and on to the subject of the British housewife's having to put up with plain white china and handleless cups for seven years after the end of the war, so tremendous was the demand from abroad for decorated wares after the long interval, and so vital the inflow of dollars. This gave the industry the boost it needed. The Greens had to buy another factory and convert part of it from the old bottleneck to continuous firing in tunnel kilns.

Crown Staffordshire is one of the few firms manufacturing service plates. (They are not generally used in England.) *Regency* has an elaborate blue and gold rim with a bunch of English flowers on the white center. Except for a delicate green rim, *Osborne* is the same. Two popular dinner services in brilliant chinoiserie are *Mandarin* and *Ming*.

Many of their patterns are also reproduced on a small scale. As I collect miniatures, I could have had a field day there. These *objets d'art,* in case you do not know, are really miniature *cabarets*—tea sets for two. They consist of a teapot, cream pitcher and sugar bowl, and two cups and saucers on a matching tray. I am always on the lookout for them. In Plummer's one day I saw two on a table across the shop, and practically pounced. Alas, they were duplicates of the two Crown Staffordshire sets I already own. The full Crown Staffordshire mark is stamped on even the tiny cups.

A set of dishes in black matt, with striking glaze, was splendid in shape also. Immediately I wanted eight of the plates for salad. When I suggested that they would be perfect for that course, Sam showed me a pattern which he thought would be better, *Black Check,* white bone china with coarse black woven threads, hand painted. This, and the black and white *Lines in Space,* were part of the range produced by the Marquess of Queensberry, a young man of ideas. Later he was appointed Professor of Ceramics at the Royal College of Art.

The Marquess also created the man-sized Queensberry ashtray with a fluted rim. Definitely conversation pieces! Decorated by means of lithograph transfer copied from old fighting prints, they depict bouts fought according to the rules laid down by the first Marquess of Queensberry. The two I ordered—you cannot buy anything at the potteries—were of a fight between Humphries and Mendoza in 1788, and one between Sayers and Keenan in 1860. On the back is the Crown Staffordshire mark, surrounded by the words, "Made to the order of the Marquess of Queensberry."

The Marquess of Queensberry rules still prevail in the boxing world, and the principles of honest craftsmanship and integrity laid down by the forefather of the present Greens—"No matter what you make, make it the best you can,"—still prevail in the Minerva works at Fenton. When you buy a May basket for a shower or wedding gift it is more than a mere gift. It is a token, making every day a May day. And when you buy Crown Staffordshire, you buy for posterity.

Chapter 7

Royal Doulton

LITTLE did I wot when I accepted the invitation to spend a fortnight on a farm in agricultural Staffordshire that I would be near the Black Country of the despised Midlands. Yet only a few miles away at Burslem, heart of the potteries, a smothering pall of smoke overhung everything. Burslem Town Hall is surmounted by a golden angel immortalized by Arnold Bennett, but the building itself and the nearby public library in the square are as black as if constructed of compressed soot.

Could anything beautiful come out of such an environment? Yes! Your favorite figurines—*Top o' the Hill, Lady Charmian, Bedtime Story, Darling*—literally thousands, for the Royal Doulton plant is there.

Over lunch, Mr. Frank W. Kerry, export manager, gave me a thumbnail sketch of the firm. The founder, John Doulton, born at Fulham in 1793, served his apprenticeship at the Fulham pottery and became an expert thrower, spending his mornings soliciting business and his afternoons making pottery on the wheel.

His second son, Henry, entered the pottery at fifteen. He had to be up at six to ring the bell and call the men to work. In two years he was making 20-gallon chemical vessels on the wheel, an accomplishment which prepared him for the revolution in sanitary procedure when porous brick sewers were condemned. To cope with that situation he built a special factory facing Albert Embankment. It was the forerunner of the numerous plants which make Doulton's the most versatile of the English pottery manufacturers.

Henry had vision. He was not content with making terra cotta garden figures and urns, and ceramic insulators for electric telegraphs. (Their big electric plant now at Tamworth is a landmark.) Deciding to specialize in figurines, both earthenware and porcelain, he worked with the Lambeth School of Art and attached many outstanding artists to his train. Three years after John Doulton died at eighty, the demand for Doulton figurines was so great that an extra building had to be erected to accommodate the numerous artists' studios.

Four years later, in 1877, Henry bought an old established pottery in Burslem where the present plant now stands. In 1885 the Royal Society of Arts awarded him the Albert Medal. Two years later he was knighted. In 1901 Edward VII granted the company the Royal Warrant.

Four generations of Doultons have been in command of the huge composite works: John, Sir Henry; his son, Henry Lewis Doulton; and now the founder's great-grandson, Lewis Eric John Hooper, who completed half a century as chairman in 1952.

Figurines are only jam to Royal Doulton. Their bread comes from their dishes—yes, they too make dishes, both bone china and earthenware, and now, after years of patient research, a new ware, English translucent china, at a price which adds to its appeal.

Earthenware patterns are infinite in number. I shall restrict myself to three: *Desert Star* with tiny stars of turquoise enamel on a warm beige background, *Debut* in soft gray and platinum, and *Pink Radiance* in a delicate rose. During the war I bought an 8-piece service of their *Cavendish,* cheerful with both center and rim flower-strewn. It was especially effective against a royal blue breakfast cloth, a spot of brightness when the war news was more depressing than usual. Because of the depredations of indifferent help, the set has been drastically reduced in number, and to my regret the pattern has been discontinued.

Present sales indicate that the new translucent china may more or less replace earthenware. It has not only its transparency and durability to recommend it, but the Doulton artists have come up with exceptionally good patterns. In the coupe plate sets are three with single sprays which suggest the consummate artistry of the great seventeenth century Japanese ceramic decorators who liked a little painting on a plain expanse: *Greenbriar,* a gauzy spray of that shrub: *Pillar Rose,* an unfolding pink rosebud and stem: *Tumbling Leaves,* a bronze leaf with two fainter leaves suggesting tapestry.

On the plain plates come five: *Reflection,* a delightful combination of stark white and soft gray with white sprays; the immediately successful *Rose Elegans,* bluish-gray rim and Billingsley-type yellow roses; *Burgundy,* a rim rich with a green vine and berries; and *Cadence* and *Citadel,* each with a simple wreath inside the rim, the former blue-flowered and platinum-edged, the latter in gold.

Fairfax, white and gold, and *Old Colony* with blue flowers, bronze leaves and a broad blue rim are already adorning many tables. *Old Colony* could be the pattern to replace my *Cavendish*.

As yet bone china holds the prior position in their production. Mr. Kerry demonstrated the strength of theirs by setting a dinner plate on the floor and standing on it—he weighs 180 pounds. After he picked it up he flicked it with his finger. It rang like a bell.

Patterns which have been successful for years are *Tracery, Meadowglow, Queenslace, Sweetheart Rose, Rondeau, Thistledown,* and *Golden Maize* all in the coupe shape. One whose sales rocketed when Kraft selected it for a colored advertisement is *French Provincial,* pure white china with the authentic French Provincial design in the best gold. It has maintained its drawing power ever since and in any of their lists invariably ranks high.

At the moment their leading number is *Coronet,* a mate for *French Provincial* except that platinum has replaced the gold. Next comes *Glen Auldyn,* surprising to no one who has seen the soft clear hues of the entwined leaves, subtle as if under water on the fluted surface. Utterly charming on the same fluted shape is *Waverley,* stylized blossoms in muted blue on the gold-edged rim. Produced in the summer of 1961, already it bids to become a runaway.

I should like to tell you about some of the other delightful patterns coming out of the Burslem atmosphere, but must content myself with mentioning names: *Cotillion, Monteigne, Melrose, Millefleur, Adrian, Strasbourg, Tiara, Summer Song, Lyric, Chatelaine, Mayfair* (brown and tinted) as well as *Arcadia* and *Chelsea Rose.* With this array of titles, you can ask for them in the shops—and revel in loveliness.

When Sir Winston and Lady Churchill were made freemen of the town of Blackpool on the former's 80th birthday, the citizens decided to give them a present. They consulted Lady Churchill. At the time, the Churchills were using a much-riveted dinner service rescued from a fire in the Tuilleries. Lady Churchill wanted to present it to a museum. She chose Royal Doulton's *Rondeau* pattern, gold on white—and could they have it for their Christmas dinner? Sir Winston's birthday was November 30th, but the whole factory worked overtime to deliver it on Christmas Eve. The following week it was displayed at Blackpool, then returned to Chartwell.

Another famous white and gold set is the late Queen Mary's doll dinner set on exhibition for charity purposes at Windsor Castle. The gold crest was done under a magnifying glass.

We—myself, Larry Parks and his wife Betty Garrett, who were staying in the North Staffordshire and making a highly successful personal appearance in Stoke that week—watched them working on an order of 8,000 cups and saucers for the Canadian National Railways, a tremendous order for the Kodak canteens, and a large shipment of black crows with white vests—they could be used later as jugs—for Old Crow Whiskey, Kentucky.

Their most exciting and "adventurous" order was a fabulous service for an Eastern potentate, a service of 3,000 pieces, including vases, for Abdul Hamid II, who became sultan of Turkey in 1876, two years before Disraeli leased Cyprus for Queen Victoria. The order was placed in 1901 and took two years to complete. It was heavily insured by Lloyds' and arrived safely, but the arrival coincided with the overthrow of the government as a result of military insurrection. The ware was unpacked and put in storage, but Doulton's doubted payment so decided to get it back. Lloyds' insisted that the firm send one of their own packers to pack it. A man named Tom Clark was dispatched. He found it in perfect condition and got it aboard a cargo boat without incident. In the Bay of Biscay the ship caught fire and was lost. The entire service, worth many thousand pounds, is presumably on the ocean bed— a salvage job for Cousteau?

Doulton's biggest seller in dishes is *Bunnykins,* involving scores of bunny-land scenes. It is called the world's best nursery pattern—*noisery,* Larry said— and many thousand sets are sold each week. One reason for its popularity may be that it was used by Prince Charles and Princess Anne in the royal nurseries in Balmoral, and now is used by Prince Andrew.

Before being shown through the plant, we visited the elegant showrooms called "The China Cabinet." In the grand manner—grand also in size—were the trio, *St. George* by the late Charles J. Noke, *The Broken Lance,* and their best known figure, *Princess Bedoura.* The exquisite young princess, arrayed in the dazzling garments of the East, is journeying, as in Scheherazade's story, to her wedding to the sultan. Her face is incredibly alive, with an expression of confidence in her own beauty, curiosity about her future with a husband she has never seen, and perhaps a slight uneasiness occasioned by her ele-vated position on the elephant—you can almost see her sway. (How one would feel in a howdah I would not know. My riding has been limited to horses, a donkey ridden sidewise in Crete, and a camel in Cyprus.) Even the elephant's stance betokens concern for the comfort and safety of the fair burden.

After such magnificence, a homely note was supplied by a Scotty curled up on the hearth. Larry stooped to stroke it. No response. It was a porcelain pooch.

England is a country of dog-lovers. (On Saturday afternoons the crowds "go to the dogs"—whippet races where live dogs streak after an electric hare and you may bet pennies.) Capitalizing on the devotion, Doulton's have brought out a full line of ceramic canines, all modeled from named champion dogs and actual portraits from life. Each model comes in three sizes, large about 7½ inches, medium 5 inches, and small about 4 inches. As gifts to take home to dog lovers they cannot be beaten, any more than their champion prototypes could have been.

Another amazing collection is that of Doulton's *Rouge Flambée* or *Veined Sung*. The story is that the ware originated when a Chinese potter, in desperation because a piece he was firing had not turned out as he hoped, threw himself into the kiln. When his survivors opened it, they found the first example of the famed pigeon-blood, supposedly a result of the oxygen consumed. None of the other potteries, using the trial and error method, has so far been able to produce it. It is the only secret at the Doulton plant, but so secret is it, kept under lock and key, that not even the senior executives are allowed in the room where *Rouge Flambée* is made.

The most popular example is the elephant, regarded as a good luck piece though given with a warning, "If you want to be lucky, keep its trunk pointing east." I felt as Betty did when she said, "If I owned a *Rouge Flambée* elephant, I'd consider myself lucky no matter which way the trunk pointed."

Another specialty to bring Royal Doulton much renown is the Toby jug, its triple-spouted tricorn making it a perfect receptacle for beer and ale. (If you would like to know about it in detail, read the lavishly illustrated, highly interesting *Good Sir Toby* by Desmond Eyles.) These drinking vessels originated in Germany and were called *steins,* as they were made of stoneware. Invariably they bore a replica of a human head as the first ones were improvised by cutting off the heads of the ornamental figures imported from the Far East.

The most celebrated mugs of the late Middle Ages were *bellarmines,* potted at Cologne for Netherlands Protestants who demanded a "derisive caricature" of one Cardinal Bellarmine. A surprising number of them were found, in perfect condition, hidden under thresholds and floors of old Elizabethan and Stuart houses. Some, Eyles says, contained handmade iron nails, twisted wire, human hair and fingernail cuttings, evidently used in the practice of magic, a belief being held that to bury a drinking vessel would give protection against "ghoulies and ghosties and long-legged beasties, and things that go bump in the night."

Gradually the bellarmine evolved in England into the best known of all jugs in human form, a convivial seated toper, circa 1770. Everyone had his own Toby jug, including the children in families which could go to such lengths of extravagance, for in those days even the weans drank "very small beer," as today the children in France and Italy drink watered wine. But it was not until the early 1930's that Charles J. Noke, then chief designer at the Royal Doulton potteries, was inspired with the idea of a twentieth century revival of the old Staffordshire Toby jug.

Noke, Sr., was an antique dealer. Many rare old Toby jugs had passed across his counter. From childhood, the son had been fascinated by them. He was a gifted modeler. His first character jug—character jugs are of head and shoulders only—was instantly popular. This was the famous *John Barleycorn.* Doulton's could not produce them fast enough to take care of their orders. From it, Noke went on to an almost unending list. *Old Charley. Parson Brown. Dick Turpin.*

Dickensians are probably the greatest collectors of Toby jugs. No wonder. All the familiar figures are there. *Sam Weller. Mr. Pickwick. Oliver Twist. Micawber. Sairey Gamp* with her umbrella. . . .

Probably next in the collecting ranks come members of the Shakespeare clubs. Needless to say, their favorite is the lovable rogue, Sir John Falstaff, so graphically described by one writer as "sensual, mendacious, boastful and fond of practical jokes, and a mountain of fat"—as the Bard of Avon put it, "more flesh than another man, and therefore more frailty," which has made him the horrible example for a current T.V. program sponsored by the manufacturer of a reducing food.

Other fictional favorites are *Long John Silver, The Pied Piper, Friar Tuck,* et cetera. From real life are *Samuel Johnson, Dick Turpin* the highwayman, *Dick Whittington* who, hearing the Bow Bells, continued on to London where he thrice became Lord Mayor, and *Drake* who played bowls while the Spanish Armada approached. A perennial best-seller is *Izaak Walton,* a jug issued to commemorate the tercentenary of his book, *The Compleat Angler.*

Doulton's have not overlooked the American market. Heading the list is *Rip Van Winkle,* with next in line *Johnny Appleseed,* the all-alive-o New England character who traveled on foot through Ohio, Pennsylvania, Indiana, and Illinois, planting appleseeds near the settlers' cabins.

If you go to Oxford, as you certainly will if you visit England at all, do not miss the collection of Toby jugs at the New Inn—it is next to the post office across from Christchurch, in New Inn Hall Street, a continuation of the Cornmarket. There are 34 in the small front bar alone. The collection was started by a former proprietress, a Mrs. Stringer, who intended to have none but old ones. By the time she had launched her project, the craze was on, and prices had soared to such heights that she had to be content with recent productions.

Beginning a Toby jug collection while in England means a great saving, for, having an open top and a handle, they go through as jugs, consequently without a luxury or purchase tax. To collect old and rare ones takes a person of genuine wealth. A Ralph Wood *Prince Hal,* bought some years ago in a Crewe antique shop for a song, is now worth hundreds of pounds. Another Wood jug, *Martha Gunn,* the Brighton bathing attendant who catered only to royalty, in 1918 brought 600 guineas, then about $3000, at an auction at Christie's.

You have also to contend with forgeries. The crazing of age cannot be simulated, but burying the jug in the ground for a while or rubbing it with coffee can achieve a disarming forgery.

Fortunately you can have a heap of fun collecting modern ones. Besides, the Royal Doultons of today will be the Whieldons and Woods of tomorrow. Time is on your side.

Figurines, as well as such hollow ware as vases, jugs, tureens, and so on, are best made by casting, that is, in molds.

The original mold, either in clay or plaster of paris, is made from the drawings of the designer, an important person who thoroughly understands all the materials and all the processes, for example, how the different clays react and which temperature suits them best. He works in collaboration with the various departments to ensure that what began as a gleam in his eye becomes a visible object in the marketplace.

His drawings go to the modeling shop where the modeler makes a perfect reproduction, though allowing for the shrinkage from wet clay to dry clay size as well as from the firing. From this original model a *block* mold is made, and from it the *case* mold, the source of the potter's working molds. Because of their water-absorbing qualities, they are made of plaster of paris. Each is used only five or six times.

A mold always consists of at least two parts, more if the shape requires it in order to be removed easily after drying. When molds are made of many parts, all pieces must fit exactly—bad joins leave raised "seams." Notches are made in one part to lock into recesses in the other.

The caster makes his cast by pouring slip, a little thinner than batter, into an opening in the plaster of paris mold. A coating of clay is thus deposited on the inside, its thickness depending upon the length of time it is left there. The surplus is emptied into a trough and returned to the blending ark for use again.

In drying, the clay contracts and can easily be lifted out when the mold is opened by separating its parts. It may be complete. It may require the luting of handles, spouts, arms, and feet which have been molded separately. Then it is *fettled*—that is, cleaned with a metal tool—until every trace of joins is removed and the lines are pure.

After its biscuit firing, it is again inspected for flaws—warping, nipping, iron marks and impurities, bad bases, and so on. Rejected pieces are destroyed. On the others, the name and mark of the firm are transfer-printed on the bottom. They are then ready for the final painting, glazing, and glost firing.

On the earthenware figures such as *The Cobbler, The Mendicant, The Carpet Seller,* better expressions, including wrinkles, as well as more earthy and primary colors can be achieved than on bone china figurines. One of unwaning popularity is *The Old Balloon Seller.* Scores of letters come from America every year asking if the original was once a famous English actress reduced to selling balloons on the streets of London.

"Was she?" we asked.

Our guide shrugged. "Your guess is as good as mine."

Up to the Doulton era, figurines such as those made at Bow, Chelsea, and Derby had been modeled on characters from the *Commedia dell'Arte*—stylized Italian comedy—which had come to Rome via the Etruscans and the Greeks. Most of the figures were inspired by ballets or masques. The favorites were *Harlequin, Pantaloon, Columbine,* and *Pierrot.* Then came the lover and his beloved. Next, the soubrette, slightly less artificial.

Royal Doulton created a new genre. Collectors of the *Commedia* figurines look down their noses at it, claiming that it is too sweet and sentimental. What if it is? It has resulted in figurines with which we can identify ourselves.

As Betty does figurines herself in her Beverly Hills home, quite large ones which she gives to her friends, she was interested in observing some of the more professional details. One young woman, on piece work, took time off to demonstrate a special process and let the visitor try it until she mastered it.

If the Hollywood star was interested in their work, the employees were interested in her. A steady procession of the younger ones crowded about Larry and his charming wife for autographs.

"The only time anyone ever wants my autograph," I said ruefully, "is on the bottom of a check."

Doulton figurines caught on in the first place because, after the ornateness and *bocage* of old Chelsea Bow, and Meissen figures, their simplicity was refreshing. There is an airiness about many of them, and not only in their names such as *Top o' the Hill* and *Autumn Breezes.* Both the *Ballerina* and the *Gypsy Dancer* doing a flamenco became the rage as soon as produced. The child figures are captivating, for example, *Little Pig* and *Sweetie*. Undeniably the favorite is the one which Queen Mary named. She saw it at an exhibition and exclaimed, "What a darling!" Now it is known as *Darling*.

At first it came as a bit of a shock to see so many *Top o' the Hills*. Somehow I had felt that mine was the only one, especially made for me. Yet it was, for each is given an individual treatment as if the only one of its kind. There is no such thing as mass production. The work is all done by hand, and the hands are the hands of artists. Even to learn to paint dresses requires that a girl be trained for six months.

Royal Doulton allows women to paint their own faces but not the faces of the figurines. That is left to the men. Women, they contend, are prone to paint an idealization of themselves, or their favorite screen star. (After that afternoon, every *Top o' the Hill* and *Lady Charmian* would have been a Betty Garrett.) Besides, no firm can afford to provide three years' training for a woman, then have her leave to get married and have children.

It may go deeper than that. Men may be better judges of feminine beauty. We asked one who was putting in the blue eyes of *Top o' the Hill*, "Don't you ever get tired of it?"

"Tired of beauty, of being surrounded by beautiful females, Madam?— Still, one might. A chap makes eyes all day long, and where does it get him? No farther," he added with a twinkle, "than a platonic friendship does."

Chapter 8

Royal Crown Derby

VISITING Derby, most men go to the Rolls-Royce works, most women make a beeline for that unfailing magnet, the Royal Crown Derby plant.

The showrooms with their plain gray walls and wall-to-wall carpet of a rich tomato red do nothing to detract from the opulence of the display pieces. They provide a chaste setting for the exquisite gems.

Outside in Osmaston Street the company's six smart green vans set out, purring a splendid and sustained publicity. Yet, little as it must seem that they have anything in common, once you have heard the legends, in your mind's eye you cannot help seeing instead of them the caravans of the English gypsy.

The English gypsy is a king, and a law unto himself. Many of the tribe are fabulously wealthy. They make money in varied and often devious ways, and pay no income tax. They do not deposit their money in banks, but secrete it in sundry hiding-places. Mr. Colin Osborne, the affable export director who received me, was in a local china shop one day when one of these Romany gentlemen peeled off a hundred and eighty-two pound notes from his roll, and laid them on the counter. At the then current rate of exchange, it was nearly $900.

He was not buying the business, merely a dinner service, of Royal Crown Derby. For formal occasions, these stiff-necked English gypsies refuse to eat off any other ware. Only three patterns at that, three that came in after the Napoleonic Wars—*Derby Japan*, the "cigar" pattern, and two similar ones known by the numbers 1128 and 2451, all Imari patterns in Chinese red, deep cobalt, and pure burnished gold, every line freehand. Imari, as you may know, was named for an Oriental factory and brought by Marco Polo to Europe where it reached perfection at the end of the eighteenth century. Of these, many gypsy families possess five hundred pounds' worth.

Careless as these itinerant folk appear to be with their household belongings—living in caravans may be conducive to that—they accord the greatest reverence to their china. What they call "washing up the good pots" is practically a rite. A single piece broken is a tragedy accompanied by heartfelt lamentations.

Yet—yet there comes a time when at a single stroke the whole set is sacrificed to tradition. When the owner of the gypsy caravan dies, the caravan and all its contents are put to the torch, a Romany version of a Viking's funeral.

"Surely not the dishes! Not the Crown Derby!"

Yes, Crown Derby and all.

Once a daughter-in-law thriftier than the others—an alien, born on the wrong side of the blanket—decided to salvage the precious set. As the old patriarch lay dying, she carried it out stealthily piece by piece. In a moment of clairvoyance he came out of his coma and sounded the alarm. Result: a feud. While the old man died untended, the tribe occupied itself in breaking the dishes over the head of the culprit and her husband. The next morning the pair was forced to toss the shattered fragments to the last shard into the blazing caravan, and not to the accompaniment of wailing but to violent imprecations. Then they were turned out to fend for themselves, forever pariah.

The Royal Crown Derby Porcelain Company, dating from 1750, claims to be the oldest of the six members of the Fine China Association.

Porcelain was first made at Derby by André Planché, born in England in 1728 of refugee French parents. His father, who had worked with the Meissen people, taught his son so ably that by seventeen he was modeling dogs, birds, and so on which won acclaim. At first, until he had earned enough money to buy himself a kiln, he fired them in a pipemaker's oven.

A Londoner named William Duesbury set up an enameling establishment in his native city in 1750. People took him plain porcelain to be decorated, the patterns exclusively their own. (The first piece he did is in the Victoria and Albert Museum.) He made such a name for himself that the manufacturers of the porcelain froze him out.

Around 1755, he went north to Derby and bought the old Derby Porcelain Factory near Mary Bridge on the Nottingham Road, and took Planché in as partner. The latter turned out to be a man of dissolute habits, and Duesbury faced bankruptcy. But he fought on, and in 1769 purchased the famous Chelsea works. Christie's disposed of his wares at annual sales, his greatest competitor and rival then being Wedgwood.

The firm was given a boost by the visit of George III in 1773. The monarch was so greatly impressed by the elegant productions he was shown that he granted Duesbury a patent to stamp his wares with a crown. Thus originated the name *Crown* Derby.

In 1776 Duesbury bought the renowned Bow works in London, but in 1784 he closed it and all his factories except the one at Derby, to which town he moved all the wares and equipment. In that northern town he died at the age of sixty-two, leaving a thriving and reputable business to his son, William Duesbury II.

The son acquired an enterprising partner in the person of Michael Kean, an Irish-born Londoner and a miniaturist. Shortly after the death of Duesbury II in 1796, Kean consolidated his position by marrying his partner's widow. His painters, in particular his two best ones, William Billingsley and Zachariah Boreman, could not get along with him, and left. Nor was there a harmonious relationship between him and his stepson, William Duesbury III, who was rapidly growing up. In 1808, when the young man attained his majority, he married the daughter of a wealthy London customer named Sheffield. Kean opposed the marriage, probably because Sheffield had tried to "buy in" as a partner and had been flatly turned down. Sheffield bided his time. When Kean retired in 1811, the firm became Duesbury and Sheffield. Unfortunately, neither was a potter. The running of the plant was left to Robert Bloor, a trusted senior clerk. He and his brother Joseph tried resolutely to halt the decline which Duesbury's waywardness and Sheffield's incompetence had set in motion.

The Battle of Waterloo in 1815 brought the Napoleonic Wars to an end. The Derby warehouses were crammed with undecorated china. Bloor revived the Japanese Imari styles which had been popular around 1700. (Most pottery firms used them, but nowadays they are thought of as distinctly Royal Crown Derby.) A selling campaign which smelled to heaven saved them temporarily, but, overworked, Robert Bloor went insane in 1828. He died in 1845. Joseph, who had carried on alone for almost twenty years, died in 1846. Robert's son-in-law, Thomas Clarke, undertook the management, but without success. It seemed inevitable that the factory would have to close.

This, a group of six potters and artists protested, could not be allowed to happen. They clubbed together and by using their own small savings, borrowing from friends, and selling personal belongings, they finally had sufficient funds to purchase the best of the models, molds, formulas, pattern books and so on, as well as the right to continue production and use the firm's marks. They established themselves in smaller premises in King Street, Derby, and kept the plant going in the face of tremendous odds. The total number of employees never exceeded forty, but they had the satisfaction of feeling that the Crown Derby factory still operated.

In 1876, three gentlemen by the names of McInnes, Litherland, and Benross, together with a Mr. Phillips formerly of Worcester, decided to revive the industry on a more substantial scale than was possible in the King Street premises. They established a pottery in Osmaston Road, on the present site— the two merged in 1935—and went after the overseas market. In fourteen years such progress had been made that Queen Victoria granted them a Royal Warrant, with the privilege of using the Royal Coat-of-Arms, and commanded that the company henceforth be known as the *Royal* Crown Derby Porcelain Company.

Some later Royal Crown Derby marks.

In 1938, the late Mr. H. T. Robinson became chairman, and Mr. Colin F. Osborn sales manager and director. By 1953 there were 450 on the payroll, 60 of whom were gildresses. Individual kilns rather than tunnels had been installed. Heated by electricity, they attain a heat of 1200 C. and could do 1400 C., a feat only equaled at Barlaston, but the ware would suffer.

Philip Robinson, the tall, loose-jointed son of the late chairman, succeeded his father as acting manager. Like him, the other directors were young, up-and-doing, and purposeful, with a capacity for combining fun and laughter with work. One of them, Peter de Waller, had just completed a tour of the Middle East and gravely handed me his calling card—in Arabic.

He had carried samples worth a king's ransom, for, he claimed, china was bought as much by tactile as by visual sense. The highlight of his trip was a fabulous order from a Middle East potentate. The latter's name was not mentioned, but a large framed photograph of that inveterate collector, Ibn Saud, was prominently displayed in the director's room. Near it was one of the plates of the set. From the amount of twenty-karat gold fired into it, it might almost be termed solid gold. From the price too, I decided later when I saw one of the six soup tureens in Tiffany's bearing a tag marked $1000.

Another time I attended an exhibit of Royal Crown Derby in Tiffany's which included fifty-two treasures dated from 1750 on. There was an inkwell presented to H. R. H. the Princess of Teck on her marriage to George, Prince of Wales (later George V) valued at five thousand dollars. A handled vase painted by Desire Leroy in 1881, with enameled Chelsea peacocks on a duck-egg blue groundlay, was marked nine thousand dollars. A fluted plate and an after-dinner coffee cup from the service commissioned by the townspeople to commemorate the eight-hundredth anniversary of the City of Derby were the least expensive—priced at fifty dollars each.

At Barlaston I had seen lithographing in color on earthenware. At Crown Staffordshire photolithographing on the Marquess of Queensberry's "fighting" ashtrays. At Spode-Copeland I had seen enough of transfer printing to arouse my curiosity, and at Minton's had been given a paper pattern of their encrusted gold. In Derby the time had come for me to see these processes in detail and get them straight in my mind.

What set me off on this tack was Roger Allen, the youngest director, who had been deputed to show me the plant.

"As a Canadian, you'll probably be interested in an order for Canada on which we are working overtime—fifty thousand pieces of china-handled cutlery, and a hundred thousand pieces of *Blue Mikado*."

When I told him that my mother had given me a *Blue Mikado* tea set for my hope chest, he had the printer run off a couple of transfers for me to take home and compare for details and size—"which means to check for the one-eighth or one-tenth shrinkage."

A pattern designed to be reproduced by printing is first drawn to fit the curves and planes of the pieces to which it will be transferred. It is then hand-engraved upon copper plates or cylinders with a sharp pointed steel graver or burin. Light and shade effects are obtained by minutely graduated punch dots. So meticulously fine is some of this work that the engraver must observe the movements of the point of his burin through a magnifying glass. The craftsmanship calls for the highest degree of skill and can be acquired only after years of experience.

When the design is complete, the soft copper plates, about an eighth of an inch thick, are nickel-plated for greater durability. Formerly they were placed over a stove and slightly heated to facilitate the spreading of the printing color over the surface with a *squeezer*. These days they are placed on an electrically warmed plate in the printing shop, or, in the case of cylinders, heated by an electric element in the center. The latest method of controlling ink distribution for lithographic printing is, of course, the nuclear thickness gauge built in the inking rollers.

The color, blended into a thick paste with various oils, is worked all over the engraved copper to ensure that each line or *channel* which represents the design has been filled. All superfluous paste is removed with a palette knife, and the surface of the copper cleaned where it is to show white.

At one time, prints were taken off the copper plates by hand. A sheet of tissue paper was specially prepared by saturating it with a solution of soap and water. Then it was carefully laid, wrinkle-free, on the copper plate which was passed between the flannel-covered rollers of a mangle-like press, and later peeled off.

Now power-operated printing machines are employed, with copper cylinders printing the pattern in a continuous roll. Several thicknesses of flannel around the rollers absorb the surplus moisture from the paper which in turn draws out the color from the channels of the plate. These long sheets, bearing a complete imprint of the pattern, are automatically peeled from the cylinder while still damp. I took a picture of them hanging on lines to dry. The room looked like a street in Chinatown decked out for the New Year.

The transferrer skillfully manipulates her scissors and cuts away all unnecessary paper from the transfers, and also separates the border design from the central pattern. With its sticky surface bearing the engraved pattern, the transfer is thus ready to be affixed to the white body of the ware. For underglaze printing, the bisque piece is coated with a fine glue or varnish to facilitate the adherence of the paper transfer.

The print is laid face down on the ware, care being taken to make sure that the joints in the pattern are neat. The back is rubbed vigorously with a soaped flannel or ball pad, then with a hard brush to ensure that the print adheres firmly and evenly, and that the color is forced from it into the surface of the biscuit.

After standing for a few minutes, the paper is washed away with a wet sponge, leaving the pattern transferred to the ware. It is then passed through an electric kiln or hardening oven at a temperature of 780 C. This fixes the color on as well as burning out all traces of oil in order that the glaze will adhere evenly over the piece. In the case of overglaze, it is done to fuse the enamel to the glaze.

Glazing the printed biscuit is a delicate process. Each piece is hand-dipped in a bath of the glaze which for the time obscures the design. Most earthenware colors are underglaze, and will last forever, though, as I shall add repetitiously, the number of colors is limited by the high temperature of the glost oven.

Many pieces are printed in outline only, and the colors filled in by hand while still in the biscuit state. Other outlined wares are fired, and the enamels added afterwards. This allows for a greater range of colors, and is usually employed with ornamental pieces. If evenly executed, it may be that the touch of the individual paintress is distinguishable.

Another process which interested me was stenciling, used when a colored background or *groundlay* is required to contrast with a printed or painted design.

A woman operative called a stenciler sketches a line to show the depth of the band of color to be produced. She covers the remainder of the article and all parts of the pattern which are not to receive the groundlay with a medium readily washed away in cold water.

The piece is then taken over by the groundlayer. She first paints a thin coat of oil over the whole surface, and pads it with a piece of silk filled with cotton wool until she has assured an even distribution of the oil. Now the color—pink, blue, yellow, red, green, as the case may be—is dusted on and adheres to the oil coating.

After a short time it is returned to the stenciler. She immerses it in water to dissolve the mixture from that part of the article not to be groundlaid, thus leaving the band or border the color desired. The article is now ready for firing in the enamel kiln. If required, further decoration is applied.

This may be done by a painter whose skill lies in her ability to paint freehand on pottery. She must possess real drawing ability, for she has to space and adapt the pattern to many different types of pieces. Again, it may be done by means of printed patterns.

These may be enriched by the addition of ceramic colors. The painting of them calls for great skill on the part of the painter also. She must exercise great care in applying them in the correct strength, for ceramic enamels, being derived from mineral oxides, may suffer chemical reactions during the firing and come out with changed tints. Fortunately, the range of onglaze enamels is unlimited, and they are made durable by firing at a comparatively low temperature in the enamel kiln.

Crown Derby has always been fortunate in its decorators. William Billingsley lived around Derby from 1774 until 1795, and designed for them under another name. A remarkable example of his flower painting is the Prentice Plate with 32 roses. Three generations of the "decorating Hancocks" served

Derby, with several from each family after the second generation. Fidèle Duvivier, a member of that famous family from Liège, did much distinguished work in the four years he was employed there. Altogether 33 stars are listed, not to mention a train of lesser luminaries.

An outstanding flower painter in a botanical style was William—"Quaker" —Pegg. At the height of his success he heard a chance Calvinist preacher and was convinced that by painting china he was pandering to mere luxury. He destroyed most of his patterns and began manufacturing stockings, Derby then being the center for that trade. Later, he married again, got out some of the drawings he had luckily preserved, and returned to his vocation.

Their chief designer now is Philip Robinson. One of his most highly acclaimed designs, *Vine,* came about by chance.

During the Second World War, the Rolls-Royce plant, which makes airplane engines, was a regular target of the Nazi bombers. One evening in 1941, as a member of the Derby Ambulance Corps, Philip Robinson was involved in a practice raid which became a real one. From 7 P.M. until 8 A.M. he was out of touch with H.Q. To pass the time in the vinery where he was stationed, he sketched the grapevine from life. The next day he started the modeling of the complete set at the factory. Fourteen days later the first plate was produced for an order amounting to £3000. It is still one of the company's most successful sellers. I am the happy owner of a coffee cup and saucer, known in the trade because of the cylindrical shape of the cup as "can and stand." *Vine* comes in blue and gold, white and gold, or, like mine, in glowing ruby red.

The popularity of Royal Crown Derby is a constant. Some patterns from the Chelsea-Derby and Derby periods of Duesbury's "thinly potted but not meagre" ware remain prime favorites. The old familiar Derby *Japan* and *Blue Mikado* keep on going, and many modern patterns take hold from the start. As an example, the dignified *Heraldic* was an immediate sellout, especially in demand by persons wanting a coat-of-arms on their dinnerware. *Paradise,* lavishly luxurious, employs its border of simulated shields in embossed, hand-gilded and burnished gold around a ruby ground with birds of paradise in raised gold.

Princess Scroll, chosen by the present Queen when a princess, and presented to her by the city of Derby as a wedding gift, is another favorite of brides-to-be. Possession of it gives them a sense of royalty, of being allied in a bond of sisterhood with the sovereign, of being queens themselves in the eyes of their new husbands.

Still another favorite is *Medway,* closely followed by *Chatsworth, Went-*

worth, Abbey, and *Lowestoft.* For dessert and gift items, the leader is *Chinese Bird,* one of Philip Robinson's own favorites.

Speaking of gifts, the boxed butter-dish-and-knife rakes in the shekels. The gift boxes themselves, also designed by Robinson, have boosted sales twelve times. Understandably! You can imagine a woman's delight when, after removing the tissue paper wrappings, she sees a box bearing the words ROYAL CROWN DERBY and the royal insignia.

A revival which is scoring a success is *Brittany.* Its pattern of raised enamel dots in bright colors stir up dreams in modern young brides. The large can-shaped coffee cup is sure-fire with her man.

When Nieman-Marcus of Dallas, Texas, opened their Derby section in 1956, they featured *Bali,* a stylized Imari pattern on the Boston Flute shape. Overnight it captured the public, and has continued to hold it. Its brilliant Derby red lotus with touches of cobalt blue and the restrained elegance of its gold rim have made its place among the Derby immortals secure.

Another recent immortal is *Rougemont,* on the same shape. It also employs the stylized lotus motif but *en camieu* in Derby red and in a geometric arrangement suggestive of the glories of Tung.

Unless I miss my guess, the new *Green Derby Panel,* in green and red, will join the ranks. It had just been put on the market when I was in the showrooms, so of course there was no report on sales.

A top-ranking dinnerware with cosmopolitan young American housewives is *Regency.* The shape, designed by Duesbury in 1760, was at that time covered with yellow roses. It did not go over, and was shelved. Towards the end of 1955 someone had the happy idea of "cleaning it up" by making it without its flowers. In plain white and gold, it is an outstanding number at Tiffany's. They had a table laid with it on the mezzanine. The center piece, a large footed and covered candy dish, was gold, as were the salt and peppers, the ashtrays, and the flatware.

Real gold? The only time I had ever seen real gold flatware was in the restaurant on the second floor of the Eiffel Tower. A friend had taken me to see the table set for a Bastille Day banquet at which the Duke and Duchess of Windsor would be present, at that date, 1938, not yet totally out of favor with the Paris public. A lace cloth extended over the edge of the table which was draped with opulent crimson plush heavily weighted by gold bullion-fringe. The flatware and goblets were of solid gold.

During the three years I lived in Kokomo, Indiana, I had become acquainted with flatware resembling gold. It was made at a local factory, and at another in Puerto Rico, of a very hard, durable metal alloy, with the "gold" color going right through. At one time it was called *Dirigold,* but this was considered misrepresentation so the name was changed to *Dirilyte.*

"Is this flatware," I asked the salesman, "gold or Dirilyte?"

"Madame!" he said in a horrified voice. "When you use that name in Tiffany's, you whisper."

Following the Sèvres fashion, Derby was the first English factory to use biscuit for figure models which, by renouncing glaze and color, simulated marble or stone. When the factory got into difficulties back in the early nineteenth century, they sold their models to Spode-Copeland, and gave up figure modeling. Fairly recently they revived the manufacture of both figurines and cabinet pieces. The latter, of course, being too valuable and too ornate for common use, are only for display.

Outstanding among the figurines are the peacocks, "high" and "low," known as the *Derby Peacocks.* They were first made in 1775, in a factory owned by Duesbury, the modeler being one John Whittaker. Each sells for upwards of 20 guineas or $60 without the purchase tax. (You can save this surcharge by having them delivered directly to your ship.) As the back view is as gorgeous as the front one, to exhibit them properly the peacocks must be placed before a mirror.

Rivaling that famous pair is another pair, the *Derby Dwarfs,* known earlier as the "Mansion House Dwarfs"—their prototype was the London sandwich man. In spite of the price, 30 guineas each, the company cannot keep up with the orders. The sales, limited only by the restrictions of production, continue unabated year after year. In wooing £.s.d and dollars into the coffers, the dwarfs have attained the stature of giants.

That is exactly what the Royal Crown Derby Porcelain Company has become in the third century of its existence. A giant among giants.

Now it gives promise of still greater growth, for the company was given a definite shot in the arm in October, 1960, when it was acquired by Mr. A. T. Smith, a well known English industrialist and patron of the arts. He occupies the position of managing director.

Although Mr. Smith has been at the helm for only a little over a year, he has gone far with his program. Part of his project, now completed, was the building of a new production wing with the last word in machinery, a new finishing warehouse and a new printing shop. Already output and exports are showing a decided increase. The pottery world, and china lovers, will watch with interest the progress of this revitalized giant, *Royal Crown Derby.*

William Duesbury, floating on his pink cloud, has reason to produce some merry music on his golden harp.

Chapter 9

Royal Worcester

UNLIKE the other five members of the Fine China Association, the sixth, Royal Worcester, has no background or tradition of family potting. From its inception, or conception, it had a "strictly commercial intention."

The idea germinated in the mind of one Dr. John Wall, born at Pewick, near Worcester. He was a Fellow of Merton, a medical practitioner with a considerable practice, the author of several medical papers, a portrait painter of some merit, and a designer of stained glass.

In 1750 he got into his hands, probably from Bristol, a formula for soft paste, of which steatite or soapstone was the basic ingredient. He interested a friend, William Davis, in the project and together they rounded up thirteen business men in forming a company in which they would become shareholders. The partnership was signed on June 4, 1751, only six years after Bow and Chelsea had been established.

The company had been launched with a capital of £45,000, the largest shareholder being a man named William Bayliss. Two brothers, Josiah and Richard Holdship, played important parts in the new venture, Joseph being in charge of the plant and Richard of decorating. The necessary publicity was taken care of by another partner, Edward Cave, editor of *Gentleman's Magazine*.

It had been decided to set up shop right in Worcester, the historic old city on the east bank of the Severn in Worcestershire, practically the middle of England. It had been occupied by the Romans. As early as 679 it had become the seat of a bishopric, and it had an eleventh century cathedral built by St. Wulfstan. It was the scene of Cromwell's final victory—the Battle of Worcester saw the complete rout of the Royalists. In short, it had atmosphere and history.

The pottery was established in Warmstry House, a commodious mansion with gardens extending to the Severn. To any but copyists, a Roman name must have suggested itself, for there had been potteries in the town in Roman days, but, seeming to feel that they must show a relationship with the Far East by incorporating the name of a Chinese location as Bow had done with "New Canton," their letterheads read, WORCESTER TONQUIN COMPANY.

No record of a financial transaction exists, but they seem to have absorbed Lowris China House of Bristol, Gloucestershire. (Originally a glass house, they manufactured some porcelain as attested by a figure, *Chinese Immortal*, inscribed "Bristoll, 1750." The same mark is on several sauce boats and butter dishes.) Apparently this was the result of manipulation by Wall and Davis, for they were awarded an extra amount equivalent to their shareholding for the secret of making steatite porcelain, also for arranging with the previous owners that no barriers be placed in their way once the transfer was effected.

The Bristol decorators had taken great interest in Chinese designs. Whenever a ship arrived from the Orient, they were on hand at the dock warehouses to borrow the imported porcelains of the East for long enough to copy them. Ships' captains were continually commissioned to bring back sample pieces for copying or adapting to speedy reproductions.

Bristol plates had octagonal, foliated, or scalloped edges. Spout cups had lids in the form of a crown with openware bows, and handles in the form of snakes or rolls of clay twisted into coiled tendrils. Sauce boats, adapted from silver plate and always with a thumb-rest on the handle, were among the principal pieces manufactured there. The wares had all the defects of soft paste, plus a few introduced involuntarily by the potters.

Having access to the Bristol material gave the Worcester Tonquin Company a head start. By the middle of 1754 production had advanced to the point of offering a great variety of merchandise at the Worcester Music Meeting. Within ten years of their opening, they had two hundred hands on the payroll, a good figure at that date.

The Worcester ware was a *pâte tendre*, nevertheless so hard that it resisted the file. Looked at against the light, their genuine old paste of that period shows a greenish tinge. Later they claimed that they had possessed the formula for bone ash china long before it came into use, but had not bothered with it as their own steatite formula was eminently satisfactory. It was suited to their glaze, at any rate—the glaze at Worcester was put on with a brush—for they had overcome crazing, and that was a great forward stride.

Their first pieces were copied from silver models with rococo reliefs painted in vignettes in reserved panels of underglaze blue or polychrome. One of the partners, Bradley, was a goldsmith in Worcester. It was probably at his behest that, to compete with their chief rival, Chelsea, such designs were issued.

93

Chelsea-wise, too, they specialized in small pieces—*compotiers,* pierced baskets, cider mugs, punch bowls, snuff boxes, perfume bottles, and tea and dessert services. As late as 1763 they had not completed a single dinner set.

Experts thought for a long time that they did not make figures, but recently records of a number have come to light. Upon investigation they were found to resemble Bow, and were probably the work of a Bow sculptor, a Frenchman named Thibault—the English spelled it "Tebo."

Some of their products resembled those of St. Cloud. They openly copied the birds of Sèvres. From Meissen they "borrowed" too, in particular the leaf-shaped dishes. But the strongest influence was French, for their favorite painters, emulated by their decorators, were Watteau, Boucher, and Pillimente, the chief exponents of rococo. To that style, Cox charges, Worcester clung long after it had been ousted everywhere else by neoclassicism. When they adopted the neoclassical style between 1775 and 1780, all originality stopped.

The famous "scale" patterns may have been derived from the Chinese, but the *oeil de perdrix* (partridge eye) and *cailloute* (pebble) were copied from Sèvres. Worcester made free with whatever they could—designs, shapes, processes, anything and everything which could be put to use.

Nor did they confine themselves to these legitimate things. They appropriated marks: the crossed swords of Meissen, the cross of Tournai, the horn of Chantilly, and the Chelsea anchor. But everybody did it, for it was not then an indictable offense. Actually it was a sort of compliment.

In spite of this sad lack of originality—when they borrowed, they borrowed well—between 1769 and 1789 Worcester contributed two decades of glory to the pages of English ceramic history. This "reign of glory" also had its inception in commercial intent, for in 1764 they decided to cater to a richer clientele, the genuine coachman-footman carriage trade. To bring this about they took as their guide the designs of Sakeida Kakiemon, the brilliant seventeenth century Japanese porcelain painter of Arita. (Arita and Imari are often confused though they are really the same, Imari being Arita's port and export center, and only a few miles away.) Kakiemon's ideal was simplicity. He loved white porcelain with delicately painted areas. His *Quail* pattern, used extensively at Chelsea and Bow, was now adopted at Worcester.

Their colors were superb, the most successful being apple green, pea green, copper green, turquoise, deep claret, manganese violet, and a beautiful pale canary yellow. But it was their blues which made them famous, and are remembered most today. Their powder blue was the old Chinese blue soufflé blown on through a piece of silk gauze. Their cobalt blue and enamel blue were unrivaled until Spode the Second reproduced them in his lively salmon-scale pieces.

Dr. Wall died in 1776, though what is known as the Wall Period lasted until 1783 when Davis died, and the Flight Period began.

This William Davis, one of the original shareholders, had taken over the management at Dr. Wall's death. Under him the quality declined. The business in which £45,000 had been invested fetched only £3000, in 1783 when sold to Thomas Flight, who had acted as their London agent.

Flight was a jeweler to the Royal Family. Putting his sons Joseph and John in charge of the works, he remained in London, controlling the plant from there. Profitably, too. Various royal personages to whom he had sold jewels ordered costly table services, his specialty being dinner, dessert, and breakfast services painted with armorial devices in full colors. Trade flourished, but quality continued to decline. While the Kakiemon ware remained good, the rest showed a lamentable lack of taste.

In 1783, George III and Queen Charlotte with three of the princesses visited the plant. The Queen selected a pattern of eight panels with a scalloped edge and much gilding. (This is not to be confused with the more familiar *Queen's* pattern with alternating panels, often arranged spirally, red on white, or white on blue, also gilt.) His Majesty ordered a blue and white set, bestowed upon Worcester the Royal Warrant, and graciously permitted them to use the prefix "Royal" in the firm's name.

Thomas Flight died in 1793 and left the business to Joseph, who took a partner named Martin Barr. The firm was known as Flight and Barr—changed to Barr, Flight and Barr in 1807 when Martin Barr II joined the firm.

In October of the following year, William Billingsley entered their employ. He brought with him his son-in-law, William Walker. The latter had developed a new muffle kiln which made firing less hazardous and results finer. It looked as if the firm were to have a new "reign of glory," for it became famous for its colors as never before. The new kiln made the cobalt blue richer, the sky blue softer. It produced a dull opaque green and a superb shade of ruby. Gilding became radiant, although in a few years it had lost that sheen and by 1820 had become brassy. Not in the time of Walker and Billingsley, however. They had left in 1813—taking French leave, the owners claimed.

Another young Barr, George, entered the firm. Under the name of Flight, Barr and Barr they carried on until 1840 when they joined a firm of decorators named Chamberlain.

The founder of this firm, Robert Chamberlain, had been Dr. Wall's first apprentice, and had risen to the post of chief decorator. In 1786, three years after Davis's death, he had set up his own decorating and enameling works in King Street, Worcester, putting his designs on china bought from New Hall, Lowestoft, Derby, Liverpool, but mostly from the Shropshire "Salopian" pottery of Caughley. Chamberlain's sons were his chief decorators, Humphrey for sporting subjects and Robert for flowers.

Within two years they found their premises not nearly large enough, and moved to the part of the city known as Diglis. There, financed by one Richard Nash, they built extensive premises on the Severn. This building is now occupied by the Royal Worcester Porcelain Works, the name of the firm since the formation of a limited liability company in 1862.

After their father's death in 1789, the Chamberlain brothers carried on, and even launched into the manufacture of bone china. They produced fine tableware. Orders poured in. But their indebtedness to Nash weighed them down, and the spate of orders taxed their limited resources. They approached Nash again for still more funds.

The new debt weighed more heavily than ever, but in 1802 their spirits got a lift when Lord Nelson and Lady Hamilton visited the plant. The famous lovers ordered a breakfast service, a dinner service, and a pair of vases. One of the latter was to have a portrait of the admiral supported by the figure of Fame, the other a likeness of the fair Emma—no mention of her being supported by Horatio.

Trafalgar in 1805, and Nelson's death, at once a momentous victory and a terrible tragedy for the country, was a disaster for the Chamberlains. The previous year they had been forced to borrow money from a family friend, G. E. Bolton, in order to make a down payment on the porcelain needed from Caughley. Now the countermanding of the commission of Nelson, plus their enormous bill at the Shropshire pottery, left them on the verge of bankruptcy.

Bolton came to their rescue. They carried on with a fair measure of success until 1828 when the firm came under the control of Walter Chamberlain and John Lily. In 1840 these two acquired the Royal Worcester Porcelain Company, and moved it from Warmstry House, where it had been for ninety-one years, to their Diglis plant on the Severn. They traded under the name of Chamberlain and Company.

The impetus given to the partners by the uniting of the two plants resulted in a creative production exceeding all their expectations. The Worcester eggshell china dates from that period, and their new apple green became celebrated for the beauty of its tint. In his book, Dr. Ernest Rosenthal mentions one dinner service which brought £4000, and many others were almost as high. Between 1840 and 1850, Worcester has been given credit for the major part of the fine china produced in England.

Then the company came under the control of W. H. Kerr and R. W. Binns, and the rot set in. The commercialism upon which Worcester was based became its all, and its proud record devolved into one of mediocrity. In 1865, five years after it had been converted into a limited liability company under the name which today stands above the door and beneath the Royal Warrant and the Union Jack, the once proud establishment made a jeweled dinner service to be presented by the city of Worcester as a wedding gift to the Countess of Dudley. If it had been the jeweled enamel of Sévres! But it was not. The gilding looked like brass, the strong colors did not make sense. To cap it all, the service was set with imitation gems—bits of glass!

Let me quote Cox:

This, a factory which had been one of the most distinguished ones of England, became one of the most flagrant destroyers of good taste. Late Worcester ware is nothing for a collector to be proud of.

Going from the museum, named for a Perrin of Lea and Perrin's sauces, to the plant bore this statement out, in so far as I was concerned.

The museum, I may say, made the trip, and the stay in the hotel, worth while. It was a treasure house. The large vases did not impress me—I had seen too many of them. Nor did I care for the elaborate decorations of the Regency period. But the early things! A "scaleblue" teapot and a pierced basket of the Wall period. Above all, a cabinet full of glorious porcelain produced between 1756 and 1780, decorated with the black transfer prints of Robert Hancock who is given most of the credit for the process. Incredible, the way each firm line and simple dot contributed to beauty. I could almost feel Hancock looking over my shoulder, and preening because the perfection of his work was being justly admired.

Worcester, in one of the most interesting districts of England, is a center for sightseeing, and the Diglis Hotel with its old-fashioned gardens sloping to the Severn, on which float armadas of stately swans, is a delightful hostelry, but when I return there it will be to see the Hancock *chefs d'oeuvres* again, and revel in them at my leisure.

My recollection of the plant is down-at-heel dinginess, dusty pottery, piles of wasters, aged and uninspired employees, and a guide who was completely indifferent once we had moved out of the sacred precincts of the past. No, at one point his face did light up: when he jubilantly informed me that, so up-to-date were their methods, they were experimenting with "airograph"—color *shot* into china.

Possibly it was that tidbit in combination with the gloom of the unlighted showroom which made apt the adjective "disheveled" used by one writer about the acclaimed Dorothy Doughty birds with what I consider their excessive *bocage*.

"Dust catchers!" I commented.

"Madam! They sell at £50 to £100 a pair in America and Canada. They do have snob appeal."

The only other current production I recall was a set of "gold" fireproof dishes also designed for our side of the Atlantic.

"They sell like hot cakes in the U.S.A. We ship them in tonloads, at £6000 a ton."

Where had I been keeping myself that I never saw them in an American kitchen?

After a long reflective walk, I dropped into a tearoom to think things over, to see what good I might say to counterbalance gold kitchenware being sent in tonloads, at £6000 a ton, to Americans and Canadians utterly lacking in taste but possessed of dollars and waiting to succumb to the snob appeal of exorbitant prices and a once famous name. I know that the plant produces acceptable dinnerware. In fact, in a shop not long ago I saw an extremely attractive set of unfamiliar design and turned a plate over to see who had made it. The mark, *Royal Worcester*, caused me to send an apology on the air.

The proprietress of the teashop showed me a lovely piece too, above her fireplace. The Queen Mother had ordered an equestrian statuette of the then Princess Elizabeth done in silver. Worcester undertook to duplicate it in porcelain, in full color, and sell the pieces the royal household did not take. In my estimation this figurine by Doris Lindner is the finest thing the factory has done for a long time.

"Very nice!" I said, feeling magnanimous.

Nice! . . . She bristled. No finer china was being made, nor ever had been made, than right here in Worcester. "My country right or wrong," I thought, and compared her belligerence with the serene confidence of the proprietress of the tearoom at Thame. "*Every* piece of Spode is an heirloom."

Her dishes were pretty. The mark on the plate I turned over was that of a Burslem potter. Naturally, a factory which was paid £6000 a ton for kitchenware would not cater to tearooms.

When I went out into the pungent smell wafted from Lea and Perrin's,

A Tiffany table setting with Royal Crown Derby *Regency* plates, shakers, small woven baskets for cigarettes, candlesticks, and center-Flemish vermeil flatware, Patrician goblets, vermeil owl salt and pepper piece. Cream soup bowls hold porcelain flowers.

A group of old bottlenecks at Derby

A turner at Wedgwood's. Working a lathe similar to that used for turning wood or metal, the turner shaves off the surplus clay with great precision to the correct line and dimensions. It takes years to master the operation.

A glazer at Spode's. At Spode's they dip each piece; all the painted pieces emerge a putty-colored beige until firing, when the colors magically reappear.

Wedgwood cooling on the rack after removal from the tunnel kiln.

The Portland Vase, Josiah Wedgwood's masterpiece in Jasper. Said Sir Joshua Reynolds in 1790: "I have compared the copy of the Portland Vase with original; I can declare it to be a correct and faithful imitation."

Wedgwood, photo by Peter Croydon

Table setting of Wedgwood's *Halford*, celadon and white with platinum trim. The celadon is right in the clay, therefore as durable as the clay itself.

Wedgwood, Woodallen Photographers

Study in charcoal and chalk: a classical black and white setting inspired by Cecil Beaton's costumes in the Ascot scene of *My Fair Lady*. Wedgwood accessories include a Parian bust of Venus, a Muse's vase, a Presentation vase, and black basalt ewer and bowl.

Wedgwood's old *Cream Colour* ware, renamed *Queensware* by Queen Charlotte, with the barbotine décor of medieval potters. In this case the raised flowers are in Wedgwood blue.

Wedgwood's *Avocado* comes in blue, as well as in a charming blend of yellow and clear brown-beige.

Spode, John Martin Ltd. photo

The Earl and Countess of Radnor with their son inspect their crested dessert service at the Spode works. With them are Mr. T. Robert Copeland (left), Mr. R. Spencer C. Copeland (center), and Mr. Harold Holdway (right), of Spode.

Spode

Spode's *Billingsley Rose*, painted by William Billingsley who because of bigamy could not travel under his own name yet made it immortal by his delicate roses. The pattern's popularity never wanes.

Spode's striking *Verdun* pattern is decorated with deep leather green and ivory or fawn in the reliefs and gold overprint.

Buttercup in Spode's earthenware is a pattern of delightful intimacy in yellow, green, and brown on a fluted ivory surface.

Colonel in Grey, Spode's swirling design based on an ancient Persian motif, is delicate gray on white, with gold scalloped edges.

Minton's gives two treatments to *Laurentian.* In the style shown the décor on white surface is raised enamel in two tones of rose, pointed up with gold.

Minton's *H 5041* has raised gold sprays on the rim and acid at the edge and below the verge. This is on a delightful gray ground.

Minton's *Ancestral* with its décor of lively yet restrained rose and blue star blossoms is in unceasing demand and promises to remain so for years to come.

Minton, W. H. Nagington & Son photo

French Green by Minton, one of the truly elegant new patterns whose discreet sumptuousness appeals to the carriage trade.

Minton

Minton's *Cameo in Grey*. Overnight this simple design in gray and white on the plain Latona shape became a favorite of current brides.

Crown Staffordshire, Hanley Studios

Black Check is one design in the range produced by the Marquess of Queensberry for Crown Staffordshire.

Crown Staffordshire, Bowen photo

At Crown Staffordshire Miss Barbara Linley-Adams, leading English sculptor, creates dainty blossoms for Sam Green's May baskets.

Among the popular earthenware figurines of Royal Doulton is the inimitable *Sairey Gamp*.

A Royal Doulton figure being released from its several plaster molds after the casting process.

Royal Doulton

Glen Auldyn, its fluted surface and flowers subtle as if seen under water, is one of Royal Doulton's most recent and best selling patterns.

Royal Doulton

Royal Doulton's new price-appealing translucent china in *Old Colony:* rich blues, warm brown, and white, employing an eighteenth century floral motif. (*Jewelry, Schreiner; fabrics, Schumacher; glass, Fostoria St. Regis; silver, Gorham Chantilly. A bride's luncheon table created for* The Bride's Magazine.)

Royal Doulton

A table setting of *Burgundy* by Royal Doulton, a translucent pattern with rich grape tones and platinum banding. (*Figurines, Royal Doulton Williamsburg collection; glass, Fostoria Classic Amethyst; silver, Reed and Barton Burgundy; candelabra, Gorham; linens, Leacock.*)

Royal Crown Derby

Royal Crown Derby *Bali,* a stylized Imari pattern in brilliant Derby red; touched with cobalt blue and a restrained gold rim. Its place among Derby immortals is secure.

Royal Crown Derby's *Rouge-mont,* on the Boston Flute shape, employs an over-all lotus motif from the Victorian tradition in a Derby-red geometric design.

The Derby Dwarfs, known earlier as the Mansion House Dwarfs. Their prototype is the London sandwich man.

Green Derby Panel in green and red, a newcomer of great promise to the Royal Crown Derby ranks.

Cobalt Heraldic by Royal Crown Derby, with a border of simulated shields in embossed, hand-gilded burnished gold and blue—or in red and plain gold.

Rörstrand's beloved Louise Adelberg designed the coffee service *Linnea,* named for the world-famous Swedish botanist, Carl von Linné.

Le Select, delicate mocha cups of translucent white porcelain, designed in her usual distinctive style by Sylvia Leuchovius for Rörstrand.

Rörstrand, Wezäta Studio

Tweed pattern, in feldspar china from Rörstrand, designed by Carl-Harry Stålhane.

Rörstrand, Wahlberg photo

Hertha Bengtsson's one-of-a-kind stoneware pieces designed for Rörstrand.

The Royal Copenhagen service, *Flora Danica*—Danish Flowers—is painted free-hand, the Latin name of each piece recorded on the back.

Painting *Blue Fluted*, the familiar and beloved Royal Copenhagen service now riding the crest of the wave for probably the tenth time.

Royal Copenhagen, Kostich Photos

A Royal Copenhagen artist giving the finishing touches to a pair of figurines.

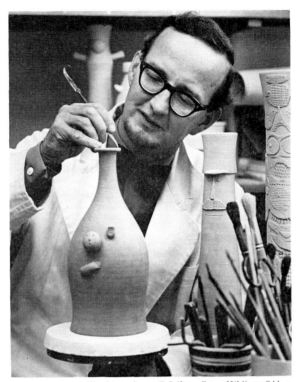

AB Gustavsbergs Fabriker, Foto Hilding Ohlson

The name now at Gustavsberg is Stig Lindberg whose faïence is known, and copied, the world over.

AB Gustavsbergs Fabriker, American Swedish News Exchange photo

Products of Gustavsberg's grand old man Wilhelm Kåge. Three pieces of his *Farsta* are shown here.

Hans Christian Andersen tells a story, a Bing & Grøndahl figurine.

Bing & Grøndahl's *Jule Aften* plate for 1961, designed by Kjeld Bonfils.

A popular new dinnerware pattern and shape. *Hazelnut*, by Bing & Grøndahl.

Arabia, three photos by Aarne Pietinen

The *Delicasy* series of jam jars and ovenproof casseroles and ramekins, designed by Ulla Procopé of Arabia.

Toned porcelain and varied colors of glasses at Arabia, the dishes in bone, pink, light blue, and light gray.

Friedl Kjellberg designed her superbly simple rice china, a "noble" porcelain, for Arabia and with it won recognition all over the world.

Porsgrund's only woman artist, Anne-Marie Ødegard, holds one of her plates. She was born Jørgensen, in case you see her name signed that way.

This Porsgrund horsewoman plate, *Myrtica Gale,* was designed by Konrad Galaaen, an artist who might be an intimate of the trolls of the countryside.

The greenhouse in which David Haviland opened his pottery in Limoges in 1842, and the factory which he built three years later.

The present Haviland factory in Limoges, where the extremely hard porcelain is produced according to the founder's standards.

Haviland

Torse White, Haviland's long-time swirled best-seller, awarded the Grand Prix at the Paris World's Fair in 1889.

Haviland

Haviland's *Bergère* on the Torse shape makes one think of the little shepherdesses who gather bouquets of wild bachelor buttons as they watch their flocks.

H-B, Quimper

Dinnerware from H-B, Faïenceries Bretonne de la Grande Maison, Quimper.

A group of Breton figures at the plant of Jules Henriot & Fils, Quimper.

"Oh dear, have I kept you waiting?"

Raymond Peynet, French painter and novelist, who has fathered The Little Lovers series for Rosenthal's, together with a cartoon and figures.

Rosenthal-Porzellan AG

Grooved vase made for Rosenthal's by the great ceramic artist Tapio Wirkkala, a Finn who has won the Grand Prix at the Triennial in Milan six times.

Rosenthal-Porzellan AG

The "2000" shape created by Raymond Loewy to skyrocket Rosenthal's American sales. The décor here is the adaptable *Gala Blau*.

Rosenthal-Porzellan AG

A table setting of Rosenthal's *Fortuna*, designed by Else Fischer-Leyden.

Lenox

The jewel-like effect on the *Rutledge* pattern by Lenox is created by hand applied raised enamel dots.

Westport by Lenox, an elegant design, features a solid border of Kingsley Blue decorated with a rim and band of 24-karat etched gold, plus a border design of gold print and raised gold paste.

Lenox's recent dinnerware pattern, *Meredith,* is one of restraint and timeless beauty, its subtle green scalloping enclosing a delicate raised gold shell.

the receiver, my first experience with an instrument of that type. As for food aboard, name it and you have it, even though a steward must go to the lowest hold. Their pre-midnight smorgasbord is an adventure in gourmet excellence, the captain's dinner a dramatic feast.

All Scandinavians are rabid individualists. This was brought to my attention vividly the first day I was in Stockholm. A friend had taken me to lunch at the famous Berns's, with its grand opera *mise en scene* and its windows overlooking the Royal Gardens. The largest restaurant in Europe, it has four dining rooms, one Chinese, as well as many small private ones.

After lunch we strolled through the King's Park where national crafts were exhibited in glass cases. (This was several years before they had opened their permanent exhibition, FORM.) The lamps took my eye. I had thought mine at home were fairly handsome but my first impulse was to take an SAS plane back and toss all but two onto the junk heap—and even about them I was not sure.

"If you go shopping for lamps," my hostess suggested, "don't just ask for lamps, but for lamps by—well, by Birger Dahl, a Norwegian, or by that clever Finnish woman, Lisa Johansson-Pape."

It struck me as odd, a Swede extolling the products of two foreign countries when there were certain to be distinctive Swedish lamps. Later, I found the same thing everywhere. All that counted was quality regardless of what country had produced it.

I also found that one bought by name. If you wanted a screen-printed tablecloth from STOBO in Stockholm, as I did, you did not go into NK and ask to be shown screen-printed tablecloths. You asked to be shown something by Nissi Skoog, Inez Svensson or Gota Tragird, to name only three leaders in that field. For silver in Stockholm the name was Sigurd Persson. At Georg Jensen's in Copenhagen either Henning Koppel or Magnus Stephensen. In Oslo, where one revels in David-Andersen's elegant store in Carl-Johansgate until one's senses swim, the name for the ravishing, and expensive, enameled silverware—*amalia*—was Theo Lie-Jørgensen. For stainless steel, the name is legion. Only for one product was there no choice—the unrivaled pewter with cutouts soldered on. In the whole world no one knows the secret of the process except the genius who invented it, the Norwegian craftsman, Mons Omvik.

When it comes to Swedish glass, you might go into such shops as Svenskt Glas at 8 Birger Jarlsgatan and say you are interested in both Orrefors and Kosta but you would prove yourself in the know if instead you mentioned Edward Hald or Sven Palmquist from the former and Vicki Lindstrand from the latter. Incidentally, when I was last in New York, Georg Jensen's were featuring Kosta, the oldest glassworks in Sweden, the glass center of the world.

Furniture allows a wide scope, for, as we all know, the northern countries make a specialty of it. To name only one designer from each country, let us choose Finn Juhl, a Dane, Bjørn Engø, a Norwegian, Axel Larsson, a Swede, and the great Finnish architect, Alvar Aalto.

Speaking of architecture, in Norway I asked my taxi driver if he could point out any examples of local design. To my amazement, he reeled off a list of architects a yard long, and casually took me to see a block of flats by Sven Brolid and Jan Walinde, and from there to a graceful, distinctive house by Anton Poulsson. Imagine the reaction if such a request were made to one of our taxi drivers.

This dissertation may seem as roundabout as the route over which the Oslo taxi driver took me, but it has an equally specific destination. What I am trying to show is the effect that this recognition and publicity has on the designers. We should try it in the United States and Canada. It may be one of the reasons that the Scandinavian countries have been able to produce dedicated artists, and make the phrase "Swedish Modern" stand for supremacy in so many fields.

Perhaps by now you will contend, as do many Norwegians, Danes, and Finns with justice, that a more comprehensive term would be "Scandinavian Modern." Yet in so far as our subject of porcelain is concerned, the phrase in current usage may go unchallenged, for the oldest name in Scandinavian ceramics is that of a Swedish pottery, Rörstrand, founded in 1726, four years before Josiah Wedgwood was born.

As you must have observed, the above lists contains no mention of ceramic designers. I omitted them purposely as you will be introduced to them in person, as it were, when we visit the other five Scandinavian potteries in the chronological order of their founding: Royal Copenhagen, 1775; Gustavsberg, 1820; Bing & Grøndahl, 1853: Arabia, 1874; and finally the lusty young one, Porsgrund, 1885.

So now to Rörstrand!

Chapter 11

Rörstrand

SWEDEN'S oldest porcelain factory originated in the minds of a group of twenty persons, officials and wealthy business men who were determined to restore their country's financial status after several disastrous wars. Meeting in the capital, Stockholm, on June 13, 1726, they formed an association, its object a factory where delft or faïence—earthenware in English, flintware in Swedish—could be produced. But while this was the avowed object of the project, their secret aim was to produce porcelain, an obsession of the kingly houses of Europe since the mystery of its manufacture had been solved at Meissen by the ex-alchemist, Johann Friedrich Böttger.

The site chosen was an old castle called Stora Rörstrand—Great Rörstrand —on western Norrmalm, at that time outside Stockholm's city limits. Their clays were brought from Devon and Cornwall, their manager imported from Germany. The first firing of faïence was carried out the following August in the presence of H. M. Fredrik I.

The next fourteen years saw three more German managers in the plant, one being the picaresque adventurer, Christian Conrad Hunger, an enameler and gilder at Meissen, whose name has gone down in infamy in the annals of the craft.

The story told me about Meissen when I was "barely knee-high to a flea" was that the arcanists and artists were kept imprisoned for seventeen years in a castle a dozen miles or so from Dresden. This was not exactly true, although being employed in the Castle of Albrechtsburg was tantamount to being in prison. Both employees and executives were under contract not to desert and take their acquired knowledge of processes and clays with them, the penalty for such defection being life imprisonment or death. In spite of this, several imbued with the idea of opening a profitable pottery of their own somewhere were willing to take the risk.

The most notorious escapee was Hunger, whose knowledge of the secret of

103

porcelain making was, to borrow Savage's expression, more than a little dubious. In 1717, lured by the promises of a Dutchman, Claudius Innocentius du Paquier, he went to Vienna as a director of their pottery at a salary of 1000 thalers with a carriage placed at his disposal.

History shows that Hunger was not one to stay put—it did not take his employers long to find out his shortcomings. In two years he lit out for Venice from whence the earliest European porcelain had come. In that city on the Adriatic he helped the Vezzi brothers to establish their third Venetian factory.

The subsequent career of Hunger is one of chopping-and-changing. Cox castigates him as an "untrustworthy disseminator of other's secrets," which he sold to the highest bidder everywhere—Venice, Stockholm, Russia. He even offered his services to the Royal Copenhagen people when kaolin was discovered on the island of Bornholm.

In 1745 he went to St. Petersburg to take charge of the factory opened by Peter the Great but then under the patronage of the Empress Elizabeth. He had been enticed there by a Russian baron who had met him in Stockholm where the faker and charlatan was trying to make contact with Rörstrand. The bait was a down payment of 1,000 species dollars, a guarantee of 1,000 rubles a year and the title of "Director of the Porcelain Factory of Her Imperial Majesty." For two years he was still making unsuccessful attempts to do something. The following year, 1748, he made exactly six little imperfect cups, and was summarily dismissed. It is claimed that the half dozen set the Russian Government back 15,000 rubles.

Hunger was last heard of in 1753 at Rörstrand. He and a man named Thelot apparently turned out some wares together. They signed some stove tiles, and also an octagonal tray painted in blue with a picture of "the feast of the Israelites at the foot of Sinai with Moses kneeling on the mountain," a subject, according to the critic Hannover, conceived in the "profane German spirit." Other pieces in blue and white were produced as well. Apparently the atmosphere of efficient Sweden was conducive to results.

By that time, the factory was in charge of a Swede trained on the premises. This was Anders Fahlström, who managed Rörstrand from 1740 until his death in 1760. From 1740 to 1750 production flourished, the ware mostly imported forms and patterns for the wealthy folk. The number of employees rose from 37 to 93. From the scattering of homes around the old castle of Stora Rörstrand a small town had emerged.

This decade was known as the First Golden Age.

But all was not gold that glittered. Finances were far from being all that could have been wished. In 1753 liquidation was avoided only by the establishment of a new company headed by one Elias Magnus Ingman, later raised to the peerage as Baron Nordenstolpe. Ingman moved house and home to the site. By dint of energy and ambition, he eventually owned the whole works.

That competition is the life of trade was never more clearly exemplified than at Rörstrand. Strangely, their greatest competition came from the Chinese, but their most feared was that of another Swedish company, Marieberg, founded in Stockholm in 1758. Stimulated by their rival's excellent output, borrowed from the rococo of Meissen and Sèvres, Ingman outdid himself. Two years later, with 128 employees, Rörstrand entered into its Second Golden Age.

Still their financial situation remained precarious. The market crash following a Whig election nearly proved fatal. Both Rörstrand and Marieberg were on the verge of bankruptcy. In 1782 the Nordenstolpe heirs bought out Marieberg. But times continued bad. Not even the astuteness of Bengt Reinhold Jeijer who became owner in 1798 could make Rörstrand-Marieberg a going concern. What accomplished it was the unexpected establishment in 1827 of the firm of Gustavsberg a few miles east of Stockholm. The new company had a dozen hardheaded business men, but men of vision, on its board. Rörstrand girded its loins for a battle royal. As things turned out, there was plenty of room for the two firms. Three years later affairs at both plants had actually improved.

What threatened to do both of them in was Wedgwood's *Cream Colour* earthenware all of a sudden sweeping Europe. It hit Rörstrand-Marieberg a smashing blow. On top of it, the English refused to ship any more clay to Sweden. That meant recourse to German clays, and they were of an inferior quality.

Before the older company went right to the wall, the English experienced a financial crisis. They were forced to sell their china clay and ball clay, and at better prices than before. Production at Rörstrand—they had dropped the hyphenated name—took an upward spurt, as well as a new fineness, for they had adopted many English production methods, and had even engaged a number of craftsmen from Stoke-on-Trent.

Another boost was their purchase of a pattern from Spode. The story is that one of the Rörstrand directors sold his daughter to get it, a piece of information I have never run across in any of the books about the great Staffordshire firm. Of course, it is claimed that history should be written by an enemy.

The owner in 1847 was Nils-Wilhelm Stråle of Ekna. In 1858, his heirs sold out to three business men who retained the name of the firm. In 1867 a limited company was formed. For the next three decades progress was tremendous, the turnover reckoned in millions of crowns. When the twentieth century dawned, there were a thousand employees on the payroll. Rörstrand had even branched out and established a factory in Helsinki.. (It was not a success and in 1916 passed into Finnish hands.) In 1923, they acquired also an old factory in Gothenburg, and formed a collaboration with another, a small one in Lidköping.* Torr Grönwall, the manager, liked the Gothenburg premises so well that he closed the old factory on the Norrmalm and trans-ferred the plant in its entirety to Sweden's great shipping port.

Grönwall was succeeded in 1939 by J. Magnus Bernström. World War II was then being waged. The owners of the small factory at Lidköping found it too much for them in the circumstances, and decided to put up their shutters. As Gothenburg was right on the sea, and in danger of enemy action, Bern-ström made a deal with the Lidköping people to carry on there for a while. It was to that small town on Lake Vanern that the present manager, Fredrik Wehtje, a lawyer, gradually transferred the whole plant, and year by year built it up into one of the best equipped potteries in Europe, with 1200 em-ployees resident in the thriving town.

Mr. Wehtje's hobby is animals. At one farm he raises horses, at another cattle, at a third poultry. His latest purchase was a farm for the breeding of swine. He claims that the idea was inspired by the little salt-and-pepper pigs designed by Rörstrand's youngest artist, Marianne Westman. When word of the new project leaked out, the potters banded together and made the manager a huge pottery porker—his piggy bank.

The first time I saw Rörstrand porcelain to recognize it, which means to fall in love with it was on the *Kungsholm*. The gift shop on board displayed ex-amples of the ware with such attractive names as *Rosemarin, Picknick, Koko, Safari*. Dainty white coffee services. Kitchenware combining utility with grace. An intriguing wall plaque, the saleswoman said, was the creation of a highly talented and imaginative young woman artist at the plant. But what really caught my collector's eye was a display of stoneware miniatures as lovely as jewels. They, above all, convinced me that a visit to Rörstrand, although deep in the hinterland of Sweden, was a must.

A train called the London Arrow connects Stockholm and Gothenburg. With a high sense of anticipation I boarded a coach pointed out by a trainman. Probably he thought I had a cold in the head, for he had directed me to a train going to Linköping (pronounced Leen-shipping), in the south towards Malmo. Into the bargain it was an express and had sped a hundred miles or so before we came to a stop. But the conductor wrote me out a cross-country

* Lidköping, pronounced leed-shipping. For "ski" the Scandinavians, and most cosmopolitan Europeans, indeed, say "shee."

schedule—five changes and it had begun to snow—and wired Rörstrand the hour of my delayed arrival. After acquiring a number of kind if nameless friends I finally arrived at Lidköping where, through the courtesy of the Stockholm head of SAL, I was met by Rörstrand's charming hostess, Margit Risberg, and taken to my hotel and fed. After breakfast the next morning—there was a rose on my tray—she came to take me to the plant. Getting lost in friendly Sweden is rather fun.

Rörstrand, buried in the country, I had visualized as small and primitive. Modern in the extreme, the plant occupied a whole city block. The parking lot across the road had a few executives' cars and 1200 bicycles for 1200 employees. The industry supports a town of 16,000 persons. Its wares go throughout the world. In the U.S.A. alone are over 500 shops selling Rörstrand china.

In the foyer my attention was directed to the huge ceramic animals of Gunnar Nyland—his being an architect may explain his working in the massive. His animal sculptures in chamotte stoneware are unique. Chamotte, let me explain here as the term will recur, is fragments of already fired clay, such as old saggers ground to powder, and used with a mixture of fresh clay. In firing, the old material serves to diminish the shrinkage.

The showrooms have been composed with effective simplicity—no array of expensive porcelain placed to "glisten" with heavy gold. With intent, Rörstrand uses gold sparingly, except in the monogrammed dishes greatly in demand since they made the handsome service with the letters OM beneath a crown for the women of Westergotland to give to their Princess Martha when she was married to King Oscar of Norway.

Modern Rörstrand marks.

Particularly to be admired were some tile tables, especially one in jade green made to order for a restaurant. The first three rows of tiles had a charming pattern of diapered flowers. Instead of a fourth row was a planter against the wall. The effect was extremely pleasant, and one which could be readily adapted to the home or patio.

107

In direct contrast to the massive works of Nyland were the stone miniatures, like those I had seen on the *Kungsholm,* but here arranged behind glass on shelves in the wall as if pieces of jewelry. These gems, as Miss Risborg rightly named them, were the creation of Carl-Harry Stålhane, peerless in that realm, and a dedicated artist who has already added immeasurably to the prestige of modern Rörstrand.

"Rörstrand" and "dedicated artists" are practically synonymous. Not that, like Topsy, they just grew. Rather were they the outcome of a rebellion.

In 1914 at the Baltic Exhibition, the company submitted a large display. If it had not been labeled Swedish, it could not have been told from any other there. Swedish artists staged a protest. Could not their country, with its intrinsic taste, evolve something of its own, not copied and imitated styles, abreast of the times though these were?

The upshot was that Rörstrand realized the necessity for artists with originality, great artists, and engaged Edward Hald, now the grand old man at Orrefors, and Louise Adelberg, who retired at seventy but still drops into her studio whenever homesickness for that environment overcomes her, or when, which happens frequently, she has a new idea.

The day I was there was not one of her days, alas! so I did not meet Rörstrand's oldest artist, but wherever one goes in Europe or America one sees her finely ribbed or fluted coffee set, *Linnea,* named for the world-famed Swedish botanist, Carl von Linné.* After forty years of production, *Linnea* with its dainty spray of flowers is still one of the most popular and profitable of all Rörstrand porcelain.

The youngest artist is Marianne Westman, versatile and prolific. Her kitchenware, immensely in demand, shows the exuberant qualities of youth and *joie de vivre.* She is the creator of the popular ovenware, *Frisco* and *Pomona,* of earthenware called *Picknick,* also oven-proof, and of artistic jam jars and spice containers which can be stacked to save space. On their white backgrounds she makes artless but not inartistic patterns in vivid enamels, attractive enough to bring gaiety to the dullest kitchen.

Before lunch, to which she had invited several other guests, I spent two delightful hours in the studio of Hertha Bengtsson. Our animated conversation was about cooking and "playing" with cooking utensils.

Hertha's empathy for the housewife—she is one herself—means that her designs are extremely practical if somewhat unconventional. She loves bowls with a design in the bottom. She likes the sophisticated effects she gets by com-

* We give him the Latin form—*Linnaeus.*

bining her undecorated white porcelain with her glazed stone ware, an exacting medium in which she excels. She derives almost a sensual pleasure from the contrast between matt and shiny glazes on the same table.

An inspired artist, she chafes at the confines of commercial necessity and occasionally stages a small revolution during which she makes something just-for-fun. One such piece was a teapot with an incredibly long spout, its only decoration a delicately engraved herring-bone. That teapot became the nucleus for one of her most successful dinner sets. Now, whenever such a mood seizes her, she goes along with it wholeheartedly. And to the management's delight. So far everything she has created in this tempestuous spiritual mood has turned out a profitable venture for the firm.

Two of her services to be found wherever Rörstrand wares are sold are *Rosmarin,* plain white earthenware, and *Koko,* oven-proof feldspar china decorated with brown bands. Featured with these services are her one-of-a-kind stoneware pieces.

For the Rörstrand exhibit at the Victoria and Albert Museum in October, 1961, the Swedes made sure of having their displays done properly by bringing over their own prefabricated units. They put on a really beautiful show. Hertha's contribution was a flameproof black coffeepot and three of her ribbed cups and saucers in a space-saving stack alongside.

When the Swedes were asked what they would like the British to display in their return engagement a fortnight later, the reply was unanimous, "Tony Armstrong-Jones." Said Diana Pollock in a recent issue of *Pottery and Glass,* "The idea of captioning Mr. Jones and sending him over with a Design label swinging from his lapel opens a vista of delicious possibilities that would, I suspect, thoroughly appeal to both him and his wife."

Another young woman artist who helps carry forward the firm's tradition and impress the name of Rörstrand upon ceramic productions of unusual distinction is Sylvia Leuchovius, a combination of head-in-the-clouds and feet-on-the-ground. Sylvia gave us tea in her studio, but I was too engrossed by her art to concentrate on any beverage, even when accompanied by the best Swedish *petit fours.*

In the showrooms I had seen her delicate mocha cups of translucent white porcelain, *Le Select,* now sweeping America, but even after falling in love with one of her plaques on the *Kungsholm,* I was totally unprepared for her magnificent wall pieces. They may be framed, hung without frames, or mounted right in the masonry. Executed in chamotte, a medium with which she is adept, and in which she achieves both novelty and conviction, they suggest a Persian or Byzantine lavishness of detail and at the same time the cleanness of design of which such Orientals as Sakida Kakiemon and Toshima Tokuzaemon were masters.

Better bring home a Leuchovius piece, collector's items all. Tomorrow's tradition, you know!

Between lunch and tea I spent a couple of rapt hours in the studio of the male designer on the staff, Carl-Harry Stålhane. The tall, blond, blue-eyed, fortyish Swede is a contemporary and was a fellow student at art school of Stig Lindberg, the prolific designer at Sweden's other large pottery, Gustavsberg. Except that each lives for his art, there is little similarity about them. Stig is gay, ebullient. Carl-Harry is calm and serious.

He has a large studio where he keeps several tables always set. His tablecloths and napkins are woven to his order. To possess any of them, most women would give the proverbial eyetooth. The predominant color is gray, with striking blocks of black, or stripes of black and white. Against these backgrounds, he does wonderful things with black and white dishes, with white and gray, or with plain white porcelain and glazed stoneware. The cutlery, of course, is stainless steel, usually the smart Focus de Luxe with black nylon handles. While he has designed much china of extreme fineness and simple form in plain white—all the Scandinavians go in strongly for white—his two most captivating services are decorated in black and gray. These are *Safari* and the severely handsome *Tweed*.

Carl-Harry cannot create anything unless it says something to him. One creation which had evidently spoken loudly was an interesting large tray.

"How on earth did you get this formless design yet one which is distinctively integrated?" I demanded.

"That was how I got it," he smiled his rare luminous smile. "On earth. Red earth."

The tray had been turned on the wheel. The cheese-dried clay—he called it earth—was scored in lines raying from the center and by a series of circles parallel to the rim. By hand and spoon, crystals of various metals had been sprinkled over it, then it had been covered thinly with clay. During the firing the crystals had erupted, each leaving a miniscule crater. Thus the design.

Carl-Harry loves red earth, and uses it in all his decorative pieces, usually in combination with a glaze. Glazes, in particular his fine matt crystal ones, are his special interest. Knowing this, H. M. Gustav Adolf VI, one of Sweden's foremost patrons of the arts, a decade ago suggested that he experiment with the Chinese process which had effected the glaze from the fired clay itself. For ten years the artist doggedly persevered. Finally, he had two pieces to show His Majesty. His first one was not quite perfect, as it had a dull mark around the top. The second one was flawless, and is now in the Royal Palace in Stockholm. You probably saw it if you attended his exhibit at Bonniers in October, 1960, an epic date for Rörstrand. The exhibit consisted of 255 pieces displayed under the title, "The Awe of Stoneware."

Two hundred and fifty-five pieces, the bottom of each with an impression in flowing script, the signature, *C. H. Stålhane, Sweden.* It did not say "Dedicated Potter." That was not necessary. Each piece said it for him, and for Rörstrand.

Chapter 12

Royal Copenhagen

EVERY young chatelaine, which means those young in spirit, too, considers her chinaware collection incomplete if it does not include at least one piece of Royal Copenhagen. Nine times out of ten the piece is *The Little Mermaid*, a prize if brought home by herself from Amagertorv 5, the old Renaissance building erected in 1616 by a burgomaster named Mathias Hansen, and really special if she watched it being made in the plant at Smallegade overlooking the charming grounds and canal of Frederiksberg Castle.

When you sail into the harbor of Copenhagen, you are confronted by the statue of The Little Mermaid gazing wistfully into space. How she became the company's most popular figurine is a delightful story.

One of the most important works of Denmark's great modern composer, Fini Henriques, was the ballet he created from Hans Christian Andersen's famous fairy tale, "The Little Mermaid." Composer and ballet master, Hans Beck, had the ballet perfected and ready for its *première* in the Royal Theatre in Copenhagen on the "second" Christmas Day—our Boxing Day. Henriques himself conducted it the first evening, when it scored a spectacular success, although he insisted that from beginning to end the credit belonged to the ballerina, Ellen Price de Planes, for her touching and poetic performance.

Among the audience was Carl Jacobsen, founder of the well-known "Carlsberg" breweries. The shy pleading glance of the ballerina—"like that of a fawn," he declared—decided him to have the lovely mermaid perpetuated in bronze. The sculptor Edvard Eriksen was commissioned to carry out the project, which he did with enthusiasm, portraying the mermaid at the moment she swam ashore, just as the love potion had begun to take effect and her fishtail to drop away. In 1913 the graceful and poignant figure was enthroned on her rock facing the beach of Langelinie.

The original bronze was bought by the Royal Copenhagen Porcelain Manufactory and duplicated in miniature in porcelain. The comparatively high price is the result of the stiff royalties which must be paid on each figurine. But that has never slowed down sales. Several times each year that section of the plant must work overtime to keep their stock up.

The figurine next in popularity is that of the Danish "deity," Hans Christian Andersen, in pure white porcelain with an incomparable glaze. (The inspiration for this *blanc de chine* came from the Chinese.) The company's famous colored figurine of the idolized spinner of fairy tales can be bought only in the small shop across from his birthplace in Odense on the island of Fyn.

The fervor of the above-mentioned idolatry may be gleaned from what nearly happened to Danny Kaye when he was in Odense making his picture. To the horror of the previously admiring crowd, he threw himself down on the bed on which H.C.A. was born. Sacrilege! Before he was quite tarred and feathered, someone luckily "recalled" that this was not the original bed. It had been sent to a cabinetmaker a few days before for repairs.

In the long list of the firm's figurines, *The Escape to America*—a boy and a girl gazing out to sea—has for years maintained a place at the top, although two new figures, *Boy with Umbrella* and *Boy with Teddy Bear*, seem to be doing a bit of tugging at heartstrings *and* pursestrings.

Perennially heading the lists, of course, are the dogs and cats, the birds and fishes in the characteristic soft colors painted under the glaze and fired at exceedingly high temperatures.

One of the largest figures ever executed in pottery, and in one piece, is the life-sized *The Potter*, the work of the celebrated sculptor, one of the truly great, Jais Nielsen. In rich blue stoneware, it stands in the garden of the manufactory at Smallegade as its patron saint. Other large pieces of his are *The Good Samaritan, Samson and the Lion, Moses,* and *Pontius Pilate,* all of which bear witness to his strong religious devotion.

On a smaller scale he has created vases and bowls stamped with his rich imagination and sense of humor. Into the bargain he proved himself an outstanding painter. In fact, he made his debut with the company by decorating a number of large vases with Biblical subjects.

Jais Nielsen has been with the firm since 1921, more than forty years. Towards the end of 1960, when he was over seventy-five years of age, he held a large exhibition at Charlottenborg in the capital. This proved to be a comprehensive selection of his rich output of ceramics and paintings. The factory, represented by its present managing director, Mr. Mark Lindgren, congratulates itself on the long collaboration between it and the grand old man.

"The association," said Mr. Lindgren, "has proven exceptionally fruitful and of epoch-making importance to both him and us."

Another Nielsen, the late Kai of their faïence factory, fashioned a grotesque, gaily colored, nursery-rhyme series of figures given the collective title, *A Feast Was Prepared in the Forest*. Holding in hand his irresistible pieces, sensitive and appealing, one is touched with sadness because so vital an artist enjoyed so brief a life.

Another group, also a collector's item, is that in Danish national costume. Inspiration of Carl Martin-Hansen, it was first produced in 1923 and given to the king and queen at their silver wedding by the women of Denmark, and has contributed to the company's prestige ever since. Another artist to do that was Gerhard Henning with his overglaze pieces, notably his first brain child, *The Nodding Doll*, and two more in the same genre, *Faun and Nymph* and *The Chinese Bride*.

The firm's specialty—many women unexpectedly find themselves returning home with a service—is dinnerware. One characteristic old blue and white pattern is *Tranquebar,* called after a former Danish colony in India. Their "immortal" pattern, *Blue Fluted,* is typical old Chinese. It comes in three styles: normal border, half-lace without holes, and full-lace with pierced or reticulated edges. *Blue Fluted* has had more ups and downs than the blue belts on the bottom, but now it is riding the waves again, probably for the tenth time. At present, customers must wait for it for eighteen months.

The most elaborate table service ever made in Denmark, and claimed to be one of the most famous historic works of porcelain in the world, is the *Flora Danica*. The then managing director, Holmskiold, a learned botanist, insisted that the illustrations in the botanical tome, *Flora Danica,* be followed faithfully. On the reverse of every piece, the Latin name of the plant is carefully recorded.

The service was originally designed for Catherine the Great of Russia, but she died in 1796—it was begun in 1790 and finished in 1802. It was then acquired by the Danish royal family, and is now on exhibition in Rosenberg Castle. King Frederic IX and his Swedish queen, Ingrid, whom the people adore, presented a set of twelve *Flora Danica* plates to Elizabeth II when she paid a visit to Denmark.

A fairly informal service, with coupe plates, is called *Confetti*. It comes in white with red, yellow, black and green confetti, the dishes interchangeable so that the housewife may assemble or compose a very interesting set in the modern manner. Compared with most Royal Copenhagen wares, they are relatively inexpensive. Gert Botelund, a young designer who takes a naïve delight in unusual table settings, had added a striking and amusing note to one which employed varied *Confetti* the day I was there. How? By tying fringed coral-red napkins into quite realistic lobsters.

Among the superb examples of Royal Copenhagen eagerly sought by those who know porcelain values are *Craquelé* and *Sang de Bouef*. The former, a stoneware product, was probably discovered as accidentally by a Chinese responsible for the first piece as was roast pork. He may have been dejected when he opened his kiln and saw the netted lines caused by the firing, for the glaze had contracted more than had the body of the piece. But when he had filled in the cracks with pigment, glazed it thinly and fired it again, he found himself the possessor of an object of amazing loveliness. Mr. H. Madslund, chief chemical engineer and technical manager at Smallegade, has brought this method to perfection. "How utterly gorgeous!" is the ejaculation of customers seeing one of his vases and bowls for the first time.

The celebrated *Sang de Bouef* or oxblood glaze, also stoneware, was the discovery of the late Patrick Nordstrøm, a Swede who had been trained as a wood carver. His glaze is made from copper oxide and, depending on the firing, may turn out red or green. When a firing disappointed Nordstrøm everyone in his vicinity knew, for he consoled himself by playing his flute.

The firing in every case is a matter of such importance to the whole pottery that occasionally the head of the factory stays up all night to watch it—"As over a cow giving birth to a calf," my guide explained.

Until recently there were seven ovens, each of which held from 6000 to 12,000 pieces. The queer cone-shaped structures, few of them now in use, are as much a feature of the Smallegade landscape as are the bottlenecks of the Black Country of the English Midlands. Some of them used coal, some oil, but in either case they were unique in that the fire was on top of the three-story oven. This device, employed by no other pottery, was the idea of Philip Schou, founder of the firm's fortunes. He introduced it against great opposition, and not without private misgivings. Recently these "cones" have been replaced by gas-fired tunnel kilns for both porcelain and faïence. For the former the biscuit firing is done at 2740 F. The glost firing can attain a heat of 2640 F. although this is seldom necessary. As underglaze porcelain requires a glost heat, only cobalt blue, green, and brown, the last composed of almost pure gold, turn out well consistently. Faïence, fired at much lower temperatures, is more generous in this matter.

The filling of the kilns takes three days, the firing forty-eight hours. Another three days are required for the cooling, and another day to *draw* the wares from the kilns. Porcelain plates are fired upright, one to a sagger. Faïence plates are piled horizontally with *thimbles* between them. This partly accounts for the price spread between the two wares.

The work is all freehand. There is no lithographing although some stenciling. It takes three years to train a girl to do a single pattern, especially underglaze. Overglaze takes longer, the minimum being four years, but in overglaze a girl does several patterns.

After a visit to the factory, one with an open eye and an open mind realizes the care which is lavished on each piece marked with either the three belts, or the three belts and a crown. *Royal* Copenhagen, indeed!

Usually the term "royal" in a firm's name means by royal appointment. Here it has even more significance.

Porcelain making had never succeeded in Denmark. Nevertheless a chemist named Frantz Henrich Müller founded a factory in the capital in 1775. It was financed by a private company though the shares were held principally by court officials. In 1779 bankruptcy threatened. The plant was taken over by the Crown, under the personal supervision of the dynamic Queen Dowager, Julianne Marie. The new name, and new trademark—three wavy lines—were an inspiration of either the Queen or a member of her Court.

These three wavy lines signify the three ancient waterways from the Kattegat to the Baltic—the Sound between Denmark and Sweden, the Great Belt between Zealand and Fyn, and the Little Belt between Fyn and Jutland now connected by a bridge of which the Danes are extremely proud. This has been the firm's mark ever since, except for fifteen years, between 1830 and 1845, when the belts were straight. (Perhaps the seas had a calm period.) The crown was added in 1889. There is no crown on the earthenware.

Müller's flair for gathering about him great ceramic artists, such as Bayer of Nuremburg who undertook the decoration of the *Flora Danica* set, was largely responsible for the firm's initial success.

Success was not lasting. First, the king demanded Müller's retirement at seventy, though he was at the height of his activity. Second, the English attack on the Danish fleet in 1801, the bombardment of Copenhagen in 1807, the taking over of the Danish fleet by Nelson, ended the shipping trade and paralyzed the life of the nation. By 1867 the "Royal" was merely a courtesy title, for a wholesale merchant named Falck had bought the entire plant with the right to retain the royal name and the markings, and to fly the royal flag.

Seventeen years later a revival took place. A great patriot, Philip Schou, bought the factory and spent his whole personal fortune in moving it to its present location at Smallegade, in modernizing it and building new kilns.

A young architect named Arnold Krog who had spent five years from 1880 to 1885 in restoring Frederiksberg Castle, and before that had studied the making of majolica in Italy, was appointed art director. From that moment, the fortune of the company was made.

Krog started underglaze decoration. His first piece was a vase showing a stork on a marsh. This gem was bought by the Duke of Sutherland whose yacht lay in the sound. The news of the purchase spread quickly, and Royal Copenhagen was on the map again, for good.

Next, Krog rescued overglaze painting from the attic. By putting together the fragments found there, and aided by vases and other objects from museums and private collections, Royal Copenhagen again began producing the best pieces from the Müller period. To them he gave the significant name, *Julianne Marie Porcelain*. Before 1900, they had opened shops in London, Paris, and New York.

For no good reason, a building containing three of their kilns was bombed by the occupying Germans in 1943. Production was further curtailed as imports were out—their kaolin comes from England, their feldspar from Sweden, their only native ingredients are Danish flint and labor.

Although it slowed them up for a time, it by no means cramped their style. I wish I had space to describe all the lovely new designs they bring out week after week, even day after day. The best I can do is list a few. In most cases the names speak for themselves.

First, take porcelain in the plain shape, flower-decorated: *Cream Fensmark, Quaking Grass, Golden Clover,* and *Golden Basket.* Also plain is *Blue Flowers* but it comes in the curve shape as well, along with the rich ivory-toned *Frijsenborg* and the delightful white *Saxon Flower.* On the fluted shape are *Clarissa* in brown and gold decoration, *Green Melody* in green and gold, and *Tunna* which is white except for a gold edge. Pure white, the Scandinavians' love, comes in the engraved *Salta* and the fluted *Georgiana.* And of course there is no letup to *Blue Fluted,* their undying pattern previously described.

Tranquebar still leads in faïence, but is closely rivaled by the yellow *Marigold* with much the same rim, employed also by the bluish-white *Gabriella* and the red-banded gray *Tureby. Fritillaria* in buff and *Floria* in cream are floral patterns which enjoy brisk sales. For deep solid color you have a choice of green *Corinna,* blue *Sonia,* and the lemon yellow *Susanne* guaranteed to bring the sun into the dining room on the darkest day of a Danish winter.

As a souvenir of my visit to Hans Christian Andersen's birthplace, Bent Nielsen, chief of the Odense Tourist Association—there's the man you must not fail to look up if you want to see Fyn!—gave me a series of the fascinating black cutouts which the fairy tale man substituted for doodling. For this reason I was more interested than I might otherwise have been when shown a set of children's dishes with decorations of the original silhouettes. Danish mothers have no milk-and-spinach problem when these bewitching mugs and plates face the youngsters at the table.

Royal Copenhagen, now company-owned, is terribly crowded at Smallegade but they refuse to give up their site overlooking the Frederiksberg gardens. With Philip Schou, the directors believe that artists, if not the bulk of the employees, too, must see beauty when they look out the windows. The artists, Schou claimed, made better use of it than the average employed person.

There are thirteen hundred employees. All wear white uniforms, supplied and laundered by the firm. Each year witnesses the twenty-fifth anniversary of many employees. Some celebrations mark fifty or sixty years with the firm. Nothing so symbolizes the tradition of loyalty as these elderly workers going about their jobs. I was introduced to an artist who was eighty, and painting as beautifully as ever.

"But not so rapidly, Madam," he said apologetically.

Sitting before me now is my favorite Royal Copenhagen piece, a vase rather like the one on which he was engaged. A charming and simple landscape, everything seen as if through a gauzy veil, unattainable yet clear. Not a line more than necessary, not an extra hint of blue. Sheer perfection!

And the glaze, the immaculate glaze. When quite young I was taught the water test for it. "If you run your finger over the surface, it should feel as if it were being languorously drawn through tepid water."

Running my fingers over the vase is just that, the water of the three belts—the Sound, the Great Belt and the Little Belt—with the royal crown above.

Chapter 13

Gustavsberg

At the Gustavsberg manufactory, just twenty kilometres east of Stockholm, some of the world's most beautiful and unique pottery is created. Through the cooperation of many great and near great artists and craftsmen, this Swedish plant has today attained a place of eminence in the world of ceramics.

Bricks had been made in the vicinity since the seventeenth century. The kilns suggested pottery to a handful of enterprising Swedes. Investigation showed them that china clay and china stone could be imported as cheaply from Cornwall and Devon as from those shires to Stoke-on-Trent. They decided to pool their resources and found a plant to produce flintware.

The enterprise took its name from the Royal Chancellor's nephew, Gustaf Gabrielsson Oxenstierna, who owned the estate of Tyreso containing the Farsta property, the present site of the works. The first building still stands. The upper hall, once a chapel, is now a museum for the display and preservation of outstanding productions through the years.

The company encountered many difficulties at first. In their own country they had to compete with the old established firm of Rörstrand, in Denmark with the famous Royal Copenhagen Porcelain Manufactory and, a few years later, Bing & Grøndahl.

In 1840 it was decided vital to put new blood into the business. From England they began importing not only the clays, but patterns, colors, and methods to assist them in their new venture. As a consequence their ware showed a decided English influence. For example, they made bone china. (They still make it, and are the only people in Scandinavia to do so.) Their Parian ware was inspired by Wedgwood's *Carrara*, understandable seeing that they had also imported Staffordshire workers. One of these, a skilled craftsman from Etruria, brought with him Wedgwood barbotine designs which he affixed to the same blue body, though shortly the classical Etruscan figures of Josiah Wedgwood were replaced by Swedish spring flowers such as snow-drops and irises.

Around the middle of the century the plant was taken over by a local man, Samuel Gidenius, whose company already had an interest in the business. He enlarged and modernized the factory, an expansion which was accelerated when Wilhelm Odelberg assumed control in 1869. At the end of the nine-teenth century, it had become a million kroner enterprise.

Odelberg died in 1924, and his two sons piloted the business safely through the stormy postwar years. In 1937 when another war seemed imminent, it came into the possession of the Co-operative Society of Sweden, its official name being AB Gustavsberg Fabriker, shortened by usage to plain Gustavs-berg. Then began a rapid expansion of the company as well as of the com-munity, which has continued. By stressing quality first, last, and all the time, by developing along their own individual lines, by the faith of their artists, they gradually reached their place in the sun.

Needless to say, a great deal of the credit goes to their present managing director, Dr. Arthur Hald, son of the great Edward Hald now at Orrefors. A vigorous, democratic executive, he is as unlike an earlier manager as—well, as stone is unlike plastic clay. This predecessor was a German named Fredrik Rohde, called "Blinkers" because of a nervous tic of his eyelids. A despot. If two employees had the same surname, one had to change. For instance, if there were two Blacks, one became White, Gray, Brown, Blue—anything but Black. Rohde was a stickler for the formalities. One day when he entered the packing room, he goose-stepped almost into a workman with a dozen valuable plates on his head. The employee, who could not bow, curtsied instead. Blinkers was delighted. "Good!" he said. "Better to break the whole dozen than to disregard the conventions. Come to my office in half an hour and we'll discuss a raise."

Dr. Hald's creed is equally intransigent, but in another way—his aspirations are for the prestige of the firm and its ultimate goals. He has expressed it in a paragraph of *Contemporary Swedish Design,* a book he wrote as co-author with Sven Erik Skawonius.

There is one quality, however, which we seek to implant in all productions, whether hand-made or machine-made, marmalade jar or necklace. This is more than a question of style and taste. It is rather a way of life which we like to call modern and democratic. Every Swede should be able to create attractive surround-ings, using the many available and beautiful objects which suit him and his habits and among which he can be happy and content.

Gustavsberg dinnerware is simple without being austere. Their blue *Elite* is tremendously popular. *Amulet* in blue, red, or gray, designed by their leading artist, Stig Lindberg, has never "rested" since it was put on the market. With the firm's policy of keeping to the fore, it is not surprising that they actually led the way in the matter of combining different patterns instead of confining the housewife to a prescribed dinner set. Into this concept Stig's *Gefyr* and *Terma* fitted well. When they were produced and for some time afterwards they were the only ceramics which could be placed directly over the flame.

Once a month, a congress of artists, housewives, and consumers is held. Sparks struck from mind to mind result in valuable ideas. (One was black *Terma* which adapts itself so admirably to many modern table settings.) If an idea which is accepted comes from an employee, he receives a bonus or royalties.

There are 1500 employees, paid by piece work. The whole 1500 were put on their mettle when the Swedish State Railways, celebrating their hundredth jubilee in 1956, ordered 7000 plates and ashtrays, all with various scenes from railway history.

The employees have evening classes and get scholarships, a privilege of which many avail themselves. They work in delightful surroundings, both indoors and out, for the factory is on a small lake. Most of them have sailboats and during the summer frequently take their lunch on board.

In the Swedish archipelago there are 24,000 islands, almost enough to provide a private island for each family in the country. The smallest ones, of course, are most in favor. Almost every family has a sailing vessel of some sort, but few have cars. Dr. Hald himself did not own one—he had to call a taxi to take me back to town. He lives in the delightful and last-word-modern Stockholm suburb of Lidingo, and rides back and forth on a bicycle. This greatly amazed some Americans who visited him, especially when he took them out in his fairly luxurious yacht.

Gustavsberg owes its distinctive character to the genius of three outstanding artists: Wilhelm Köge, Berndt Friborg and the aforementioned Stig Lindberg.

Köge, known as the grand old man of Gustavsberg, was for the first twenty-five years of his career the only artist there.* He began as a poster artist, but when in 1914 the Baltic Exhibition came in for unfavorable criticism, he set artists searching for new materials with which to express themselves, and himself departed on a long tour to get ideas. Greatly impressed by Persian

* Wilhelm Köge died in October 1960, after a short illness.

wares, he introduced his famous *Argenta,* silver deposit on a green background. It became, and remains, one of the firm's most popular productions.

Next he introduced *Pyro,* the heat-proof service, and followed it in 1933 by *Praktika.* Two years later he brought out *Praktika II,* in which he had reduced not only the size of dishes for small apartments, but the number of pieces in a service.

During the thirties, he created also the lovely white *Carrara* ware. That accomplished, he turned his attention to what proved to be his real love, stoneware. To it he gave the name *Farsta,* the name of the Gustavsberg site. It showed the influence of the countries he visited, notably China, South America, and Mexico. In the company's museum is an outstanding collection of Mexican pieces he brought back, as well as those of his own showing the exotic influence of that brilliant and brooding republic.

Köge did not hold his artistry above the creation of dinnerware for the people. In 1891 he designed the dishes for Berns's, the restaurant to which flock tourists in the know. He also designed a dignified pattern with raised crowns around the rims of the plates for the Swedish Foreign Office. His foremost dinnerware, *Gray Bands,* still going strong, has been copied abroad times without number—and without mention of royalties! In 1905 he made a service in typical *art nouveau* style and called it *Marguerite* in honor of the king's first wife, Margaret of Connaught.

Berndt Friborg, in his bright intimate studio, is a cheerful man in a cheerful atmosphere, and fully conscious of the responsibility his talents have laid upon him. He is a master craftsman rather than an artist, and as such started out in 1934 making lowly jampots and carrying out the designs of others.

Yet he has been called both the servant and the master of ceramics. In 1941 he surprised everyone by showing wares of his own composition, stoneware pieces, in the Sung tradition where he feels he has his roots. In stoneware, in which form and glaze are inseparable, he excels. His glazes are his own, and he has a great variety of them, ranging from strong tones to shadings made up of distinct and separate parts, their wealth achieved by an infinite manipulation of metal oxides.

Without fanfare, he showed me the lovely things in his sunny studio where flowers bloom in brilliance along the windowsills. He was subdued when he held up his treasure, a vase in yellow. Its purity of line, its glowing golden hues, especially its feel, tugged at whatever is touched within one by beauty in a really exquisite form. Out of curiosity, I asked him its market price.

He smiled and shook his grizzled head. "No price will be put on it, Madam, in my lifetime. After that—." He shrugged.

The Gustavsberg catalogue for 1830 lists a set of child's dishes, of 40 pieces, English designs painted on Swedish shapes. The next outstanding tea service was made in 1867, and had not only English decoration but English form. In 1956, Gustav VI wanted a miniature bedroom set for Princess Margareta, but in Swedish form and decor. Friborg was asked to make it for her. It is one creative effort in which he takes great pride.

His Majesty, by the way, is an avid collector and a Friborg enthusiast. Every time his favorite potter has an exhibit at the great Stockholm department store, NK, King Gustav goes there before the crowd is let in, and takes his pick of the wares.

"The yellow vase is still the most beautiful thing you have shown me," I said when the potter escorted me to the door of his studio and shook hands—a long friendly handshake. "I don't mind that you refuse to sell it. It is already mine. I have it here," I explained teasingly, touching my forehead with my free hand. "Such a convenient way to carry it! No tissue paper, no packing it in a suitcase, no bother of custom officials. Best of all, no matter where I am, I can take it out and look at it. Inviolably mine."

He chuckled, and drew me back into the room. For a moment he stood in reflection before a shelf, then handed me—a bowl? A vase? A tiny thing which fitted into the palm of my hand. An oblate spheroid piece with the tiniest opening in the top—of the most indescribably clear cobalt blue with a thousand infinitesimal patternings in rust oxide, on the bottom his signature and the mark all three Gustavsberg artists use, a hand rising from a sickle-shaped **G**.

What is it? Actually a primitive lamp, of the sort the Scots call a cruzie. Filled with oil into which a wick is dipped, it gives off a faint gleam of light.

Whenever I cup this valued possession in my hand, and run my fingers over the more-than-satin surface, it becomes an Aladdin lamp transporting me back into the flower-filled studio. And not only there, but from pottery to pottery, back down the ages to the beginnings of the art, casting a floodlight on the first potter's wheel I ever saw, in the open-front shop in remote Turkey, the country from whence the Crusaders brought the first porcelain treasures of the East, and laid them at the feet of their kings.

Occasionally when browsing, one comes across something which fairly takes one's breath. In Svenska Tenn, a gem of a specialty shop overlooking the sea from the Strandvagen, was a tall vase of white stoneware. The top looked like nothing so much as a distorted eggcup. Yet in its simplicity and grace the design was compelling. But the price tag!

"Seventeen dollars!"

"It's a Stig Lindberg," the proprietress explained.

Stig Lindberg, artist, ceramist, and sculptor, is the man on whose shoulders now rests the destiny of this prosperous and important industry in so far as the arts of design, form, and color are concerned. And the responsibility is happily placed, for with his advanced and singular imagination, anything is possible. His designs are his alone. Arms become branches, hands grow forth instead of horns, and two Narcissus heads sprout from one neck. Anything is possible, from Adam and Eve in the Garden of Eden, Daphne pursued by Apollo, and Young Love in 2000 A.D.

The Gustavsberg mark and two signatures by Stig Lindberg. The stylized hand through the large G, with designer's name shown, is typical.

Stig was born in Umea on the northern part of the Gulf of Bothnia in 1916. To study sculpture, he enrolled in the art school in Stockholm—same class, you may recall, as Rörstrand's dedicated Carl-Harry Stålhane. In 1937 he went to Gustavsberg to work under Wilhelm Köge, and became interested in porcelain.

He first attracted attention with his stoneware at its première showing at NK in 1945. He specialized in vases, arresting in form but with no embellishments to detract from the flowers they contained. His irregular forms, a protest against conventional symmetry, made an immediate appeal, and at once began to exert an international influence.

In dinnerware, his prolific imagination has evolved more individual shapes and designs than it seems possible one man could devise. Three-cornered plates. Boat-shaped bowls. All sorts of odd pieces which upon familiarity and study reveal not only functionalism but an arresting beauty.

When Köge retired, Stig succeeded him as head of the plant, and he now has ten artists and more than fifty craftsmen under him in the design department. Younger artists with names to bear in mind are Hibbi and Arne-Carl Breger, and Kärin Bjorqvist whose dinnerware, *Vardag,* made such a hit.

Though not on the staff, the well-known sculptress, Tyra Lundgren, whose birds are celebrated, does some work there. The artists are paid by the month, and given so many days a week for their own ceramic pursuits, but must design some commercial products, the idea behind this being to raise the general standards of good taste. Stig also teaches at FORM, the recently established school and art center of the capital. It is a spot you cannot afford to miss.

Less than a year after he took over he created a service which he named *Servus,* with only half the number of dishes in the old master's reduced *Praktika.* From that point he got the cooperation of Berndt Friborg and the heads of the research laboratories, and developed the fast-selling *Gefyr.* In it, as he had scrapped the common round forms, the oval predominated.

What has probably brought Stig his greatest renown is his faïence, his own version of the old Spanish majolica which reached its peak in the Italian city of Faenza and Nevers in France. Introduced to the public in April, 1941, under the title *Painted This Spring,* Stig's exhibit made history. In this medium the artist who has been termed the "playboy of ceramics" plays seriously with form, color, and decor. A vase opens at one side, from the opening peers a face, the exterior is decorated in "drops." Another, patterned with "bobbins," has the form of an old-fashioned dressmaker's dummy. And here is an oval bowl which seems to have been pinched grotesquely just before it hardened to the cheese stage. Styles and decoration assume a variety of shapes and designs such as zigzag, saw, spool, leaf-veins, and flowers in monotone. His series called *Domino* is regarded as a classic. Colors are strong and clear, his favorites being yellow, turquoise, mulberry, green-brown, yellow-green and a good French gray. His *Colorado* service in earthenware, angular in shape, is glazed in turquoise, green, yellow, and black. For informal affairs, it is without a peer.

The last time I visited Gustavsberg, Stig had developed a new fireproof stoneware with rattan handles. He showed me a soup pot with a lid which fits in and can be hung by the edge to catch the steam, an idea that came to him as he watched his wife walk from the table back to the kitchen with a casserole lid. And naturally I asked to be shown the brown and white striped bone china for which he was awarded two gold medals at the California State Fair Exhibition a year ago. Call for it by name, *Ribb.*

Another recent venture is playing cards, the first to be exported from Sweden in fifty years. They are not porcelain, of course, but are of his design, and have afforded him an immense amount of amusement. England has requested a license to produce them.

His latest interest is a new white stoneware thin as an eggshell—so thin that he had made dozens of pieces but, when I was there, had finished the fine engraved lines on only one without piercing it with his graver. He insisted that I accept one of the earlier bowls as a souvenir. (I was not hard to persuade.) To the casual observer it might appear to be a bowl you would pick up in a dime store to hold a narcissus bulb. To anyone in the know it would say "Stig Lindberg" as unequivocally as would the initials "**SL**" and the hand and sickle-shaped "**G**" impressed on the bottom.

If imitation is the sincerest form of flattery, Stig should feel sincerely flattered, for there has been an immense pirating of his designs. Yet never does the imitation deceive the initiated. No one else can achieve the quality and glaze, the artistry and skill which mark the work of this distinguished potter, Stig Lindberg, artist, ceramist, and sculptor, *par excellence*.

The Exchange of Peace**
Post Communion Prayer:
    God our help, we thank you for this supper shared
    in the Spirit with your Son Jesus who makes us
    new and strong; who brings us eternal life. We
    praise you for giving us good gifts in Him, and
    pledge ourselves to serve you even as in Christ
    you have served us.   Amen.
*Hymn: "Beneath the Cross of Jesus"   #162
*Benediction   *Chimes
Choral Response
Postlude
Congregation Standing   + + +Organ Interlude

                    * * * * *

GREETERS: Inez Reis, Hazel Bickley

The Exchange of Peace** - This is a time of expressing the unity that God has given us in Jesus Christ.
In an appropriate manner express to your neighbor
the greeting 'May the Peace of the Lord Jesus Christ
be with you.'

The Deacons Fund is being received this evening.
You may use the plate in the rear of the Sanctuary
on leaving.

The present sanctuary building will be 50 years old
this Easter. It was first dedicated with an organ
recital by Prof. Friederichs of Cincinnati. There
then followed nightly services all week with the
Pastor, M. F. Balleu, visiting ministers and the
Choir.
                    * * * * *

    PLEASE LEAVE INSERT 'THE THANKSGIVING' ON PEW.

The head of the Crucified Christ shows His humanity: His pain, suffering, and death. He suffers still as He looks upon our world where hate, cruelty, and injustice are so prevalent. "Father, forgive them; for they know not what they do." (Luke 23:24)

Original Woodcut by Carol Nelson

anchor/wallace ©1975/Mpls. 55435   Ptd. in USA   No. A-4153

MAUNDY THURSDAY

April 16, 1981   7:30 PM

Prelude

Call to Worship:

Pastor: Our Lord has invited us to commune with him, even though we are guilty of betraying him.

People: We would not "sell" our Lord, yet we have betrayed him for less than silver.

Pastor: Our Lord knows what we have done. But he still invites us to his table in hope that, unlike Judas, we will accept God's forgiveness.

People: We come in confession of our guilt, and in acceptance of the forgiveness our Lord offers.

*Hymn: "In the cross of Christ I glory"   #154

Prayer of Confession   (in unison)

Forgive us, Father, for we have betrayed your sacred gift of love. For the price of enjoyment in sinful pleasures, material gains to satisfy our greed, and acceptance by our friends, we have denied our allegiance to you. We are unworthy of your love, but we confess we cannot live without it. Receive us back into discipleship as we come to your table this evening. We pray through your Son, our Savior, who shed his blood for us.   Amen.

Prayers of Silent and Individual Confession

Declaration of Pardon

The Good News: John 13: 1-15

*Hymn: "Let us break bread together" Page 5
                (20th Century Hymn - Gold Cover)

The Sermon: UNBROKEN FELLOWSHIP FROM JESUS CHRIST
                      Reverend George L. Reed

Cantata: "Jesus Death - Upon the Cross"

The Sacrament of the Lord's Supper
   * The Invitation
   * The Thanksgiving   (See Insert)
     The Distribution of the Elements

Chapter 14

Bing & Grøndahl

ALL December a steady stream of parcels leaves the Copenhagen post office. The wrappers are stamped with three blue towers, trade mark of Bing & Grøndahl, porcelain makers to His Majesty Frederick IX of Denmark. Each parcel contains a plate. A *Jule Aften* plate.

Jule Aften? A man's name? Or the nickname of a girl?

Neither. It is simply Danish for "Christmas Eve."

For over sixty-five years, each Christmas the famous firm has brought out a new plate depicting an event in Danish history, the spirit of Yuletide, or merely a beautiful winter scene. All the plates are characteristically blue and white underglaze—heavenly blue, the color of the Madonna's robes, and white for purity, symbol of Her Son who knew no sin.

When the last plate has been made for the year, the mold is broken.

To many a Danish family, the current *Jule Aften* plate is the most prized Christmas gift. In two Copenhagen houses where I was entertained, the parents had started a collection for each of their children the year of its birth. When I asked a precocious small girl how old she was, she said, "I'm as old as Kronberg Castle." I had visited the sixteenth century castle twenty-eight miles north of the capital the previous day. If the child had not pointed to her birth-plate on the wall, I should probably still be wondering what inspired that whopper.

Not only Scandinavians, but many on our side of the Atlantic, are collecting these fascinating plates. From time to time, advertisements appear in the newspapers specifying one or more numbers wanted. For example, "1899—Crows Enjoying Christmas," or, "1938—Lighting the Candles." Apart from the collection in the Bing & Grøndahl museum, the only complete one, so far as their curator knows, is that for which they depleted their own scanty reserves. This was to fill out a series which the former American ambassadress, Ruth Bryan Owen, was taking back as a personal gift to President Roosevelt.

How Bing & Grøndahl started the Jule Aften plates—give the "J" the "Y" sound—is a story. For that matter, there is a story in the founding of this major Copenhagen pottery itself. Unfortunately, except in the eyes of the experts and informed, until recently it has been overshadowed by its great rival, the earlier established Royal Copenhagen Porcelain Manufactory.

That royal project, as we know, came under the patronage of the Queen Dowager, Julianne Marie, in 1779. Early in the nineteenth century the Crown Prince took over, but, having more engrossing affairs, gave it little attention. In no time, it went into a slump.

At its lowest ebb, one of their ambitious and patriotic young artists, the sculptor Frederick Wilhelm Grøndahl, approached the management. He was bursting with an idea for getting the business back on a sound basis. This was to make biscuit copies of the sculpture of the famous Albert Bertel Thorvaldson. Son of an Icelandic wood carver, Thorvaldson had settled in Copenhagen and become a national figure. When he died in 1844, he had been buried in the courtyard of the museum which was named after him, his grave almost a shrine.

Grøndahl's scheme was regarded coldly. Undaunted, the enthusiastic young man sought out the owners of an enterprising high-class stationery shop where art was appreciated and encouraged. This business had been founded in 1820 by H. J. Bing, a poor but well-educated Dutch immigrant. Favored with a royal license, but fighting bitter and stubborn competitors, he and his two sons, first his partners and later his successors, had worked their small stationery to a rich and extensive repository of fine arts.

Art itself, they claimed, possessed a commercial value. They set out to encourage the public to decorate their buildings only with fine objects. By facilitating the purchase of such things, they would cement for themselves a solid financial status. They arranged exhibitions of Danish artists. They bought their pictures and paid well for them. The policy proved farseeing. By 1853, the Bing establishment had become an important cultural feature in the life of the city.

This was the year Grøndahl approached the brothers. His proposition appealed to them. But in order to make the project pay, would it not be necessary to manufacture more than merely art objects? It was decided to produce glazed china for the housewife as well.

A pottery, officially known as The National Factory of Porcelain, was set up at 149 Vesterbrogade. At first they had trouble getting skilled laborers to work so far out of the city—now it is practically downtown. Many of the present employees are descendants, with the same name, of the original employees of 1853. By chance, I was there for the celebration of the fiftieth anniversary of their master modelmaker.

Grøndahl worked out the technical and artistic problems. The Bing brothers supplied the money and developed the market for their useful chinaware, as well as the art ware dear to their young partner's heart. As Thorvaldson's spirit was still alive among the people—he had been dead only nine years—the biscuit figures were an immediate success.

Suddenly tragedy struck. Grøndahl died. It was a staggering blow. But the enterprising Bing brothers knew they had a good thing and decided to carry on, expand, even include export. Able artists were found who adopted the firm's motto, "The First with the Best." The great aim of Harold, the younger brother, was to ennoble the craft. (In the end his ideas paid off in solid cash as well.) He shrewdly signed up their first good artist, Peitro Kroken. His heron set, combining blue underglaze with gold, became one of the most decorative wares of all times. Shown at the Paris Exhibition of 1889, the year the Eiffel Tower was built, its acclaim was unprecedented.

Six years later the business had grown at such a rate that reorganization was necessary. A new firm was incorporated with the Bing family owning the controlling interest, as they still do. To commemorate their second opening, in a greatly enlarged plant, a spectacular product was demanded. Prizes were offered for suggestions. The winning idea? Yes, you have guessed. The *Jule Aften* plate.

The plates caught on like wildfire. Potters everywhere copied the idea, but none achieved the same renown. The *Jule Aften* plates are not only a definitely Danish tradition, but they are definitely Bing & Grøndahl.

To make these plates, the requisite clay mixture is molded on a jigger to the desired shape, and placed on wire shelving to dry to a cheese consistency. (Even with currents of warm air blown on them, it takes from one to three weeks to remove 80 per cent of the moisture.) The cheese is fired, and emerges strong enough to be painted by the artist and signed. Then it is dipped in the glaze, B & G's only secret process. Next the plates, now resembling putty, are stacked in saggers and fired at an exceedingly high temperature which restores the colors. If they have not burned through properly, the examiner rejects the piece—with underglaze painting no retouching is possible.

The competition for the honor of signing a *Jule Aften* plate is terrifically keen. Barely has the mold been smashed when the firm's artists, and ambitious free lances, begin submitting their ideas for the following year. The award is made early in the summer. Immediately the manufacture in ever-increasing quantities gets under way.

The first plate, in 1895, was "Behind the Frozen Window," by F. A. Hallin who designed the next two, "New Moon over Snow-covered Trees," and "Christmas Meal of the Sparrows." Some artists have produced only one. For example, S. Sabra in 1901 with "The Three Wise Men from the East," and H. Plockross in 1907 with "The Little Match Girl." On the other hand, Achton Friis did fourteen from 1917 to 1929, and another, "Arrival of Christmas Train" in 1931. Among his titles are: "Fishing Boats Returning Home for Christmas," "Pigeons in the Castle Court," "Eskimos Looking at the Church of Their Little Village in Greenland," and "Fox Outside on Christmas Eve."

Another with a prolific imagination was Ove Larsen who, except for two years, had an unbroken run from 1936 to 1945. His most popular plate was "The Lillebelt Bridge Connecting Jutland with Funen." (Funen, or Fyn, is the island on which Hans Christian Andersen was born.) The Danes are justifiably proud of their "Little Belt" bridge, 1,178 metres long, and spanning a strong current in water so deep that some piers measure 30 metres. Crossing it by train, I felt suspended in space.

Larsen's 1943 plate depicts Ribe Cathedral, the oldest in Denmark if not in Scandinavia. Ribe was the hometown of Jacob Riis, a young writer who came to the U.S.A. in 1870 and took an active part in improving the schools and tenements in Lower New York, and in introducing parks and playgrounds in congested areas.

The plate which made a hit with the Danes, and the opposite with the Nazi occupants, was Larsen's for 1944, featuring the "Sorgenfri." This is the castle outside Copenhagen where the Nazis kept King Frederick a prisoner during three miserable years.

Borge Premwig signed his name in 1952 to "Old Copenhagen Canals in Wintertime," and, two years later, to "Birthplace of Hans Christian Andersen at Odense." The latter was a sellout, for the man who wrote the simple fairy tales for his friends' children is a national figure in Denmark. His statue is everywhere. His picture is even on some of the bank notes.

A comparative newcomer, Kjeld Bonfils, submitted for the centennial in 1953 "Boat of His Majesty, the King of Denmark, in Greenland Waters." This marked only the second time the Crown Colony had been so honored. When the royal yacht, *Dannebrog*, docked at Gidthaab, Greenland's metropolis (population 1,300), the people turned out en masse to greet their sovereign and Queen Ingrid with the traditional nine cheers.

Bonfils repeated his win in 1955 with "Kalundborg Church," and in 1956 with another best seller, "Christmastime in Copenhagen." His plate for

1961 was "Winter Harmony," a charming scene featuring a squirrel with a nut on a branch of pine, a church in the snowy distance.

An artist whom I had the pleasure of meeting in her attractive studio at the plant was Margrethe Hyldahl whose work is in museums and galleries all over the world. As a young girl in 1903, she did her first piece for Bing & Grøndahl, a *Jule Aften* plate, "Happy Expectations of Children," inspired by memories of her own childhood eagerness to open the annual flat parcel.

Margrethe appeared on the roster again in 1946 with her "Commemoration Cross" in honor of the Danish sailors who lost their lives during World War II and in 1950 with "Kronberg Castle at Elsinore," where Shakespeare's *Hamlet* is performed each summer in the courtyard by one of the outstanding theatrical companies of Europe. Naturally, Sir Laurence Olivier was one star to shine in that firmament. Margrethe's 1951 plate, her sixth, shows "Jens Bang, New Passenger Boat Running between Copenhagen and Aalborg." Aalborg, on North Jutland, is the home of the famous beer and the even more famous Akvavit.

The 1960 plates, "Osterflars Kirke," is especially charming. The church is at the end of a snowy road, beside it a lovely old tithe barn, above, a star-pricked blue sky. Nostalgia flooded me that day in December when mine arrived. If only I could have been parceled and sent to Copenhagen by return mail, there to spend Yuletide, the Dane's most festive season. I could almost hear the fervent, *"Valkommen!"* on every side.

Still, if one cannot return, one will have made some really good friends— as their brochures say, "Meet the Danes and Make Four Million Friends" —and your beaming postman will hand you, from one of them, a flat parcel with three blue towers above your name and adress.

Your *Jule Aften* plate! *

Throughout its history, the factory has been fortunate in its staff of exceptionally fine artists—sculptors, modelers and painters—who have devoted their unhampered skills to producing the ceramic art work on which the establishment has invariably laid emphasis.

At the beginning of the twentieth century, a revolutionary young artist, Carl Petersen, appeared on the horizon. He had rocked the pottery world by publishing an article which reflected with asperity on contemporary Danish porcelain products, hitherto considered sacrosanct. "He is for us," Harold Bing said, and engaged him. Petersen was mainly interested in stoneware, but

* Credit for many details in the above must be given to Mr. Aaron Ritz, export manager of B & G, and to the reprint he gave me of an article by Dorothy Divers, "The Danish Christmas Plates," which appeared in *Christmas,* an American Annual of Christmas Literature and Art, published in Minneapolis.

his Chinese-inspired cylindrical vase in rice porcelain occupies a place of honor in the Copenhagen Museum of Fine Arts.

In the Paris Exhibition of 1900, Bing & Grøndahl showed the work of two truly great artists, Kai Nielsen and Jean Gauguin, the latter the son of the famous French painter who abandoned his banking career and family—in fact, all western civilization—and went to live in the South Seas.

Kai Nielsen's *Venus* was a life-size figure of the goddess, very lovely and also unsettling in its allure. Even when broken by a drunken woman who reeled against it at the fair, the sex-appeal was apparent. Another dramatic piece of his was a *Venus with the Apple*.

Two of Gauguin's pieces at the same exhibition were a bull of the power one would expect to find only in bronze, and a satyr reeling on the back of an ass which is shrieking and stumbling to its feet. Cox gives Gauguin the palm as one of the greatest artists at that period. Another authority, Gordon M. Forsyth, claims that he is the greatest artist who ever worked in pottery.

In the Paris Exhibition of 1925, a new name appeared—Hans Tegner, with a group of small figures in hard porcelain representing various characters from the Andersen fairy tales. These have become immensely popular with collectors.

At that exhibition Gauguin showed a number of pieces in chamotte, in which medium he proved himself a gifted artist. Nielsen's display included *The Grape Gatherers* and *The Birth of Venus*. His last work, *The Sea*, was full of life and charm. His death in 1934 was an incalculable loss.

By the way, you will see the murals and friezes of a third generation Gauguin, Paul René, and those of the brilliant Knut Rumohr, when you stay in the big friendly Viking Hotel, Oslo. Their attractive booklet, given on request, says:

To guide one's footsteps to the bar Gauguin has placed a number of his popular and characteristic cocks along the walls, some strutting arrogantly, other flapping their wings in panic flight. Above the bar itself a golden cock welcomes the thirsty traveller.

The Bing & Grøndahl shop is at 4, Amagertov, next to the stately establishment of Royal Copenhagen, complete with doorman. After such pomp it is pleasant to enter the more intimate atmosphere of the B & G store, presided over by their Miss Thistad who moves among the lovely things with justifiable assurance. Ask for her. If she is not actually engaged elsewhere, she will be delighted to show you around.

You will love B & G's simple, un-busy dinnerware designs. *Falling Leaves*, misty gray and muted brown foliage against a softly shaded groundlay of

Copenhagen blue. *Sea Gull,* an enchanting hand-painted pattern. Another hand-painted one, *Butterfly,* ornately classic. For their centenary they featured *Demeter,* cornflowers on a blue-sprinkled body.

They have no large assortment of patterns. Mr. Ole Simonsen, their manager, says their present ones are sufficiently in demand to keep the plant busy the year round. Nevertheless, two exciting new ones are in production: *Hazelnut,* a cluster of filberts and leaves in natural colors on a handsomely modernized old shape, and *Bernadotte,* designed by the well-known Swedish designer, Count Sigvard Bernadotte. (You will recall him as the prince who married a commoner, thereby forfeiting his claim to the throne.) He made one request of B & G, that he be allowed to give the first set they made to his father, the Swedish king, as a gift on his 75th birthday. In the plain white porcelain beloved in the north, *Bernadotte* has proved a sensational success.

Among the charming birds and animals are those designed by their current leading modeler-artist, Svend Jespersen. They include stately cats, adorable kittens, huggable cocker spaniels, smug robins, and, their top number, the bearded titmouse.

The figurines of children are legion, and appeal to the heart as much as to sight and touch. You will be captivated by *Gentleman,* a young fellow of five or six helping his small sister on with her coat. *Mary* cuddles a doll. In *Youthful Boldness* a gallant of ten or thereabouts presses a kiss on the cheek of a reluctant maiden of the same age. Sitting on my desk as I write is the one which outsells them all in America, *Children Reading.* You can almost see the tiny tots' lips move. To add to buyer appeal, each piece is initialled or signed personally by the artist.

Naturally B & G do not encroach on their neighbor's territory by reproducing Edward Eriksen's *The Little Mermaid.* On an elegant square plate is their version of her, dreaming her life away, the background a sailboat and the royal yacht.

My first purchase was a *Bleu Royal* urn of simple lines. For decoration, two little gold roses on a raised gold-rimmed oval, outside it a not quite diapered scattering of infinitesimal gold blossoms. Sèvres could have done nothing finer. But I wanted something essentially Danish as well.

"A piece every tourist does not take home," I requested of Miss Thisted.

That twinkly-eyed lady—you will agree with the appellation on both counts —turned serious and gave me a long speculative look, then from somewhere in the rear brought a figurine, a young girl resting after a swim. With me, it was love at first sight. I call her my mermaid, though she is not truly one, for the seductive figure, pensive on the sea wall, lacks a tail. Yet a veritable mermaid is suggested by the incomparable glaze, the B & G secret glaze—you touch it, then fondle it—and the way the soft tones, gray and ivory-beige, definitely but deliberately indeterminate, give a sense of mist and recession, as if, landlocked, Undine mourns her haunted and poignant sea.

Even after I had adjusted myself to the price, Miss Thisted was not sure about selling it to me. It had been designed for the Christmas trade and was not yet on the market. But she would find out. . . . The answer was yes. A great many tourists have returned with the lovely Undine by now, for her sales have risen steadily from the onset, but mine was the first to cross the Atlantic.

I was still a mere browser when Miss Thisted arranged my visit to the factory in Vesterbrogade. In the old part of the plant built in 1863 I was greeted with true Danish warmth by the export manager, Mr. Aaron Ritz.

What did I wish to see first? Their museum?

Mr. Ritz showed me pieces made by Grøndahl himself, and the early treasures of the great Kroken, Petersen, Nielsen, and Gauguin. (Bing & Grøndahl are their own best customers, for they have agents out all the time to buy back "first editions" at many times their original value.) Of definite museum caliber was the color work of a modern artist, Miss E. Heffermann-Lindencrone who died in 1946 at the age of seventy.

And next on the agenda? The making of our famous figurines?

The method was not unlike that of Royal Doulton. Slip was poured into a hole in the mold and the surplus poured out. The mold was turned upside down, left for six minutes, then opened. To ensure that all parts had the same humidity, they were left on a wet foam rubber cushion for 24 hours. The next step was "repairing" the various parts at room temperature, luting them with slip, and prebaking the assembled piece at 1200 C.

For the perennial favorite, *Hans Christian Andersen,* ten large molds are needed, and over a hundred small ones. For example, a separate one is required for the upraised index finger. In the case of assembling this figurine, the repairer's task makes child's play of a jigsaw puzzle.

Some large molds cost 200 kroner—about $29. One may be used fifteen times, twenty at the most. After that it fills with water and is inexact.

"If someone could invent a single mold, what an expense-saver it would be!" Mr. Ritz said.

He gave me a fresh slant on colors. All except cobalt blue and green must have gold in them to get the exact shade. Take the sweater, hair, and shoes of my *Children Reading.* They are mixed with 24 karat gold. It comes as pure gold from the Bank of Denmark, and is bought in quantity to the value of half a million kroner a year—around $75,000. Gold which would otherwise be wasted is stopped by a filter, and can be salvaged by chemical process.

Their only secret, as I have said twice before, is the composition of their glaze. I watched the glazer dip three dozen of Jespersen's titmice. She wore a chemical glove to protect her hands. (Silicosis, bane of potters, has been ended at this factory by a suction device.) In went the birds painted in their ultimate tones. Out they came an all-over dull putty, as if a wicked fairy had cast a spell upon them. But after being fired—baked, they call it—the good fairy takes over and just as magically the colors reappear.

Biscuit pieces, though plain white, are baked twice. Underglaze figures get only two firings, the second at 2700–2800 F. Coal is used for figurines, but dinnerware is baked in electric kilns, in one of which I intrepidly stood.

Intermittent kilns, not continuous ones, are used. It means that the wares are fired for 24 hours, then cooled off, and the process repeated. The kilns are filled twice a week, three times in the rush season. *What about wastage?* Sometimes it amounted to as much as 7 per cent, but their firing system was the only one they had yet found to give the perfect results they demanded.

Some "seconds" or "rejects" are sold, but the only allowable defects in such cases are of beauty and color. Three plates, on which the gold had overlapped the line, were marked down to 300 kroner, an appreciable loss as the markdown was far from perfunctory. Pieces with glaring defects, or with cracks or chips, are not allowed to leave the premises at any price, no matter what they had cost. In fact, they have one man, their highest paid employee, to smash them.

"Hm! He must have a smashing good time."

No. Too great care is taken in the manufacture for that. "Smashing" is a sporadic activity occurring as a minor part of his executive position.

Mr. Ritz admitted that the potteries did not contribute appreciably to the nation's economy, unless in the matter of tourist takings—they do attract great numbers of women tourists. Of materials, 94 per cent must be imported. The only native product is flint from Bornholm.

"Our edge is in having skilled labor. If ever the unions raised wages high enough, the industry in Denmark would be killed. That was what happened to Swedish textiles."

"However," he volunteered after a minute, "the intrinsic value far exceeds the monetary value. The potteries definitely contribute prestige and culture. And will continue to do so. Because of the national pride which all of us Danes take in our outstanding potteries, our wares, as one writer put it, have withstood the withering effects of industrialism. We shall not easily lose our national pride."

Chapter 15

Arabia

FINLAND—its own people call it Suomi—is a spellbinding country, with a strange, haunting yet somehow serene beauty which touches every facet of life and makes an artist of every Finn. Women predominate by 10 per cent, for 80,000 men out of a population of 4,000,000 were killed in the "Winter War." Nevertheless, the Finnish women, even the professional ones, remain extremely domestic and wholesomely feminine.

Aulanko, three miles from Hämeenlinna where in 1865 Jan Sibelius was born, is the finest tourist center of this Land of a Thousand Lakes. The hotel was designed by a young woman, Marta Blomstedt, an architect of excellent taste and clear-cut imagination. Even if I had the space, I could not do justice to its ingenious conveniences and unusual charms. You must see it for yourself.

In one of the private dining rooms we were shown tables elaborately laid and flower-decked for a crayfish banquet being given for a group of touring celebrities. The large dinner plates were black, highly glazed. The salt and pepper shakers and other condiment dishes were coral-red and white to match the meter-square napkins.

"The china, of course," the manageress said, "was made for us at Arabia." She pronounced it the Finnish way, the second "a" short as if followed by two "b's." "If you are interested in porcelain, and Finland, you really should go there."

The Arabia Porcelain Factory is in a suburb of Helsinki, which, except for Reykjavik, is the most northerly capital in the world. The bright, pleasant, busy-to-bustling plant covers a floor space of 31 acres. With over two thousand on the payroll, Arabia is the largest employer-firm in Scandinavia. Its production of household goods includes feldspathic porcelain and earthenware dishes; *objets d'art* individually made by their world-renowned potters, paint-

136

ers, and sculptors; exclusive hand-painted gift ware; vitrified sanitary fixtures; façade tiles; refractory bricks for home and industry; electric porcelain; and a great many other articles designed for specific purposes. It is easy to credit the claim that Arabia is one of the best efforts Finland is making towards an economic comeback after the country's unequal war with Russia.

ARABIA
MADE IN
FINLAND

In the ceramic field, it turns out approximately a quarter of a million finished pieces a day, which means a great selection of underglaze and onglaze patterns in an abundance of shapes to cover all possible requirements of the table, the kitchen, and the home in general. Undoubtedly, this mass production must result in a great deal of ordinary, everyday ware, but such is the soundness of taste and material that all the products are well designed.

Arabia is proud of the fact that the scientific efficiency of its ultramodern laboratories, the creative genius of its famous artists, the technical knowledge of its engineers, and the manual skill of its artisans have helped to bring a touch of elegance to more than thirty countries in the two hemispheres to which Arabia quality china is exported. Unfortunately, even including the other Scandinavian countries, they send abroad only about 20 per cent of their products. The best customer is the U.S.A.

In June of 1960 a design center resembling the Swedish FORM was opened on the fifth floor of P. Esplanaadak, 25 B, in the heart of Helsinki. Thirty-two leading manufacturers of outstanding Finnish products, including Arabia, exhibit there. Unlike DEN PERMANENTE in Copenhagen and other permanent exhibits, nothing is on sale, but you will be given information about prices and places where you may buy these treasures.

Mr. Gunnar Ståhle, the slow-spoken, undemonstrative, and indomitable managing director, gave me a brief outline of their history.

The porcelain factory was founded in 1874 by Rörstrand. It took its name from a nineteenth century villa built in Helsinki by a general who had lived in the Arabian countries and there had developed a love of Islamic art. Rörstrand did not make a go of it. In 1916 it was taken into the cooperative movement then sweeping the four northern countries.

Once World War II got into full swing, the struggle to survive was monumental. By 1946 the market for porcelain was dead. The directors were desperate. Were all those employees to be laid off?

"We had no idea how long the firm's resources would last, but while they did we decided to give our people work, making anything at all—let their conscience be their guide," he added half-seriously.

The materials were there. The machinery was available. They made things. Some you will see in their museum. Some found a ready sale immediately after trade reopened. One piece, a huge vase over three feet tall, stands on the floor by Mr. Ståhle's desk. It is a constant reminder of the parlous times they went through, and also of what close cooperation eventually achieved, knitting employers and employees more firmly together than ever. Above all, when a disgruntled employee comes in with a complaint, or is called upon the carpet, the vase acts as a silent yet effective mediator.

Mr. Ståhle was more interested in showing than in telling. He led me into a studio where once a week children of four and upwards were allowed to experiment freely, thus encouraging and keeping alive the sturdy folk art. One tiny tot was modeling a horse. It had four legs, a large head, neat ears, and a spot from which a tail could sprout. When asked why it had no tail, the shy reply, translated for me, was that the horsey sat down too hard and rubbed it off. Occasionally these odd little creations of childish imaginations and fingers have a quality, a sort of spontaneous wistfulness, which appeals to collectors.

Enthusiasm showed through the crust when the managing director produced a series of gift boxes he had originated. Varied in shape and size, they stood out by reason of their gaily splashed motifs, many employing red and black on a white ground. This modest contribution had boosted sales enormously, especially in the export countries.

Every week a selection is made of half a dozen housewives from hundreds of names sent in. These six women are given every facility the plant can offer in the matter of setting tables according to their personal taste. Of the current six tables, I thought four were fairly good, one terrible, and one excellent. The last was laid for five, two at each side and one at the head. At the foot was the so-called centerpiece, a group of four "organic" vases, one holding autumn leaves, one some grasses, one just a few stripped and varnished branches, and the fourth, in ceramic birch bark, a loose grouping of clusters of full-ripe rowan berries. Looking as if they had been tossed there by a careless but loving hand, that crimson fruit was the slight but exciting decor of the plates, beige to resemble the most beloved of the Finnish marbles.

The housewife responsible for the setting was probably one of the better Finnish cooks, for it evoked the smells of the viands: Carelian steak put in a brick oven to "do" all night, pike with egg sauce, or the popular lamb and cabbage "steamed" in layers in an iron pot. A teacart beside the table held a thick lead-glass decanter and five matching liqueur glasses for the renowned Finnish Mesimarja, made from cloudberries.

Each week the heads of the various departments go into a huddle over the six tables to see if a germ of an idea may be gleaned from any of the arrangements. Rarely do they fail to come up with something. Even the table I had pronounced terrible had given them a clue to a need of that particular woman —children's dishes with suction cups. As for the women themselves, they become so interested in the project that they do not stop with their visit, but continue to send in suggestions, usually highly practical.

"For instance, one came in the mail this morning. Why not roughen the handles of earthenware casseroles to make them less slippery in soapy dishwater?"

Americans certainly get around, yet I was startled when in the first studio a pretty girl in a smock raised a pleased face from the vase she was painting and called out cheerfully, "Hi, America!"

What on earth was she doing in a Helsinki pottery? Who was she?

She was from Los Angeles, had gone to Royal Copenhagen for a year on a fellowship, and was now on salary at Arabia. She loved it.

"Can you imagine an artist being paid for doing exactly what she wants to do? No strings whatever!"

It was because artists in Suomi were given an absolutely free hand, she went on, that the country was making its mark in every line—not only in ceramics and glass, but in weaving, woodwork, lamps, architecture.

"So far I have done nothing world-shaking," Nancy replied to my question about her work, "but between my 'divine discontent' and the way the ideas simmering in my brain box are suddenly on the point of boiling up, I have hopes."

She had nothing of her own ready to be shown. Instead, she took me to the adjoining studio—from it, she was sure, inspiration would seep into hers. It belonged to a genuine artist, Miss L. Mickwitz, seventy years old. She had not come in that morning, but her young disciple pointed out her porcelain troika with driver, three horses, and two passengers crouched so convincingly against a blizzard that with only the feeblest sort of imagination one saw snow.

"Makes you shiver, doesn't it? Miss Mickwitz has had dozens of offers for it, but she keeps it to remind her of past glories. It will probably end up in the museum here."

Arabia employs fourteen artist-craftsmen on the same basis as Nancy's, each with his or her own cheerful studio. Assured of a steady income, and the freedom to call upon the experience of the firm's technicians, some of them have produced the finest pieces to come out of the north. I did not meet all fourteen, but never have I seen happier persons than those I did meet. Creative artists, spurred by encouragement and close association with others traveling the same path.

Unfortunately for me, I missed Francesca and Richard Lindh. Francesca, born and educated in Aversa degli Abruzzi, Italy, and Richard, a native of Helsinki, met at the School of Arts and Crafts in the Finnish capital, married, and proceeded to set up their own ceramic workshop. In 1955 they joined Arabia. The following year Richard was appointed head of the Applied Art Department, from which vantage point he occasionally plans the factory's stands at various exhibitions. Both he and his wife won first prizes at the Museum of Contemporary Crafts in New York.

Doing an entirely different type of ceramics is Toini Muono who went from the Industrial Art Institute in Helsinki to Arabia in 1931 and has been busy gathering honors ever since. She does her things in the robust Finnish way yet with no sacrifice of subtlety. Her tall curved vases, her small thin bowls, her large rough dishes and her brilliant wall plaques are equally strong in form and glaze. Toini's infallible intuition has achieved fascinating results.

In contrast again is Aune Siimes who joined the staff in 1933. She makes exquisite eggshell china vases with an intense relief pattern of changing transparency, although what made her name in ceramics in the first place was her white, pink, and cobalt-blue-and-white porcelain of elegant simplicity. Her costume jewelry is also noteworthy. Some of her pieces are shown in the International Museum of Ceramics in Faenza, and some are in the collection of the King of Sweden. One day I hope to own an Aune Siimes striped bowl.

Michael Shilkin, at Arabia since 1936, was born in Petrograd and made his first statues in snow. His talent sets his sculptural ceramics apart. From a naturalistic manner his animal figures have developed towards a more cultivated stylization, but are still powerfully masculine. One of his reliefs is at the main entrance of the plant.

The ceramic artist with the picturesque temperament is Rut Bryk, Stockholm-born but an "Arabian" since 1942. Her dark radiant colors are unique, her rare juicy glazes give deep-toned richness to her wall plaques of chamotte.

Her birds and fruit, and above all her figures of the Madonna possess a grace and allure pronounced irresistible.

Probably Kyllikki Salmenhaara who went to Arabia in 1946 is the foremost name in Finnish ceramics. Finnish to the core, she gives her bowls and softly shaped vases a surface which conjures up a vision of the loveliest thing in her country, the bark of the white birch. (A Finnish birch grove in sun and shade has to be seen to be believed.) She has a predilection also for surfaces of autumn leaves, reindeer lichen, and native granite. In spite of this artistic chauvinism, her art is universal, purely a ceramic creation. Everything about it—mass, form, and glaze—combines to make an integrated whole. Barely forty, and with a stack of honors behind her, Kyllikki has many years to forge herself an even greater fame.

A latecomer to Arabia—she joined them in 1949 when, at twenty-six she had barely been graduated from the Art Institute—is Raiji Tuumi. Her style has been termed "harsh and solid, sparse and fascinating." She prefers large forms to which she gives the roughened surface of stone. Her glazes are mostly green and a warm rusty brown.

Kaj Franck, in his 40's and bubbling with good humor and inventiveness, is their leading designer for household ceramics. He is a modern and inclined to the bizarre, although that is the wrong adjective for his much-in-demand *Kilta* cups with saucers and lids, and definitely so for his even more-in-demand *Decor Polaris*, its patterned blue as cool as Finnish spring water.

Years ago, he declared war against matched table sets for any meal. His "services" are made up of supplementary pieces in different colors, with the stress on black.

"Black," he contends, "gives a striking note, and goes with almost any color, including strong ones if properly used."

Ulla Procopé creates the flameware *Liekki*, the set of nine useful yet extremely ornamental plates in white faïence with a cobalt pattern called *Valencia*, the gay *Samba* cups, the arresting large *Fiesta* cups for coffee, and the captivating spice jars with texts in four languages.

Purposely I have left to the last an artist of long-assured position, Austrian-born Friedl Kjellberg whose name has been signed to Arabia porcelain since 1924, the year she launched out on her celadon and *sang de boeuf* glazes with notable success. But where she fulfilled one of her own aspirations, and incidentally more than justified the firm's investment, was in her white ware, the bowls and mocha sets in the difficult "rice grain" technique. Known as "rice china," it has won her recognition all over the world. Superbly simple, and with a clear warm luster, it has been described as "noble porcelain." In 1960 she designed dark-glazed saucers and bowls with dark stands to provide effective contrast to the eggshell-thin white ware.

As my friends have begun to regard me as something of a china specialist, I was not surprised when a young Westchester matron called on me for help. Her brother was going to Stockholm and had offered to bring her back a dinner service if she would tell him what she wanted. She knew nothing about Scandinavian porcelain, except its excellent reputation, so how could she give him a manufacturer's name and a particular design? We strolled along Madison Avenue and turned into Bonniers. We were barely in the dinnerware department when her choice was made. She had seen one of Friedl's rice china cups and saucers. Even when the salesman figured out the cost of a full service for eight, she refused to look at any other ware.

"We could sell our second car," she said reflectively.

From a truly economic standpoint, it is doubtful that it pays Arabia to employ all these artists. But they bring prestige and publicity. Loaded with medals and honors, they would do credit to a country with many times the population. Fortunately, through exhibits and art magazines, their work is becoming familiar throughout the world.

What is more important, as Wendy Hall sums it up in her excellent *Green Gold and Granite,* is the satisfaction Arabia must feel. Far from allowing the machine to kill creative effort, they are making it serve the artist under the best possible conditions.

Chapter 16

Porsgrund

On a late October afternoon I went to Porsgrunn. It rained all the way from Oslo. In the rain-spattered fjords past which the express flew were islands where trees, struggling for existence as had the invincible people of this rigorous land, grew precariously in the crevices of the rocks.

We made a stop at Drammen, hallowed ground to me because there Peter Hofnagel, the greatest name in Norwegian ceramics, had founded a pottery, and there had created some of the immortal treasures I had been shown in the Kunsindustrimuseum in the capital. His masterwork is an enormous centerpiece with cruets, mustard pots, and salt cellars grouped around an almost naked boy holding a pierced basket for fruit.

Hear Warren E. Cox's opinion of it:

The modelling of this object is surely overdone and the anatomy of the boy is none too good but what gives a peculiar charm is the vigorous painting and the bubbling overjoyed intoxication of the boy as he prances through the scrolls and scallop-shells, the foliage and the pots, as though gaily bringing the *pièce de resistance* to the whole dinner. This work of art has been called the "jolliest figure in the whole work of fäience."

He concludes by saying that it has a quality which "the copyists cannot catch any more than they could lay hold of a sunbeam."

For the quarter-hour the train stopped, I stayed out on the platform, trying to breathe in a whiff of Hofnagel's air.

For years Peter Hofnagel was a round peg in a square hole. He began his career as a lawyer. Deciding to take up agriculture, he bought an estate near a town called Arundel, but being disappointed at not being given the appointment as postmaster there, he became a merchant. He was well on in his forties before he realized what he wanted to do—make things with his hands, make ceramics.

143

In 1757 he founded a tile factory at Herrebøe. Discontented with it, he founded a second for making stoneware stoves. In 1758 he opened a third and switched to faïence. *Ah, this was it!* His half-Scottish stepsons did the decorating and signed their name, *Large*. The wares found no market. To keep the factory going he had to sell them below cost. He closed his doors and opened a plant at Drammen, with even less financial success.

In 1763, as the Seven Years War ended, he founded a factory at Osterbro in Denmark. A series of lawsuits, though he won the final decision, left him with insufficient funds to carry on. He returned to Norway. Six years later he died, only aware that he was a sad and disconsolate failure.

Yet in 1900 when the Kunsindustrimuseum had an exhibition of ceramics, his pieces brought anywhere from 4,000 to 12,000 kroner, about $600 to $1,700. How one such sale would have encouraged poor Hofnagel! It is to be hoped that some stray atoms of his ego have survived to float in the ether and pick up Cox's eulogy on the waves.

By the time I was installed in the ultramodern hotel, the rain had slowed to a heavy drizzle. From my wide window the view outside, a row of lighted shops backed on a river, resembled a Joseph Pennell etching.

So this was Porsgrunn. A port on an inlet of the Skaggerak. A town in Telemark County, the district famous for its skiing and roses. Porsgrunn, noted for its fine porcelain.

Mr. Jacob A. Möller, the proprietor of the Porsgrunds Porselænfabrik—Porsgrunn, formerly Porsgrund, is only one of the confusions resulting from the Norwegians' many spelling reforms—had met the train in his Kapitan. With his wife, he was returning at half past seven to take me to dinner. It was then not five. I had lunched lightly in my Oslo hotel at eleven. Reaching for the phone, I asked to have toast and tea sent up. It came. My eye was caught by the dishes. Not the usual hotel ware. Had the hotelier sent his own personal china? Even more than the delicious hot toast and fragrant tea, the charming and whimsical horse-woman on the plate raised my morale.

If there had ever been a day, as other Scandinavians claim, when the Norwegians subsisted on a soup made by boiling a rusty nail in a gallon of water, that day was past. Dinner in the other good hotel, the remodeled and modernized New Vic, was a gourmet meal, served on attractive porcelain. "From the restaurateur's own china cabinet?" I longed to ask. Instead I admired the smart lamps in the dining room. From the pride with which my host informed me that his factory had made them, I knew why we were dining there rather than in my hotel. It, I found the next day, served gourmet food too, and also had attractive porcelain.

After breakfast in my room—again I had the dishes which I had named "Lady Centaur"—Mr. Möller came to take me to the plant. En route we detoured frequently at points of interest, also to give him time to fill in the gaps in the story of Porsgrund he had told me the previous evening over coffee in the Möllers' delightful treasure-filled home.

Porsgrund porcelain came into being in the third quarter of the nineteenth century. A local shipowner named Jeremiason Johan had gone to Carlsbad in Germany to take a T.B. cure. When he saw feldspar and quartz together being shipped from there to various porcelain plants of Germany, he was set thinking. If he could get kaolin and ball clay from England, he could make porcelain too. His ships could carry timber, the chief natural resource of Norway, to England, and fetch clay back. Coal, too.

The idea stimulated him. By 1885 he had his plant in operation. From the start it gave great promise, for he had managed to inveigle several truly good artists into his employ. Unfortunately, he lived only a year to witness his success.

His widow decided that perpetuating his work was the best memorial she could erect to him. For ten years, this gallant woman stood at the helm. She saw her artistic products sold everywhere in her native country and farther afield, amazingly even in Sweden which prided itself on the aesthetic quality of its own creations.

At her death, the management was taken over by her niece's father-in-law, Hans Möller, father of the present owner. Under him the factory continued to win acclaim for its really fine and original wares. Orders began to trickle in from America, then flow in a steady stream. The dollars made 1900 to 1910 Porsgrund's golden decade. Unlike both Jeremiason Johan and Peter Hofnagel, Hans Möller lived to see the fruit of his efforts. And, alas! to see it lie rotting beneath the tree when the First World War burst into flames, even though his country had remained neutral.

For some time Norway had been in a state of political upheaval. Little Norway, with the third largest merchant marine fleet in the world, with its outstanding explorers such as Fridtjof Nansen and Roald Amundsen, had long been demanding its own flag and government, and wanted them before the emigration to America became too widespread. Southern Norway effected its withdrawal from Sweden in 1895, when Christiana became Oslo, but the rest of the country remained under the neighbor's thrall until 1905, the year Prime Minister Mikkelson achieved an amicable separation.

The period of transition persisted almost to the opening of World War II, when the German occupation left Norway no choice but to get into the fray. Hans Möller's son, Jacob, a lawyer, was elected police-master of the underground in Telemark. A year later he was put in charge of the group formed to ferret out fifth columnists and quislings. Possibly because Vidkun Quisling was one of the intelligentsia and born in Porsgrunn, these comprised roughly 25 per cent of the people of the district.

Porcelain and patriots suffered alike. The Nazis forced the factory to deliver the goods or else! "Else" meant that they goose-stepped in and helped themselves. Hans Möller died. The new manager and his son, the latter a no-good at the best of times, were ardent Nazi sympathizers. This made things tough for the underground, for it had to have money. Jacob Möller had depended upon the factory to supply the necessary funds. Now that was out.

"Secretly, the local bank gave us the money we needed. And each time, for the various sums, I insisted upon signing a note. Those cancelled notes are among my most precious souvenirs, for they are evidence that, after all, the family factory supported the underground financially."

The war had left Norway in a desperate financial plight. Sorely in need of dishes as the people were, porcelain was a luxury item. For it there was no money. Worst of all, the company had no funds for advertising in America, the country with the dollars.

"As if there were anything to advertise, the way everything had been allowed to go to rack and ruin!"

In 1946 Jacob Möller was asked to take over the plant. Porcelain manufacture was to him by no means unfamiliar territory. His wife was the niece of the former owner, and he had been a member of the board during his father's regime. But his law practice in the town and district provided generously for the education of his four children. Would it be fair to them to give it up? Would it be fair to the employees not to?

When his business friends learned of his decision they protested against his foolhardy step. The situation was hopeless. They begged him to resume his legal practice before it was too late.

The pottery wheels were barely turning again when out of a blue sky he was hospitalized with a ruptured appendix. He chafed at the inaction, and lost his appetite. He admits now that it was partly because of the coarse "institutional" dishes on which the food was served. One day his wife brought china from home. He cleaned up the plate.

"A good thing all our patients have not fine dishes," teased the matron who removed his empty tray.

"They should have," he insisted.

She agreed. They had to replenish their stock, too, and immediately. But when they could barely afford flintware, porcelain was out of the question.

"The initial cost may be slightly higher," he admitted, "but porcelain is chip-proof, altogether more durable, especially in the new electric dishwashers. Put off ordering for a week or two. I have a scheme in mind."

The problem, he knew, was not confined to Telemark. It was nationwide. The moment he could travel, he went to Oslo and contacted the government hospital authorities. They gave him a sympathetic hearing. In so far as they could they would fall in line with his idea of a subsidy, though, because of the condition of the national exchequer, it would take some doing to pry the smallest sum out of the treasury.

Tired to the point of exhaustion, he proceeded to a restaurant. The heavy dishes used in these eating places had bothered him before, but not to the same extent. Excellent food did not have to be served on a dingy chipped plate, and even earthenware did not have to be ugly. He pushed the plate away. The proprietor rushed over and asked what was wrong. Jacob Möller is a persuasive gentleman, and soon made his point: People who came in tired and hungry needed food for their souls as well as for their bodies.

The restaurateur was definitely interested. He was about to redecorate the place, had already chosen colorful table linens and draperies. If Porsgrunds Porselænsfabrik could make him some dishes to go with them, at a reasonable price, the order was on the books.

Mr. Möller called a meeting of the executives and put everything he had into his speech to them. As conditions did not warrant their continuing with the manufacture of their characteristic aesthetic luxury porcelain, they must adjust their machinery, *and their egos,* to wares for which they could find a market. Two potential categories of customers, hitherto scorned, were hospitals and restaurants. Hospitals suddenly found themselves bulging at the seams, and restaurants had queues. The tourist traffic had chosen as its Number One vacation spot the magic-landscaped northern country whose valiant people had stood against the invader. Hotels were springing up like mushrooms. Good hotels, not jerry-built. As modern and as comfortable as were to be found anywhere. For instance, the Alexandra at Molde, the "City of Roses" which had been razed by the Nazis because the court had taken refuge there.

When approached, the management of most of the better hotels had shown a keen interest in finer dinnerware. Porcelain if the price were right, and naturally from Porsgrund.

"As artistic as is compatible with the price you have quoted us," they said with one accord.

"Artistic regardless of price," Möller told his executives. "Our motto! Nothing ugly or imperfect must go out of the plant. As for demeaning ourselves, we shall demean neither ourselves nor our traditions if we send tourists home talking about our fine Norwegian ware."

He inspired his staff. The technicians applied themselves to evolving short-cuts and economies without loss of quality. The artists burned the midnight oil. Some of their conceptions were extreme, but at least they were original, and, with a bit of eventual editing, not too revolutionary.

The response was amazing. The new patterns were snapped up almost hot from the kiln. (New kilns, of course.) The number of employees, many of them third-generation Porsgrunders, rose to 200, then to 350, with another 150 in the department making sanitary porcelain.

Two Porsgrund marks. The one at left was used in the 1940's to 1954, the one at right since 1954.

Seldom now in Norway are you served your food on coarse, undecorated dishes, or, if decorated, merely with the initials or name of the hotel. For the throngs who flock to the North Cape 1100 miles away to see the midnight sun, Porsgrund designed dishes with such amusing and whimsical decorations that a shop was opened for souvenir hunters.

As yet the factory is not going in for novelties. One special order they filled was "Peer Gynt Riding on a Pig," made as a penny bank for the Minister of Finance. Another, which they turned down, was for a plate decorated with a picture of the late king's face. A rival pottery manufactured it, to the royal perturbation.

"Are those plates to be used on the table?" the monarch demanded.

"Oh, no, Your Majesty! They are merely to hang on the wall."

"Good!" he sighed in relief. "I'd hate getting gravy in my nose."

Displayed in the showroom were ravishing examples from the days when Porsgrund's only aim was to create beauty. On one handsome vase an artist had reproduced a flying squirrel picture by the famous animal painter, Kittelsen. A sculpture of a young ermine seemed to breathe. To come from that room to one with purely utility wares saddened me.

The utility wares saddened me, too, but for a different reascn. Too few of these essentially beautiful everyday pieces reach our shores. Our hospitals and restaurants, and our homes, could benefit from the dishes which Mr. Möller termed "ordinary." In what could coffee taste better than in a "Lady Centaur" cup?

The inspiration for this horse-woman motif by the young artist, Konrad Galaaen, was the historic narrative about a nunnery, Ginsöy Kloster, which in the Middle Ages was situated not far from Porsgrunn. The figure represents a nun returning from a flowery meadow. In her hands she holds a bunch of moor myrtle, sometimes called "sweet willow" or "gale,"—botanically *Myrica gale*. As the Norwegian name for it is *pors,* it is quite likely that the town was named after the herb.

Galaaen, at Porsgrund since 1948, looks the artist. No beard or velvet smock, but a sense of a palette-shaped halo above his fine handsome head. From his twinkling eyes and lively expression, he might be an intimate of the trolls through whose charming countryside my train had passed.

This artist has designed exquisite porcelain with a half-transparent pattern, delicate pieces compared to those which have made his name known throughout the ceramic world. His huge stoneware wall decorations have put Galaaen in a class by himself. Outstanding examples of them are a magnificent plaque with four stylized Norse ponies and chariot, and a great sculptured fish. Both pieces, at the entrance of the Philips Building in Oslo, are targets of camera fans.

Tias Eckhoff, after five years on the staff, was promoted to art director in 1953, the year he won the coveted Lunning Prize. The following year at the Milan Triennial he was awarded two gold medals, and in 1957 two more. Skillful at combining colors, one of his most striking productions is a coffee service of fine white cups, the coffee pot, cream, and sugar in black. Unfortunately nowadays he cannot achieve a good black as the basis is uranium, in demand for atom bombs. In heavier ware is his popular fireproof *Glohane,* meaning firecock, a name still in use in the north. Eckhoff also designs silver and stainless steel for Georg Jensen in Copenhagen, and door handles for the Norwegian Trio Factory.

The latest studio to be opened is occupied by a practical young pipe-smoking gentleman, Eystein Sandness. He proved himself at once with his first mocha set, the decor geometric in alluring soft tones. It has been suggested that one of the artists, and possibly Per Nordberg, the sales manager, visit America to acquaint themselves with our preferences. For example, do we or do we not like the undersized saucers with the outsized cups? If the practical Sandness is chosen to make the trip, I can just see him, pipe in mouth, his tall figure leaning against the rail, one eye cocked for the State of Liberty, the other scanning the famous skyline and maneuvering it into an embellishment for a dinner plate.

The only woman artist, now that Beth Möller is a designer with the Royal Copenhagen Manufactory, is Anne-Marie Odegard, *nee* Jørgensen. I first saw her work in the Porsgrund store in Oslo when I bought a pair of her salt-and-peppers, "Mr. and Mrs.," attractively boxed and sold under the name of *Madame Condiment Set.* The salt shaker was designed some time ago, but the pepper shaker is recent.

In Norway House, New York, I was surprised one day to see women recently returned from the Land of the Midnight Sun buying so much. It turned out that they had failed to bring back enough souvenirs to give to their friends. In half an hour, I saw four *Madame Condiment Sets* borne away—at three times the Oslo price.

One might describe Anne-Marie as a young woman of joyful exuberance. She favors pitchers and coffee pots without handles to break off, yet like the medieval *albarellos* of Spain and Italy, more or less cylindrical but with concave sides, to be grasped by the body where the "waist" curves inward to fit the hand. Bursting with ideas, she feels held back by having to perform routine jobs. Not that she is limited by her employer, she hastened to add. No one could give his artists more latitude than does Mr. Möller. While she is expected to design plain pieces to satisfy customers in the lower money brackets, she is always given time to develop her own specialties when the spirit moves her.

"Don't think I am grumbling when I say that I am looking forward to the day when exports pick up and our staff is increased. More jobs can then be specialized. For instance, I'd like an assistant to do the transfer printing, and save hours of my valuable time. Frustration is death to an artist's inspiration." She laughed ruefully, and in all humility added, "Artists are born, you know, not made, but anyone can be taught to transfer-print."

The born-artist was in the ascendant when she designed the bowl Mr. Möller asked me to accept as a reminder of my visit, and a much-treasured souvenir it is. On the pure white surface are blue birds as stylized as mythical birds of ancient lore, their crest and wings formed of leaves with clear veins. In the background, stars and fishes. As for the glaze—let us call it supernal.

It is in Anne-Marie's feminine studio that the artists congregate at teatime every afternoon for conferences. Often Per Nordberg sits in, also Mr. Möller when he can get away from his office.

"One way of keeping my ear to the ground, rather than having it bitten off by these rarin'-to-go artists!"

That characterizes them perfectly. Chockful of youth, enthusiasm, and eagerness. One reason that the products of Porsgrund are so strongly Norwegian—or in other words, independent, is that each is an expression of a distinct character, yet all with a universality resulting from the whole staff's interest in and their knowledge of the great world reached by their merchant marine.

Added to these is the spirit of Hofnagel, still alive in every one of his country's fellow artists.

Chapter 17

Haviland

RECENTLY the W. H. Block Company of Indianapolis had an exhibit of Haviland china, with some of their original productions, and some coin-new. Mr. Frederick Haviland, then of the New York company, was present, affably discussing the date and value of old pieces being shown him by women from all over the state. Talking with him, I might have expected to be mentally in the Fifth Avenue showrooms. Not so! Without any volition on my part, I was in the quaint north Portugal town of Aveiro, because of its canals known as the Portuguese Venice.

Aveiro has a porcelain factory, which was why I had gone there. It, Vista Alegre, has a small but precious output. Strolling through the streets late the first evening, I chanced upon a gift shop. In its dimly lit window was a miniature cabaret gay with roses and gold.

Half fearful that the *objet d'art* might have been spirited away during the night, I dashed around immediately after breakfast. The cabaret was there, but not such a prize in the bright morning sunshine. The roses were daubed on, the gilt hewed to no line. Could that tawdry set be Vista Alegre? I turned the tiny pitcher over to see the mark. No VA—Limoges. There it was again, just Limoges. But which manufactory? Twenty-four porcelain fabriques in that French town—producing quality ranging from superb to nondescript or worse. Except that you group only twenty-three. One you automatically counted out as very special. Haviland—*Aviloŋ* they pronounce it in Limousin, with pride in their voices.

The manufacture of china brought prosperity to Limousin as it had to Staffordshire and Saxony. *Porcelaine* and *faïence* contribute over 440,000,000 francs annually to the country's coffers. As money-makers for France, they rank first, even ahead of wine. And the leading pottery, producing the most notable French porcelain since the halcyon days of Sèvres, is Haviland.

Haviland

The de Havilland family had gone from Normandy to England with William the Conqueror in 1066. One branch, still in the United Kingdom, includes Olivia de Havilland (cinema) and Geoffrey de Havilland (aircraft.) Another branch emigrated to America in 1640, almost in the wake of the *Mayflower*. They dropped the "de" and one "l" from the name, built their first American home at Haviland Hollow, in Putnam County, sixty miles out of New York City, and settled down to become dyed-in-the-wool Americans.

In 1831, two hundred years after his ancestors had left France, a young Haviland, David, opened a retail china shop in his native city, New York. His wares, selected with both shrewdness and an eye for beauty, were imported from England. Prominent families patronized his emporium in fashionable Barclay Street. Such a clientele was a source of great gratification to the young merchant burning with a desire to succeed. Yet even more than financial success, he desired the prestige which could come only from satisfying his customers. To achieve this end, no trouble was too great.

One day a valued customer brought in a broken cup. It belonged to an old family set. Could Haviland replace it?

Haviland took the cup in his hand. At the contact, a sixth sense told him it was not English. Probably French. Yes. It said "France" on the bottom. Nothing more. Not a mark of any kind. What French pottery had produced, created, such an exquisite piece? If he knew, he could not only duplicate the cup but add their fine china to his stock. Yet how was he to know? It said only "France."

You have heard the story of Bernard Palissy, the great French peasant potter of the early sixteenth century, the course of whose life was changed by a plain white cup put in his hand? Now a broken one was to change the course of David Haviland's life. Night and day it haunted him. He had to go to France. There could be no peace of mind for him until he found out where the cup had been made. Finally, leaving his brother to manage the store, he booked his passage.

Crossing the Atlantic in 1839 meant a tedious voyage of many weeks duration. He was seasick the whole way, a streak of bad luck which threatened to persist, for, once in France, he found himself traveling down blind alleys. Again and again he thought he had a clue, only to find that it led nowhere. Time after time he returned to the statue of Palissy before the Sèvres museum in the Paris suburb, and practically prayed to the resolute man in bronze to hand him the magic key.

"Why not try Limoges?" the curator suggested to the dispirited merchant. "Porcelain has been manufactured there for seventy-five years."

In Limoges he found the match for the broken cup. He berated himself for the time he had lost. The veriest dolt should have known that Limoges was the logical place to look. Not only was it the center of porcelain manufacture, but it was at the nearby town of St. Yriex that the indispensable kaolin had been found in the intensive search after the Jesuit priest, Père d'Entrecolles, had sent his furtive sample home from the Orient around 1705. Bursting with triumph—he had his customer's cup—Haviland sailed back to New York.

He was bursting also with optimism, for he had arranged to have the superlative china of that particular Limoges fabrique made according to his specifications, and shipped to his store in Barclay Street. His fortune seemed assured.

Unhappily, things did not work out that way. The French potter found it impossible to change his methods and processes merely to produce shapes and decorations to suit "crazy" American tastes. But it was not for nothing that David Haviland had early adopted the motto, *Nil desperandum.* Give up? Never! Rather would he go back to Limoges and himself make china for the "crazy" American market. Two years later, in 1842, he took his whole family there, and established a small pottery in a greenhouse at the edge of town, the address, 72 Emile-Laboussière.

His troubles had only begun. The French artisans grumbled incessantly about the new shapes and designs. When they saw their jobs imperiled by young apprentices being taught to work out the *outré* forms and patterns, they staged demonstrations. Both teachers and pupils had to go about in groups to protect themselves from attack. One innovation in particular aroused their ire. Up to that time local potters had made nothing except plain ware which they sent to Paris to be decorated, one of the reasons the cup had been inscribed only "France." Haviland built his own decorating shop, and installed the equipment needed to change from plain to decorated ware.

Little by little the magnetic personality and tact of the intrepid proprietor ironed out most of the differences, a feat completed when, on a momentous day in 1842, the first consignment of Haviland china was shipped to New York, and became an immediate success. The artisans all about-faced. They took such pride in the glowing sales and prestige reports, they boasted so immoderately about what *they* had done, that for a time they had to go about in groups to protect themselves from the craftsmen in the older potteries.

It was not long until it was obvious to everyone that Haviland was producing better china and in greater quantities than had ever been attempted in Limoges before; that his porcelain was so hard that it lived up to the claims of indestructibility made by the sales force. Within three years, by 1845, buildings in addition to the greenhouse had to be erected to cope with the growing trade.

Even at that, their capacity was taxed. The vogue had spread to England and Scotland. Throughout the nineteenth century it was the thing to make what British humor twisted into the "Grand Tower," especially on one's honeymoon. Rare was the bride visiting the continent who did not inveigle her bridegroom into 72 Emile-Laboussière, Limoges, the mecca of the truly discriminating.

An elderly Edinburgh friend has a 24-person service, practically intact although much of it is in constant use, souvenir of her parents' honeymoon in 1875. Each piece has their monogram etched in gold. A costly procedure as five separate layers of acid-etched gold (consequently five firings in the kiln) are required to make the design stand out in relief. Present day tourists, alas! have their initials or monograms merely stamped.

From the outset the shrewd David Haviland had maintained a staff of technicians and engineers to keep him abreast of the times and ahead of his competitors. Even though it meant trying out some they had to discard, he insisted that the firm give ear to all new ideas.

One which his son Theodore adopted was lithographing. Until 1873, when this process for decorating china was originated by three Frenchmen, patterns had all been hand-painted, a costly undertaking and slow, for the artists refused to work anywhere but in their own homes—many still do—and followed their own temperamental schedules. Decorating two plates in a day by hand was a cause for marvel. A larger piece took a week.

Theodore Haviland not only instantly recognized the merits of lithographing but set about improving the process. Later he introduced chromolithographic decorating, subsequently taken over by practically every china manufacturer in the world. It was an interesting process to watch. At magic speed, the girls in the Emile-Laboussière studio pressed the paper patterns on with rubber rollers, and removed them with pincers. My guide told me that, in the old days, two hundred women were employed doing decalcomania, and Theodore himself, wearing a tall hat, would come in and bow over each table. It made the workers feel very important.

By 1890 Haviland's had again outgrown their quarters, and on the same site Theodore, now head of the firm, supervised the construction of one of the largest and best factories in Limoges. Up-to-date methods and machinery were introduced. Coal ovens were replaced by the cleaner gas kilns. Skillful technicians, for which Europe was scoured, were put in charge of the various departments. In the grounds, studios were provided for the great ceramic artists who now joined the staff.

Nine years later, Theodore was able to turn his attention to the needs of himself and his family. He bought 300 acres of land on the edge of a small village named Ambazac ten miles out of Limoges, where he planned to build a modest chateau and settle down as lord of the manor. Warning him that even a modest chateau with only thirty bedrooms would require years to build, the architect advised him to put up a smaller house in the interim. Later, this small house proved a valuable investment.

World War I struck Limoges a crushing blow. All the potteries were in a desperate plight, though hardest hit were those producing luxury goods. It is not surprising then that, faced with closing down, many of them flooded the markets with cheap souvenirs, such as the tawdry minature cabaret I saw in Aveira more than four decades later.

Haviland's had its own difficulties. In the early years of the 1900's it had been routine for them to ship 150 casks of porcelain a week to New York. Between 1914 and 1918, they did not ship that many a month, and with no assurance that any would reach its destination and be paid for. Their staff of over a thousand dwindled to 360. The resultant hardships and hunger were heartbreaking. Although feeling that such a step was a blot on their escutcheon, they too decided to try novelties in the hope of making a quick comeback. A kiln-load of delightful ducks was produced. They did not sell, I was told by the oldest employee—ex-employee, rather—René de Jacques, introduced to me by Harold Haviland in his attractive office opening off the board room. Finally the whole consignment was unloaded on McCreery's of New York who almost gave them away.

"When customers wanted Haviland," René said, "they meant dishes, not ducks."

After that episode, Haviland made dishes, and only dishes, manufactured according to the high standards laid down by the tall-hatted, bushy-bearded Theodore Haviland whose portrait looks down on you from the rear wall of the board room in Limoges. If Haviland porcelain was to be anything, he had decreed when the new factory was opened in 1890, it must be dignified and appeal only to persons of refined taste. That is the creed to which they still adhere.

Time moved forward. Beloved and respected by all, Theodore handed the reins to his son, William David—class of Harvard, 1902—and retired to the small house to watch from the sidelines. He was not on the scene when in

1927 the plant he had built with love and pride was struck by lightning, necessitating the building of a new one along even more up-to-date lines.

Much as William David loved the family chateau and its gracious life, his tenure was intermittent. The American trade had grown fantastically. He was spending more time in America than in France. Something had to be done about it. Besides, by 1936, the world was rife with wars and rumors of wars. France would inevitably become embroiled. Supplies from Limoges would be cut off. So, nearly a hundred years after his grandfather had established his fabrique in a greenhouse, William David found himself embarking upon an even more revolutionary step, that of establishing headquarters in New York.

He looked about for an American potter willing to manufacture porcelain according to the Limoges formula. Ultimately three independent ones were chosen—at Antioch, Illinois, at New Castle, Pennsylvania, and at Cleveland, Ohio. The first consignment demonstrated that the domestic line was worthy of the famous Haviland name. Today American Haviland is a leader on our side of the Atlantic.

Their ovenproof ware, in twelve different colors and patterns, is a true china, and is guaranteed for a year against any kind of breakage. *Riviera Casual* was purposely designed to meet the growing trend of outdoor living. Dramatic in color and design is *Portofino*, created for them by a Puerto Rico plant. In that pattern an especially attractive cheese plate with a wide polished teak rim has found a harmonious companion in my stainless steel Norwegian cheese slicer.

The rapid success of the American venture made it impossible for William David to manage affairs on both sides of the Atlantic, no matter how carefully he apportioned his time. The American company, a separate firm in spite of its importing a great deal from Limoges, was put in charge of his eldest son, Theodore Haviland II, and a younger son, Frederick, the fourth generation to carry on the tradition. The fifth generation is represented by Theodore III, Theodore II's son and assistant. The Limoges plant on its time-honored site was, until his retirement a few months ago, under the direction of another son, Harold—*M. Avilon*—a big, handsome gentleman with personality plus.*

If in its productions, the factory has leaned towards the conservative, M. Haviland's life has by no means followed suit. "Never a dull moment!" said

* Theodore Haviland II is president of the whole enterprise. Frederick is vice-president, and managing director of the Limoges plant.

René. "His biography would read like fiction, sufficiently colorful to be melodrama."

All of the Havilands have been educated in America, the sons at Harvard. Each paterfamilias saw to it that his sons met and married American girls. With one exception—Harold. Graduated from his alma mater, he returned to Limoges footloose and fancy free. But only until he met a charming and talented French girl. They were married just as soon as he had won Any's consent, and that of her parents.

His parents' consent was not forthcoming. His father stormed. It was bad enough that the girl was French, but a Roman Catholic to boot! For a while the marriage caused a division in the ranks. When a granddaughter was born, William David unbent slightly. He capitulated unconditionally when a grandson appeared on the scene.

Both children were born in the house in the village of Ambazac. Nicole is an American citizen. Christopher, born in August, 1941, shortly after the American Nationality Act of 1940 went into effect, is French in the eyes of the law. When he ultimately takes over, the Haviland circle will have completed itself, the family reverting to the nationality and the religion of the early de Havillands.

During World War II, Limousin was one of the main theaters of guerilla warfare in France. On June 10, 1944, the whole population of the small town of Oradour-sur-Glane was murdered in retaliation by German troops of the S. S. Division, *Das Reich*. In Limoges itself, once the occupation took place, a German regiment paraded the streets daily. The French inhabitants went on their way without noticing them. That stung.

"But," said René, "they could hardly post bills or carry banners saying, 'Look at us! Look at us!' "

At first, Harold Haviland fought with the American Army. Later, joining the French underground, he had one hairbreadth escape after another. He was on Hitler's death list, and was actually on the point of being handed over when he became suspicious of a guide who was leading him and a party of British airmen into Spain. The guide, found with Nazi papers, was shot without ceremony or compunction. Finally, M. Haviland ended up in London, and, under an assumed name, directed parachutists by radio to chosen destinations in France.

The war over, he settled back into the life of Limoges, and continued his patriotic duties by contributing to his country's treasury an export total of over 120,000,000 new francs a year in U.S.A. trade alone. As the average wage for an ordinary artisan in the States is $2 an hour, while in France it is only 35 cents, he can still pay the 45 per cent duty and compete with American-produced wares. Of all French porcelain shipped to America, two-thirds is Haviland.

In 1957, when his father retired, Harold took over as head of both the French and American companies. The next year he added to and further streamlined the "new" factory with "1927" on the cornerstone. Gas kilns were replaced by electric ones capable of a temperature of 2800 F., I was told, a heat guaranteed to produce porcelain of peerless durability.

"If like Rip van Winkle," René said proudly, "David Haviland could come back after his long sleep and see the mighty tree which has grown from the seed he planted in his greenhouse a hundred and fifteen years ago, would he not rub his eyes in amaze?"

René de Jacques has been associated with Haviland's for more than half that period. He started with the firm in 1896, when he was sixteen. Now at eighty, but an alert eighty, and retired on a generous pension, he is never so happy as when called upon to show an overseas visitor through the plant.

"I'm as much a part of Haviland's," he said twice, "as if they had impressed the Haviland mark on the soles of my feet."

René had not started in the Limoges factory. As a result of his proficiency in English, which he learned at the Lycée, the government of France gave him a scholarship for further study in America. There he found employment at Haviland's in New York. He stayed for thirty years.

Haviland's was proud of him when he enlisted in the U.S. Army in the First World War. When he rose to the rank of quartermaster sergeant, the management shipped him a whole cask of porcelain for use in the mess. This caused trouble with the officers. They were never done protesting. "Why should noncoms have better dishes than we have?"

In 1920 René went to France to visit his mother. He stayed so long that he forfeited his American citizenship and could not go back to the United States to live. Not until 1947 did he return for a visit, his object to seek out his old friends, especially in Brooklyn where he had made his home. After such a long interval few remained.

An article published in the *Saturday Evening Post* mentioned him as Haviland's oldest employee. It got him into touch with people of whom he had not heard for years. One letter, postmarked Sarasota, Florida, was from the widow of Captain Heilich who had been in charge of his detachment in the army.

"Are you," she wrote, "the quartermaster sergeant who was given the controversial china?"

Letters went back and forth. The correspondence gave fresh color and interest to his life.

"As, Madame," he concluded with old-world courtesy, "our porcelain brings fresh color and harmony into the lives of many housewives."

During the century and a quarter of its existence, Haviland's have taken special orders as a matter of course. Among these have been services for emperors and kings, VIPs and millionaires. One for Ibn Saud, a 2700-piece service, set that monarch back a cool $60,000. Haviland made the dishes for the royal train when the late George VI and his queen toured Canada and the U.S.A. before World War II. *Each tea setting had to have ten cream jugs.* A bit puzzling! Of course, as the continentals claim, all English, royalty not excepted, were mad. In this case there was a simple explanation. On previous trans-Atlantic tours, guests had "pinched" the pitchers as souvenirs. The result had been an embarrassing shortage.

"Having nine extra ones," the envoy concluded, "will allow for a jug to be *given* to the guests."

This catering to royalty and potentates did not blind Haviland's to their main occupation, what René had called, "bringing fresh color and harmony into the lives of many housewives." For these important persons—personages in their own domains—countless pleasing forms have been created.

Two basic shapes are Louis XIV and the Torse or Swirl. The former was inspired partly by the famous boudoir of Mme. de Montespan, mistress of *le roi soleil.* The latter, twisted fluting achieved in the finest of translucent white porcelain, was introduced at the Paris World's Fair in 1889, and received the distinguished *Grand Prix.* Both have sold steadily ever since. Indeed the company has no better seller than the plain white Torse.

As for patterns, anyone who is harmony-conscious can choose her service merely by the sound of the romantic names—playing it by ear, as it were. For instance: Auberge, Bagatelle, Chantelet. . . .

Auberge, the French word for inn, owes its origin to the weatherbeaten sign over the door of *"A l'Arbre Vert,"* or Green Tree inn. *Bagatelle* was named for *"la Rose Bagatelle,"* a rose as popular in France as our American Beauty here. *Bergère* makes one think of the little shepherdesses who gather bouquets of wild bachelor buttons in the fields where they watch their flocks; and *Floreal* of the rich harvest of August, a month which took that name in the nomenclature of the calendar adopted by Napoleon. *Orsay* comes from the Jardin d'Orsay in Limoges, for it was there that Jean François, a Haviland designer, enjoyed the perfume of the sweet peas he was capturing with his crayons on his block of paper. *Sheraton,* a classical gold band, has been chosen by so many brides that it is usually referred to as the "Wedding Band." In platinum it is called *Versailles.*

Their best seller in 1961, Mr. Theodore Haviland told me, was *Ladore*, revived. The fine gold tracery of this classic patetrn is a modification of the ornate carving found in wall panels in the Chateau de Fontainebleau.

Vying with it are three in blue: *Bergère* with its bachelor buttons; *Mistral*, a new and charming pattern with odd sprays of softly delicate flowers on a platinum-bordered Louis XIV shape; and *Strasbourg*, also revived, its roses blue.

One thing about Haviland patterns—conservative designs for chatelaines of good taste—they revive.

Not so conservative was the coffee cup and saucer suggested a year or two ago by an American buyer. The saucer would be oblong, with a well for the cup in one end, in the other end an ashtray. Harold Haviland considered it an extremely doubtful number, but out of deference to a good customer manufactured a hundred or so. They did not sell.

A word about the Haviland shop. You will not find "rejects" there as in most plants. Nothing is carried but quality ware. Their "seconds" are picked up for a song by dealers who sell them—for two songs!—in the Saturday morning street markets to be encountered throughout France.

And wherever you buy, do not be deluded by a mere "Limoges" on the bottom. All American Haviland is stamped THEODORE HAVILAND—NEW YORK, and all French ware THEODORE HAVILAND—FRANCE. The word "Limoges" may or may not appear.

MADE IN AMERICA

Haviland marks: left, for French china and now with phrase "Made in America" for American; right, former mark for American china.

Any Limoges china not bearing these marks has been made by a firm which has no connection with the Havilands. If it says *only* "Limoges" you may be assured that it has been made by a factory with no standing, for the reputable ones sign their wares either by name or mark.

Don't say "Limoges"—say "Haviland."

161

Chapter 18

Quimper

THREE hundred and fifty miles west of Paris, as the crow flies, is the department of Finistère—End of the Earth—in Brittany. Brest is the principal port, but the capital, Quimper, lures most women, for it is there that the charming peasant pottery, *Quimper* is manufactured, and has been continuously for nearly three centuries. Records show that primitive pottery was made there in 1420, seventy-two years before Columbus set out in search of India.

With so many people doing things in ceramics these days, I decided, seeing that I was in Paris anyway, to visit the *fabriques* making this peasant pottery de luxe, if one might coin the phrase. Friends who collect this type of thing would prefer a piece brought home from the point of origin to a piece picked up in a shop. Besides, I had never been in that delightful part of France—Brittany, land of traditions, is known as the French Cornwall. Into the bargain, one of the publishers who have given me such encouragement with this book is himself a collector, and thought we might include a chapter on *Quimper* even though it was not porcelain. Could I appreciate the ware adequately without meeting the potters, seeing Bretagne and the Bretons, and finding out for myself how much the environment and the natives had influenced the products? Ah, if you want to go somewhere badly enough, you never have any trouble finding good and sufficient reasons for the trip!

In the captivating old-world town with its main street running along both sides of the scenic and navigable River Odet the two leading potteries are: Jules Henriot et Fils, and Faïenceries Bretonne de la Grande Maison, H-B.

In the former I was received by *le fils*, Yves Henriot. With obvious pride he told me that the pottery had been in existence, and in the Henriot family or its forebears since 1690. How much farther back its roots went, he did not know.

162

Records exist of a charter of brotherhood signed on July 6, 1493, by one Jean Dumaine and twenty other potters in the church of Ger, viscounty of Mortain, Normandy. History jumps nearly three centuries to 1774 when Guillaume Dumaine from La Josserie near Ger, where his family made earthen pots for the butter merchants of Isigny, set out on a tour of France. He settled in Quimper, shortly became owner of a rundown pottery bearing the date 1690, and in 1778 married the daughter of the proprietor of the hostelry, Croix Blanche, near the cathedral. In 1821 their granddaugher, Marie Renée, married a potter named Jean-Baptiste Tanqueray. In 1864 the name Henriot appears on the parish register when, on September 27th, their granddaughter, Marie-Augustine, became the wife of Pierre Henriot. He was the son of Captain Jules Henriot, an engineer with Napoleon Bonaparte's *Grande Armée*. Later he was knighted for his share in building the famous bridge over the Berezina River across which Napoleon escaped when retreating from Moscow. Pierre managed the factory until 1884 when he died and was succeeded by his son, Jules. His son, Joseph, was the father of Yves Henriot, who became head of the firm in 1951.

Yves is very proud of his wife and helpmeet, the former Yvonne Kerner, from Laval, Mayenne, where her father, great-grandson of the German poet and musician Albenezins, is a musical instrument maker. That may partly account for the many ceramic instruments on display.

The keynote of the numerous showrooms through which he conducted me was not the expected simplicity, but volume and variety, and a sensation of exciting ornamentation which ennobled the lowly cock, the lordly crane, the suckling pig, the heavy farm horse, and ever and always the peasant himself. A thin fellow in blue was perched on the handle of a stein. A Falstaff leaned out of a beer keg. A winsome child attacked a huge striped apple with gusto, her free hand stirring among the half dozen on the ground beside her. Each piece of earthenware was symbolic of Breton folklore.

The variety was incredible. Lovely square plaques to enliven a wall, or to protect one's table from a hot dish. Delightful coffee cups doing double duty as drinking vessels and conversation pieces. Novel top-selling chocolate sets. Made to order for a shop in New Orleans, that city a fit setting for the exotic pair, were a vivid red pitcher and jardiniere. The jardiniere and a tray with oil and vinegar bottles in black with brilliant rose and blue decor, would be welcome in my home. Had I not been afraid that M. Henriot would think I was hinting, I should have suggested buying them. Stores importing them were Ogilvie's of Montreal, Marshall Field, and Saks Fifth Avenue. I went to Saks later, but they had sold the last set.

Two other places where you may see wares bearing the HENRIOT-QUIMPER mark are Carbone of Boston, a customer since 1905, and Bloomingdale's of New York, since 1919. At these shops you may choose a striking and arresting dinner service in gaily decorated white faïence, or a complete fish course in black showing countless varieties of marine life in natural tones.

An attractive planter took the form of a covered well. An ornamental figure was that of a domestic-of-all-work seated before the hired man on a horse. One end of a pair of book ends was a hearth where the man of the house relaxed, the other the kitchen range where his good wife labored. A useful tray had crayfish handles.

As the Bretons are a seafaring people, the potters specialize in dishes for seafoods. They manufacture more of them than of anything else. Each is designed for one particular fish or crustacean, or even for the specific way it is cooked. I took a picture of M. Henriot with a World's Fair prizewinning oyster plate. It had compartments for two dozen oysters on the half shell. As *huitres* abound in the waters of Finistère, oystering is one of the chief industries. An American artist who had taken up his abode for a year in picturesque Guilvinec, a nearby fishing village, told me that all months of the Breton calendar must have had an "R," so consistently were the bivalves on the menu. Still, once you have eaten the delicate Belon oyster washed down by a bottle of Muscadet, you will not be surprised.

M. Henriot drove me to the fabrique of his chief competitor, and left me in charge of a young director, another Yves, surnamed Bolloré.

Faïenceries Bretonne de la Grande Maison, H-B, is, he said, the oldest factory making *Quimper* at the present time. It claims to be the original one, the first to produce the ware of distinctive character which made the name of the small Bretagne city known wherever pottery is prized. Its trademark is a joined H-B, the initials being those of the two families, Bousquet and Hubaudière, identified with the growth and prosperity of *la Grande Maison* during many of the alleged 530 years of its existence.

The pottery first came to general notice under the direction of Jean Bousquet who had come to Quimper from the famous faïence manufacturing town of Moustiers, and began making the ware in 1652. Either in direct line or through marriage, his dynasty lasted until 1915 when the last scion was killed in action during World War I.

In 1685, Bousquet turned the management over to his son, Pierre. He extended the business on an ambitious scale. Retiring in 1708, he handed the thriving enterprise to his son-in-law, P. Bellevaux, formerly a master potter at Nevers, one of the greatest names in the history of faïence. The plant then took the name of Bellevaux.

The name changed again, this time to the Caussy Faïencerie, when Belle-vaux's daughter, Marie-Jeanne, in 1749 married Pierre-Clement Caussy, son of the director of the royal factory at Rouen. His tenure brought more changes than merely that of name. It brought dynamic progress, for he was able to introduce all the decorating ideas, plus many of the secrets of Rouen manu-facture.

In 1771, Caussy's daughter Elizabeth became the wife of Antoine de la Hubaudière, an aide to the king in the province of Bretagne. When he was killed at the massacre of Fougères in 1793, his widow carried on with the as-sistance of her twenty-year-old son, Jean-Marie.

His son, Felix, became the factory's head in 1853, and was active in the firm's affairs until his death in 1881. It was his grandson, Guy, in whose veins ran the blood of the original founder, Jean Bousquet, who died on the field of battle in 1915. This ended a dynasty begun almost two and a half centuries earlier. At Guy's death, the company was formed as a syndicate under its present title.

H-B proved to be a much more pretentious fabrique than that of Henriot et Fils. For example, they had executed a number of pieces in the style of Etruscan ware, some of enormous size. An imposing dining table made of decorated tiles which formed a complete and harmonious picture was also very effective.

The Brittany phase had not been neglected. H-B has created figures and faïence of truly characteristic quality. The credit for most of it must go to the famous sculptor and painter, R. Quillivic, chevalier of the Legion of Honor and a member of the jury of the Autumn Salon. He and his artists have drawn freely on the lives of the fisherfolk for ideas. The peasants of Brittany in their colorful costumes have a whole display room to themselves. They are all modeled by hand, and faithfully reproduce the brilliant hues of the everyday attire of the villagers.

The headwear which interested me most was the Breton *coiffe*. Of crocheted lace, it resembles a tall cylindrical bun on which white-of-egg frosting has been spread with a heavy hand. No lady felt properly dressed without one, especially on a Saturday afternoon, I was told by a pleasant girl of eighteen or so who shared my seat in the bus going to Guilvinec. It was Saturday afternoon then, and she invited me to her home in one of the hamlets the bus stopped at to see her mother's. It sounded like fun but I wanted as many hours as possible at the fishing village, so I went on. And was lucky enough to get some color shots of a coiffed woman pushing a handcart, a second one a pram, and a third pedaling her bicycle vigorously to the glee of the tiny tot perched on the handlebars. Another woman, without idling her crochet hook for an instant, came out of her doorway to pose on the cobbles. That done, she unbent and showed me how the lace structure was kept on. One pin secured the front to her hair. Her back hair was wound about a roll of the stiffly starched lace, then pinned.

Many of the women attending the service the following morning in the medieval cathedral—St. Corentin dates back to the 13th century—wore the distinctive *coiffe*. The men, especially the older and markedly prosperous ones, had their distinctive headwear too—large broad-brimmed black felt hats with a wide velvet band fastened at the back by an enormous silver buckle. As I felt diffident about taking pictures of the devout coming from church, and the Bretons are devout, I was grateful to have a pair of the hatted pottery figures presented to me on Monday morning as souvenirs.

H-B makes complete dinner services in peasant style. In Altman's I saw one in sunny yellow with brilliant peasant decor, perfect for today's patio dining. The set comes in brown and green as well, and all three can be harmoniously combined. A table there, covered with a coarse handwoven oyster-white cloth, had brown plates, yellow cups and saucers, and green serving dishes.

As all H-B's work is done by hand, standardization of pattern or pigments is impossible. Each piece stamped with the mark H-B is individual. The slight differences, even irregularities, give these dishes a peculiar fascination and allure.

If you cannot visit the Quimper factories, many stores throughout the land can bring you their peasant pottery de luxe—*Quimper*.

Chapter 19

Rosenthal

THE last stop on the European pilgrimage proved to be not only an extended one, but one which aroused a tremendous amount of interest and controversy. Once my women friends learned that I had visited the Rosenthal plants in Bavaria, they buttonholed me. "How did you like Rosenthal porcelain?"

About a competitor to be reckoned with, potter friends made their questions carefully casual. "How did you like Philip Rosenthal?"

But it was the business men who made it tough. "You have been to Selb and met Rosenthal on his native soil, and should have some of the answers. In a country beaten to its knees fifteen years ago, and in a district on the border of a Soviet satellite state, how has the 'Empire of Rosenthal' been brought about? Is it because Rosenthal has virtually cornered the world's ceramic artists, or has he the Golden Touch?"

These three questions I shall try to answer in my own way.

Philip Rosenthal II, potentate of this empire with its capital in Selb, northern Bavaria, would be a playboy de luxe were he not a dedicated potter, for he applies the same single-mindedness to sports that he applies to industry. Besides being an amateur pilot, he is a sports car enthusiast, a mountain climber, and a cross-country runner. "If you see a tall man in shorts running from the factory, and not pursued by the police," he said, "it is probably me going home to lunch." He makes this two-and-a-half-mile run part of his daily routine, whether in London, Paris, or Selb.

He refuses to become a slave of schedules, teletypes, and phone calls. One of the greatest catastrophes which can befall an executive, he contends, is "manager disease" resulting from an inflexible mental attitude. He vowed never to become a victim of it, and insists that luxury hotels and cocktail parties must be planned in life in a reasonable ratio lest business life take over with its resultant one-sidedness.

Against this fatal malady, he claims that the best precaution is mountain climbing, for which he now and then has a compulsive urge. When he had to go on a business trip to Africa, he grasped the opportunity to climb Kilimanjaro. On similar trips he scaled Mont Blanc, Monte Rosa in Switzerland, and Aconcagua in the Andes.

Born with a gold spoon in his mouth, but in the midst of a war which spelled ruin to his then Fatherland—he is now a British subject—he can make do with a silver spoon, even with a pewter one in a pinch. As a regular utensil, no! Rather, bigger and better gold spoons. For just as efficiency is one of the main tenets of his creed, so is crescendo, not diminuendo, the directive for the music to which his life is attuned.

An expert in feminine psychology, and a perfectionist—he has been married three times, each wife a woman of great charm plus cosmopolitan good taste—he knows what discriminating hostesses demand in chinaware.

In its field, Rosenthal-Porzellan AG has the greatest sales in the world market. Being head of a firm with such a record would more than satisfy most men. Not Philip Rosenthal. In his bright lexicon, the big phrase is "the American market." Rosenthal sales, which at one time dropped to eighteenth place in the U.S.A., still come only second. Their technically perfect porcelain remains a notch below that of the English bone china of Wedgwood.

Much of Wedgwood's enviable position Rosenthal credits to their inspired slogan, "A Living Tradition." If he could come up with a better one, he is convinced that he could outsell his personal friend and keenest competitor, Sir John Hamilton Wedgwood of Barlaston. Of course, Sir John had a head start in the industry. For eleven generations there have been Wedgwoods potting in Stoke-upon-Trent, Staffordshire, and for six generations Wedgwoods have really been in there slugging. Philip Rosenthal is only a second generation potter.

On most maps of Germany, if you look in upper Bavaria where it abuts on Thuringia, and in the extreme east of Czechoslovakia, formerly the German province of Bohemia, you can find Selb, the important little porcelain city, capital of the great "Empire of Rosenthal."

A hundred years ago, "porcelain city" would have been a misnomer. Then Selb was not much more than a village, with a single industry. In 1858 it burned almost to the ground. The people were left destitute.

That one industry was weaving. Moved by stories of the extreme poverty following the fire, a weaver named Lorenz Heutschenheuter went to Selb to help restore trade. Then he stumbled across a deposit of fine white powdery clay—kaolin. Since the triumphs of the alchemist Böttger in 1708 at Meissen, so many porcelain factories had sprung up in adjacent Thuringia that the district was known as the German Staffordshire. Heutschenheuter decided that potting might be more profitable than weaving, especially since the craft was threatened by the introduction of mechanical devices. Without more ado he opened a china factory in Selb. It was the first privately owned one in Germany. (Previously all had belonged to the state, to princes, or to the nobility.) This gave it popular appeal. Its fame spread.

In 1879 the factory was visited by a young man, Philipp Rosenthal, from America. German-born and able to speak the language, this shrewd head of the glass and china department of a Detroit store had been sent to Selb to buy china. Only twenty-four, he had packed thrice that amount of living into his life. Son of a Westphalian china merchant, at seventeen he had run away from home, and worked his passage to the U.S.A. In that land of freedom and opportunity he had been cowboy, dishwasher in a restaurant, elevator boy in a hotel, and had even ridden horseback on the mail routes in Colorado.

Young Rosenthal had not been many hours in Selb, when, with his uncanny instinct, he realized that the big money was made not in selling china but in producing it. On the spot he decided that the time had come for him to settle down. He would remain in Selb and become a potter.

His first problem was living quarters. In an old rundown mansion in the nearby village of Erkersreuth, he rented a room, fortunately a large one as it was both home and factory. There he and his young wife, Maria, his only worker, painted the white china bought from Heutschenheuter. Maria went from house to house with a small cart and sold each lot as it came from the kiln. Soon the single room had to be abandoned for a small factory in the hamlet of Ploesburg a mile away.

Philipp Rosenthal was not unmindful of the debt he owed his wife. A few years after her death, he expressed his gratitude by naming his first complete dinner service *Maria Weiss,* or White, a white ware bordered with small roses in relief. On two counts the factory claims it to be the biggest dinner service in the world: first, according to the number of pieces in a set, 156 instead of the usual 98; second, according to the number of services sold since its introduction in 1914.

Another steady seller dating from that time is the rococo *Sans Souci.* The embossed portions of the various pieces are copied from the design on one wall of a charming room in the palace Frederick the Great erected at Potsdam.

The ex-Kaiser, Wilhelm II, gave the potter permission not only to copy it, but, when the artist added soft blue and rose flowers and a basket of posies in the center, to name the service after his grandfather's dream palace.

These two and *Moosrose*—mossrose—at prices to suit everyone, were created by artists of high standing and repute. That was more than could be said of much of the heavily gilded porcelain being manufactured by other potters for the palaces of oriental princes and the mansions of the *nouveau riche* at home.

This was no accident. From the beginning, Rosenthal had two aims in view. One was to make money by catering to the desire of the well-to-do for luxury china. The other, following the example set by Josiah Wedgwood a century earlier, was the more idealistic aim of devoting his real talents to the production of good china for everyday use.

Philipp Rosenthal's motto, one to which his son adheres today, was, "My first care is for the customers of good taste and not those with fat pocketbooks." Strangely, it found a remarkable response in his homeland. The Germans, aware of their reputed lack of good taste, were willing to have one of their own people impose it upon them in the hope that some semblance might seep in through their pores. Even today the informed German housewife shows more pride in the mark on the reverse of her dinner plates than in the quantity of decorative gold. That Rosenthal mark is every customer's guarantee of elegance. Knowing Philipp's aims, and his skill in executing them, can

you not see why the business grew from a husband-and-wife concern to one of the greatest organizations in the history of the industry?

Of course, as is often the case, his artistic genius or flair may have owed something to a heritage of remote Jewish blood. Because of it, Geheimrat—privy councilor—Rosenthal was driven out by the Nazis, several of whom had insinuated themselves as members of the board of directors. Thanks to the good reputation of his name, and to his second wife, an influential woman of "pure Aryan" stock, his exile was postponed until 1935. By then, he had ten companies and 5000 employees.

A dozen years later, when the rest of Germany was still reeling from its defeat in World War II, Rosenthal-Porzellan AG issued its 250-millionth piece of china and its 100-millionth to go overseas. Unfortunately the founder did not witness this astronomical attainment. He had died in exile a decade before, on March 30, 1937, at the age of eighty-two, and was buried at Bozen —Italian *Bolzano*—the center of the German-speaking part of the South Tyrol.

Philipp Rosenthal was genuinely interested in politics, in particular touching the field of porcelain. In 1898 he founded the Society of Bavarian Porcelain Industries, and was its president. He was one of the founders of the Kaiser Wilhelm Institute for Silicosis Research, and, in 1914, of the Association of the German Export Industry of which later he became president. He also played a major part in promoting one of the world's most famous fairs, that held at Leipzig, now in the Soviet Zone. In fact, he was called its second founder, and well deserved the honor of having a street named after him, a name which, in spite of Nazis and Communists, still stands.

At the age of 61, Philipp Rosenthal had married another Maria, surnamed Frank. (Now Comtesse de Beurges, she is a member of the board of directors.) She provided him with a son and heir, the present Philip Rosenthal—he spells his name with one "p," the English way.

Philip was born in Berlin on October 23, 1916. His early education was undertaken in France and Switzerland. In England he attended a public school, Laurence, then Exeter College, Oxford, where he majored in political economy and philosophy. To this he added travel, and he planned after graduation to cover the earth, with a specific expedition to Mongolia to make its people the subject of his thesis for his doctorate.

The beginning of the war changed this. Already an amateur pilot, he joined the Scottish Air Force, a civilian outfit which made short shrift of the Messerschmidts and Heinkels invading the country north of the Tweed. Later, he attached himself to the British Foreign Office, but his German name and nationality were against him. (His British citizenship, though applied for in 1938, was not granted until 1947.) To carry on his fight against Hitler, he went to Paris. Frustrated again, he was permitted to join only the Foreign Legion. When France collapsed, he enlisted in the Sahara Company to do underground work in North Africa. Prison and concentration camp sentences resulted. His fourth attempt to escape was successful. He managed to get to Gibraltar, from there to England.

He became a baker's assistant, then tried journalism. Under the name of Rossiter he visited POW camps, and attempted to teach the prisoners the rudimentary principles of democracy. Suddenly he found himself back in the Foreign Office where, until V.E. Day, he "dished out" political intelligence. Then the war ended. Now his one desire was to take over his inheritance, enter the firm which had been his father's life work, put into the business his comprehensive foreign experiences and widespread connections, and help restore the firm of Rosenthal to its international reputation.

The Rosenthal factories had suffered no bomb damage, but, after six years of war, materials and machinery were out-of-date and buildings inadequate. The production of the main plant at Selb was jeopardized by its situation on the border of the Soviet zone, a proximity which slowed up construction and greatly increased expenses.

The newly drawn frontiers deprived Rosenthal-Porzellan AG of conveniently situated sources of raw materials. Saxon and Czech coal could not be obtained. Kaolin still came from Czechoslovakia, but the quality had deteriorated and shipment was difficult. Fresh sources had to be opened up in West Germany. Even new materials were tried. For several years indispensable china clay came from Bursala, northern Spain, and in 1956 the firm astutely purchased the site.

It had suffered staggering trade losses. When the Iron Curtain hermetically sealed off the states of Eastern Europe, Rosenthal's lost the important Henningsdorf plant near Berlin as well as two others in Czechoslovakia. Big markets behind the Iron Curtain had disappeared overnight. Worst of all, sales organizations everywhere had been disrupted, and depots, particularly abroad, lost.

This was the situation when Philip Rosenthal, at twenty-nine, stepped into the picture.

What counted in his over-all scheme was America. Week after week he watched the overseas sales drop with alarming celerity. It was not merely a matter of postwar conditions, either. Psychologically, the war had changed the world. Young people everywhere were in revolt against the conservative. Not yet thirty, he was young enough to understand and sympathize.

His eye was quick to perceive that, except for a few old and established favorites such as *Maria Weiss, Moosrose, Sans Souci,* and *Pompadour,* an American favorite, their designs were outmoded. He went into a huddle with himself, then attacked his confrères.

Porcelain must be brought up to date, must make a true if modest contribution to the culture of the times. Without entirely scrapping the old traditions they had to find new means of artistic expression. To his father's motto on customers of good taste he added a line, "From the old take the well-tested, from the new take the best."

Regardless of expense, he engaged Europe's top artists: Tapio Wirkkala

172

from Finland; Jean Cocteau from France; Bela Bechem from Germany itself. Europe quickly took their creations to heart. America still turned a cold shoulder. Bone china sales continued to soar, but even with the postwar clamor for dishes, Rosenthal sales tobogganed until in a final plummet they reached a new low of eighteenth place.

The day that figure was shown to him, he telephoned New York for an appointment with the only person in that city of eight million who counted with him—Raymond Loewy, a Frenchman who had lived in the U.S.A. long enough to know American tastes. If only as the designer of Coca-Cola bottles and Studebaker cars he had made his name a household word to Americans.

The next day Philip Rosenthal flew to New York City, was met and taken to the studio with its staff of selected artists whose designs go throughout the whole civilized world. Loewy promised to design medium-priced dinnerware which would strike a responsive chord in current American taste—on a strictly royalty basis, of course, which is how he works with all his clients.

The sequel reads like the ending of a fairy tale. American sales jet-rocketed They jumped to second place. Only Wedgwood, scion of the Prince of Potters, continued to outsell his friend Rosenthal, Prince of Selb.

The shape responsible for this was one which, without being *outré,* had discarded the traditional in favor of today's elegance. It was named the "2000" shape, as if its popularity were envisioned carrying forward to the dawn of the twenty-first century.

Truth to tell, this "Classic Modern" was actually a modification of a shape created by the medieval potters of Spain and Italy, the *albarello,* an easily grasped, thin-waisted jar which could be removed from the apothecary's shelf without disturbing the rest.

Few porcelain shapes have appealed to the feminine imagination as has "2000." One reason is that it lends itself readily to decoration. Besides Loewy himself, probably a round dozen artists have contributed, among them Otto Hoffman with *Semiramis,* and Margaret Hildebrand with *Graser* and the coarse tweed effect, *Seidenbast.*

The "2000" which finds markets all over the world is *Gala Blau,* decorated as a result of teamwork in the Selb studio. It has a narrow cobalt rim edged on both sides by a fine gold line. Although the blue is that of the very heavens, *Gala Blau* is symbolic of more than mere color, and of more than mere line, sweeping to the skies though it does.

Perhaps *Gala Blau's* greatest merit is its adaptability. Its simplicity fits it into any period, ancient or modern. It assimilates with any color scheme. It is particularly successful in a friend's dining room with crimson draperies against an off-white background, and Carl Malmsten furniture in limed oak with blue chair seats. Satin-finished silverware, and glasses also in the "2000" shape—they were made by Rosenthal's at their Frankfurt glassworks—effectively complete the ensemble.

With this fingerpost pointing the way, Philip Rosenthal called another meeting of the board, and announced his intentions of getting the best designers from the four corners of the globe.

"While porcelain manufacture cannot actually be classed with the plastic arts," Herr Rosenthal told me, "ceramic designers must be able to make the clay follow the tendrils of their vision and flights of fancy. The dream in their minds must become the reality in porcelain. Even kiln-fired to rigidity the lines must flow. Short of that we refuse to accept."

Fortunately, this quality has been attained by every artist on the staff. It is particularly noticeable in the gamut of the young Danish designer, Bjørn Wiinblad, and in a less subtle but more puckish form in the merry pieces created by the inimitable French painter and novelist, Raymond Peynet, who romantically combines picture and tale.

Wiinblad works in both glass and ceramics. As a centerpiece for a table in the New York showrooms, the display caught the buyers' fancy with a set of five of the Dane's candlesticks named *Tulipa*. Of various heights ranging from about two to almost twenty-two inches, they are in clear crystal with black-tinted tulip chalices borne airily on slender weighted stems. At Georg Jensen's the prices range from $12.50 for the shortest one to $32.50 for the tallest.

Wiinblad's most recent decor, an outstanding success which has proved a magnet for dollars, is *Quatre Couleurs*, gold in four different shades. His decorations for the Royal Danish Ballet suggested scenes from his *Commedia dell' Arte* series for a complete coffee, tea, and dinner service in the "2000" shape. On another dinner service of that form he depicted the four seasons.

Perhaps where he reached his peak and made himself recognized as the spiritual brother of Denmark's most celebrated son, Hans Christian Andersen, was in his *Symphonie Pastorale* ensemble, nymphs conjured up in his little hut in the woods on the outskirts of Copenhagen to the recorded background music of Grieg. Merely looking at the airy figurines, as one writer said, you hear the faint elfin strains.

Raymond Peynet, as might be expected of a close friend of Arthur Rank, the English film producer, is a dramatic person, bubbling over with *joie de vivre*. His decoration on plates, boxes, ashtrays, and vases is only another form of storytelling, his characters the shy whimsical figures floating into existence from his world of phantasy. His best known figurines, *Les Petites*

Peynets—a lover and his lass—are definitely compounded of moonlight and gossamer, "such stuff as dreams are made on," yet too tactile to be tongue in cheek. Positively alive, they dance a minuet or a saraband to the strains of a porcelain violin over which, one is willing to take oath, the bow moves seductively.

"Peynet's pieces are irresistible," said the young executive who was conducting me through the showrooms in Selb. "No one can look at them and not smile."

Not I, at any rate. I felt my face wreathed in smiles then. Now, at home, I can achieve the same effect any time merely by glancing at my favorite Peynet, *Song of Spring*. A kneeling lover plays his flute—or is it the Pipes of Pan?—from the score on his demure sweetheart's garter, his audience an entranced and diminutive hedgehog at her slender feet.

A Rosenthal artist of tremendous acclaim hails, as might be expected, from Finland. Tapio Wirkkala is, by many European authorities, considered the world's greatest designer. If this takes in a lot of territory, they back up their statement by pointing out that the Finn has won the Grand Prix at the Triennial in Milan six times.

Like all his countrymen, Wirkkala is an individualist. His form, Finlandia, has the grace, harmony, and strength of the composition of the same name by his late compatriot, Jan Sibelius. But he stubbornly insisted that its decor be only plain gold bands—"Let the form speak for itself." As a selling proposition, it was a flop. Direktor Rosenthal tactfully called a conference of the studio personnel. Finally Renate Rhein submitetd an all-over stylized four-leaf clover in a color between jade and *feuille morte*. It was given the name *Rusticana*. No sooner was it put on display than it became a runaway with incredible sales, the supply barely keeping pace with the demand. Not to be outdone, Wirkkala evolved his *Blue Rose,* its sales second only to those of *Rusticana*. One of the artist's admirers has described it as a "Finnish fairy tale with the aurora borealis shining through."

Frau Else Fischer-Leyden of Berlin designed another best-seller, Fortuna. Hans Theo Baumann's popular Berlin shape carries designs with names like *Dahlem* and *Grunewald,* and other lovely suburbs of that great drawn-and-quartered city. In the Munich studio, Lise Müler's fancy runs riot, but the moment she feels a brush in her fingers it is brought to heel. At first, the results may be startling, but ultimately they assume a rare exotic witchery. The "Empire of Rosenthal" got its authentic touch of royalty a couple of years ago when Sigvard Bernadotte, son of the Swedish king, joined the assembly. His productions are drastically unorthodox, and highly acclaimed.

A designer who cannot be overlooked is the modernist, Professor Hans

Stangl of Munich. Evidently he has taken as his maxim, "Life begins at seventy," for that was his calendar age when he began creating his unique figures in gray clay subtly suggesting a soft but vital jade or celadon in its exquisitely glazed depths.

Each figure is nothing but a series of solid curves, no angles anywhere. The faces are featureless hollows, yet warm with vitality. Even untitled, the pieces tell their own tale. One which lingers in heart and memory is *Mother and Child*, a name you would give it instinctively, for all the yearning of mother love is inherent in the flowing form.

The most recent factory, opened a year ago, is only a pleasant drive from Selb, on the outskirts of the small town of Speichersdorf-Plössen. Across the road from the plant is the hangar where the Herr Direktor garages his English sports plane—the reason, probably, that the site was chosen. The Kulm plant it is called, for distantly behind it, an effective background, is a mountain named Kulm, said to have been the anvil of Vulcan.

The plant is the last word in streamlined efficiency. The main building is set well back in the grounds. The wall facing the main road is of concrete slabs which can be removed at any time it is necessary to enlarge the plant. There are few windows, yet the place is remarkably bright, for long rows of glass in the roof provide ample light. This glass is slanted to screen sun-glare. Also, important in that latitude, it sheds rain and snow. In the two-story section of the building, where the air conditioner is housed, is the inhalatorium. There silicosis, bane of the potter, is, if not eliminated, at least nearly screened out.

Neither step nor motion is wasted. Between one process and the next, everything follows as on an assembly line. For example, in the basement are three miles of kaolin pipe to feed the clay to the pug mills. From the latter it comes directly upstairs to the potters' wheels, jolleys, jiggers, and casting equipment. Transport belts have virtually eliminated the conveying of anything manually.

Naturally, the pieces to be fired have to be arranged in the kilns by hand. There are five of these, the last word in kiln construction. The chinaware is placed in carriages and sent continuously through the tunnels, which have three different zones: preheating, firing, and cooling. Completely electrical, their system of controls is theoretically foolproof, but a skilled electrical engineer is always on hand. A single error in judgment, a moment's failure of machinery or controls, could result in incalculable loss.

The employees commute in buses from Selb, or cycle from the nearby town. At Kulm 400 persons do the work which requires 1200 at Selb. At first, it was feared that the new labor-saving devices would prove another spinning jenny. In towns with a single industry, layoffs spell tragedy. Fortunately, the output is porcelain of a less expensive type, not exactly cheap but in the middle-price bracket unfailingly in demand. So far, the unemployment bugaboo has been kept at bay.

Visiting the potteries, guests stay in the Rosenthal Casino, a charming private hostel with three double and fourteen single rooms. Instead of being numbered, beside each door is a tile with a Rosenthal design. The dishes used in the dining rooms are *Maria Weiss*.

The staff consists of the manager, Rudolf Zuhl, his daughter who acts as housekeeper, plus a cook, two maids, and two waiters. Zuhl, a blend of dignity and affability—he might be the butler in a stage drama—is a perfectionist like his employer. The headwaiter, Wolfram Kienast, a youth of eighteen, runs him a close second.

One noon time the big dining room was invaded by a number of young men and women. The executive who was lunching with me explained their presence. In fact, he had to rush as he was lecturing to them in half an hour.

One of the firm's pressing problems is getting enough young people to fill executive positions, in factories, sales organizations, and in Rosenthal's stores and departments all over the world. Above all, young men are always in demand to replace those who are retiring.

For this purpose Philip Rosenthal inaugurated congresses known as *Nachwuchs,* literally translated as "recruits" or "rising generation." They are held for 14 days two or three times a year. At each between twenty and thirty recruits are in attendance. (When I was there, they numbered 25, one an East Indian.) Most of them stay in hotels or with private families. Those who are resident in the Casino have been selected for special grooming. Many of the leading executives look back with pride on their fortnight as guests in the old Casino. Conscious of the early recognition of their talents, they tell you with satisfaction. "Yes, indeed, Madam, I was one of the fortunates who enjoyed the hospitality of the Casino."

An executive from each department takes his turn giving a lecture in his particular field. The students visit the various factories in order to familiarize themselves with the technical processes. The most rewarding phase of the project is the exchange of ideas, for the students come from all parts of Germany, and even from points outside, if they have been recommended. Both young executives assigned to me were outsiders, although Herr Weber of publicity was only from so far afield as Westphalia. Herr Noteborn of the export department was from Holland. Great things are expected of these two young men, so much so in the Dutchman's case that he has taken out German citizenship papers.

The Herr Direktor believes in catching them young, while still of an impressionable and plastic age, and letting them grow up in the firm's employ.

One's visit to a pottery begins with the showrooms, probably the least enlightening department of the plant. One is shown museum pieces and the firm's outstanding services, but these bear little relation to the average housewife's needs.

For example, the first Rosenthal service pointed out was for a thousand persons, and had been made to order for Ibn Saud at a cost of half a million Deutschmarks, $125,000. The second was for Pope Pius XII and though the devout Bavarians would have enshrined it, not a single piece could be duplicated.

An extremely ornate set in blue and white, with lavish gold, had been designed for the Shah of Persia. For Soraya, his former wife, was a simple but elegant set in white with a broad band of fine gold lines raying inwards from the rim. The Eisenhower service had a wide engraved gold border with the coat of arms of SHEAF—Supreme Headquarters Expeditionary Allied Forces. The Grace Kelly set had a gold leaf border inside a narrow encaustic gold band. For the scholarly was a service called *Odyssey*. Greek characters in a narrow gold border related part of the story of Odysseus. Each set was accompanied by a key plate in German, English, or French.

Distinctive dishes were designed for the Hilton Hotel in Berlin. The plates have a broad band of beige luster, soft and lovely, edged with gold. They bear no relation to the form Berlin, though this was the shape chosen by the wife of the courageous mayor, Willy Brandt, when she was appointed to select a service for the City of Berlin. In this task she was assisted by the wives of most of the ambassadors. It was unanimously agreed that the china should carry the arms of the city, a black bear on a silver ground, and should be named *Kurfurstendamm* after West Berlin's handsome shopping boulevard.

All these details and many more I had accumulated during a pleasant round of sightseeing and festivities while I waited the return of the chief actor from Baden-Baden where he had been attending a directors' annual conference plus vacation. "We ate too much and we drank too much," he told me later, "but we had a marvelous time. Into the bargain, one of the group started an argument which may add a new line to production."

That was when he showed me a number of paintings on porcelain, boxframed, which had resulted from one of these conferences abroad. They were executed by famous portrait, flower, and landscape artists, and were beginning to be regarded favorably by discriminating buyers. One advantage they have over canvas is that they are easily cleaned.

The Herr Direktor has his office in The Studio, a self-contained building, mostly glass, not far from the main Selb plant. To it my two young executives escorted me the morning Philip Rosenthal returned.

He uncoiled himself with effortless grace from his swivel chair, and greeted me with a firm handshake. Galvanic and vital, had Harold Haviland of Limoges told me? He exudes magnetism. Rarely does one encounter such an *alive* person, integrated, at the same time intransigent and amenable, as hard as his own technically perfect porcelain and as soft as the butter on the small *Maria Weiss* butter pats on the Casino tables, and behind it the driving force of a jet.

He apologized for detaining me so long in Selb. "I hope my people entertained you in an adequate manner."

"Never a dull moment," I assured him. "My week in Selb has been as serene and brilliant as the scene from this window."

The Studio, mostly glass, afforded a breathtaking view of the Bavarian countryside, the woods then blazing with the multicolored foliage of autumn. Cutting the horizon a mile or more away were the chimney stacks of the original Rosenthal-Ploesburg plant.

"If all goes well," the founder's son said, gesturing towards the rolling terrain, "next year we shall have a swimming pool and refreshment stand out there."

Sitting in the uncluttered office, we chatted informally, though never without point. About the role of the chief executive he said, "He should be informed about all important decisions, but never bothered about bagatelles. It is generally conceded that our designers are responsible for our unprecedented success. I admit our debt to them, no one more sincerely," he added with unexpected vehemence. "But over the years I have learned that it is not so much a matter of the designer as of the design, back of which is the realization that it is to a woman's five senses—yes, and her sixth—we must appeal.

"How many stop to think of the array of personnel who shared in the manufacture of the dinner plate set before them? Not a dozen, not a score—more like five score! The designer is only one person, working in a single capacity. . . . The plate is the result of teamwork, of cooperation all along the line. Polished and burnished, it is only half done. It still must be displayed, sold, packaged, and shipped. Each process requires its own specialist."

179

On that subject he is uncompromising.

"This is the age of the specialist, not only in the professions, but in industry. In ours particularly. One man may have a flair for form, shape, and line, and for putting it on paper. Another's forte is executing the shape, bringing it to life in clay. Yet it does not follow that either of these artists, though master of his own genre, may also be a master of pigments. They *could* be color blind. Actually, one of our sculptors cannot tell red from green."

He conducted me through The Studio then, and explained why it was apart from the main plant—"to ensure that its production does not impinge upon, conflict with, nor become familiar to the general factories. It is specialized specializing, its staff of artists engaged upon ideas for anything to do with the production, display and sale of porcelain and glass."

In Germany alone over two hundred shops sell Rosenthal china exclusively. In addition are Rosenthal departments in many large stores. They operate under definite restrictions. For example, they may not display another manufacturer's wares in the same window or on the same shelf, nor may they reduce the price. Outside Germany are 477 outlets in stores and shops.

The outstanding world market, though it accounts for only 10 per cent of their exports, is the U.S.A. This is the result of the perspicacity the designers have shown in catering to the tastes, demands, and aesthetic requirements of a nation which has outgrown its adolescent lack of cultural standards, and can afford to indulge in both novelty and quality. Admittedly, many now in the money are influenced by the snob appeal of Rosenthal's high prices. Nevertheless, of one thing they are assured: porcelain of lasting value. As in the founder's time, the "Rosen-thal" divided by crossed swords beneath a crown is still every customer's guarantee.

It was when I was leaving the Rosenthal's—from the rundown mansion in Erkersreuth where his father first lived the son has created a charming chateau—that I was handed the subtitle for this book.

"One of these days," my host said with a twinkle—and from the resolute set of his chin I should have known that Wedgwood's top place in the United States was in his mind—"one of these days Rosenthal-Porzellan AG will scale the export mountain in the U.S.A. and plant both feet on the peak. *Today's treasures, tomorrow's traditions!*"

Chapter 20

Lenox

IRISH blood is persistent. Although mine stems from five generations back, and only on the distaff side, it is still sufficiently undiluted to reproach me for not visiting the famous Belleek pottery in Ireland, especially as I have been within reasonable distance of it many times. With true Irish inconsistency I rationalized by saying that I could watch Belleek being made any time right here in America. I did recently, incidentally adding to this book, intended to be exclusively European, a chapter on an American pottery, Lenox, probably as much for the poignant story of its founder as for its quality wares.

The pioneer Lenox in America was Samuel, born in 1784 of Scottish parents in County Antrim, Ireland. At the age of twenty-two, he and the blithe colleen he had married sailed from London for the U.S.A. They landed in Baltimore, proceeded to Philadelphia, and thence to the small industrial city of Trenton rendered historic by Washington's crossing the Delaware at that point.

Samuel became active in the Delaware trade and acquired a number of sloops which carried on commerce up and down the river. Later his brother James joined him and the name of Lenox began to be well known among the river men. Subsequent members of the family were expert captains, and owners of warehouses and boats.

Proud fatherhood came to one of Samuel's sons, Hiram, a hardware merchant, in 1859. The offspring was grandiosely named after the great Scottish novelist and poet, Sir Walter Scott. Apparently, if Hiram hoped to have his son eventually join him in the firm, the gesture had been a mistake. Although the lad helped around the store in his spare time, he displayed little interest in the business, or, as his cousins did, in boating. It might have been less regrettable had he aspired to emulate the laird of Abbotsford and become a writer, but he showed no literary inclination. His gift, one of which no sensible parents could boast, was a "not manly" artistic talent with crayon and paints.

How he nearly got it "licked out" of him was one of the stories which he loved to chuckle over years afterward.

"At school the other pupils enjoyed my little knack of drawing. Our second-form teacher had a Poll Parrot head and a nose in keeping. I could not resist making caricatures of her on my slate. One day she pussyfooted up behind me, and—Wow! What a whopping I got!"

Before long it was evident that the talent was to be channeled in one direction—china. By that time, several small potteries had sprung up in the New Jersey capital, so many, indeed, that the city was coming to be called the "Staffordshire of America." On the way to and from school, young Walter had to pass one of these. The sight of the potter's wheel fascinated him. The smell of the potter's clay was incense in his nostrils. That I understood, for immediately J. Stephen Neale of Lenox's publicity staff opened the door to the pottery proper, the nostalgic smell engulfed me, and—Lafcadio Hearn was right when he said that of the senses smell was the strongest emotionally—caught me up in the excitement of my first pottery, Barlaston.

Soon, when not attending school or clerking behind the counter, the youth began to hie himself to a large vacant room above the store. There, with his father's grudging permission, he indulged to his heart's content in experiments with clay, and in modeling thinly potted pieces which, when fired in a local kiln, he decorated with patterns of his own fancy. Finally, having set up a decorating studio in the room, he became associated with several other like-minded artists.

Not for long was he content with decorating other potters' wares. His interest centered on the china body itself. One reason for that was his detestation of the thick ugly dishes his father displayed on his front shelves and at times actually in the window. Coarse hotel ware! Two decades later he admitted that it was not much worse than the current manufacture, for even in the '80's most American china was still of crude design and pretentious decoration. If a potter achieved an unusually good piece, he gave it a Staffordshire mark, mostly Wedgwood, for nobody who was anybody would use the native ware, unless belowstairs. The fastidious housewife would not be caught dead with it on her table. It was set with dishes imported from England or France.

Walter was well aware of this. The handsome young man, tall and slender, his perfectly shaped head crowned with thick curling black hair, his countenance radiating intelligence, honor and friendliness, was welcome in the better Trenton homes. It was in one of these that he was served tea in a cup of such fineness, such whiteness, such a glaze as, except in his most exalted dreams, he had not known could exist. The instant he had the cup in his hands he realized that here was the ideal china body, the one he had been seeking all along. For the rest of his life he was never to lose the feel of the exquisite china in his delicate sensitive fingers. Without knowing it then, he had joined the company of Palissy, Böttger, Billingsley. . . .

"Belleek!" he said over and over again as, walking on air, he returned home. "From Ireland!"

The Irish pottery had been opened in 1857. The gentleman responsible for what grew to be the chief industry of Belleek, a village on an island in the River Erne, County Fermanagh, was the owner of a nearby estate. Out riding one day when the sun was exactly right—not always the case in the Emerald Isle which depends upon rain for the "Emerald" in the name—he noticed how dazzlingly and brilliantly white was the newly whitewashed cottage of one of his tenants. The source of the paint proved to be a limepit in the neighborhood. Consequent investigation showed that the whole estate was on a stratum of feldspathic clay.

Two interested countrymen, David McBirney and Robert William Armstrong, crossed the Irish Sea and traveled to Worcester where they made some preliminary trials with Cornish clay and Fermanagh feldspar. In 1857 they established a pottery at Belleek.

Their first product was Parian ware—unglazed biscuit. It was the joint effort of the manager, William Bromley, a modeler named Gallimore, and a number of workmen hired temporarily from the Stoke-on-Trent factory of one Walter H. Goss who claimed to have invented the process.

It was not until 1863 that they began to manufacture the ware which was to bring them name and fame, their porcelain with an iridescence obtained by the application of metallic washes. One writer describes it as "notorious for a curious slimy nacreous lustre which glistened like wet barley sugar." Actually it resembled a mother-of-pearl luster which Böttger, the "alchemist," had stumbled upon at Meissen, the secret formula of which had been stolen by the renegade Hunger when he ran away from the great German plant. The Belleek formula was no secret. The metal they used was lead. Their finest luster consisted of white lead, red lead, flint, and borax, and required four firings.

As was inevitable with a pottery right on the sea, such as Capo di Monte at Naples and Quimper in Brittany, many of their products had a marine flavor. Ornaments were mermaids, sea-dogs, coral, and shells. Dishes and bowls were made in the shape of shells, definitely rococo.

Like the earlier Lowestoft of 1757 to 1802, Belleek became immediately popular along the eastern seaboard upon its introduction to America, the demand taxing the resources of McBirney & Armstrong. It became a clamor in the '80's when, at the death of the two partners, the Irish company suspended operations for an indefinite period.

This spelled opportunity for Lenox. His first step was to serve an apprenticeship in the local factory of Ott & Brewer. There, aided by William Bromley, Jr., son of the manager of the Belleek plant, the junior partner, John Hart Brewer, had been experimenting with the challenging porcelain. Later, Bromley suggested that his father be sent for. Bromley, Sr., came, bringing several of his workmen, probably those who had been lured from the Goss Pottery in Stoke-on-Trent.

In no time Ott & Brewer were turning out American Belleek of great beauty and extreme lightness in weight—twenty-four pieces tipped the scales at just under a pound. (Their first piece is the property of Lenox, Inc., and bears the inscription, "W.B. 1887 to W.S.L.") Owing to differences in the clay used, and to their glaze, American Belleek is less lustrous but warmer in tone than Irish Belleek. Its look of highly polished ivory, however, gives it its own distinction.

Bromley soon left Ott & Brewer and went to the Willets pottery to aid in the development of their eggshell china. (A Willets Belleek vase with decoration of wild roses in high relief may be seen in the collection of the Pennsylvania Museum.) Jonathan Coxon, a Staffordshire-born craftsman, became superintendent, and appointed Walter Scott Lenox head of the decorating department.

By 1889 Lenox, then thirty, was ready to form his own company, and in Coxon secured an able partner. At this time, Lenox did not have the money to put up his half of the deal—his total cash assets amounted to less than $4000. Since a number of attempts by others to make fine china had failed, borrowing capital for the venture proved difficult. Finally a friend named William Hancock lent him the money to erect a block-square building at the corner of Mead and Prince streets, but with the prudent stipulation that it be constructed in such manner as to be readily convertible into an apartment house should the venture fail. Lenox had no alternative but to accept the harsh and unencouraging terms.

He was forced to import two skilled potters from Ireland in order to learn their methods, but from the beginning Lenox himself worked night and day to perfect his "American Belleek." The first piece, an enshrined exhibit in the display room, is a cup and saucer now copied as a souvenir for persons like me. (You will love it.) On the bottom of the saucer is the inscription, "Reproduction of first Lenox piece #1. Designed 1889. Limited edition." Both pieces bear the Lenox mark, an "L" in a wreath above the name "Lenox."

As was said, many American potters when they produced a good piece, stamped it with an English mark. From that first cup and saucer until the present day, Lenox china has been stamped with the Lenox name.

"Let the world pass judgment," Walter Lenox insisted, "on its intrinsic worth."

Within seven years, by 1896, the intrinsic worth had been recognized to such an extent that Lenox was able to buy Coxon out and became sole owner. Financially, the going was still rough. American-scale wages saw to that—about 70 per cent of the cost of fine china is labor, much of it skilled. What stood Lenox in good stead was his ability to make friends. Many a time he borrowed $500 from one friend to meet the payroll, or to pay back what he had borrowed from another. Harry A. Brown, secretary of the company, often stood by as ware was taken from the kilns, then, if it had turned out well, rushed to New York to collect in advance enough money to buy more potting materials. Nevertheless unqualified success seemed assured.

Social success, too. The handsome bachelor, living gracefully, was known as something of a Beau Brummel in Philadelphia and New York where he was always made welcome by his many friends, especially those in theatrical circles. Yet, when he was only thirty-six, the man who apparently had the "world by the tail and a downhill pull," was stricken with locomotor ataxia, a calamity which would have crushed a less indomitable individual. Paralyzed and almost blind, for twenty-five years he had to be carried into his office on the back of his personal attendant and chauffeur.

As a result of his affliction there developed one of the most affecting human relationships in American records. Harry A. Brown became his alter ego—"Dominie," the blind potter called him. Though the mind of the stricken Lenox miraculously remained as brilliant and resourceful as ever, he saw only through the eyes of his loyal associate—and his own sensitive fingertips.

Until near the end of the century Lenox products had been principally ornamental pieces. Then the firm decided to experiment with dinnerware. But their Belleek was too fragile. It lacked the durability of English bone china and other imported ware. They were forced to develop a new formula, which they did with such success that the whole plant operation was switched to it. As the famous jewelry firm of Tiffany's had strongly encouraged the project, the first complete set was displayed in their store, at that time at 37th Street and Fifth Avenue in the beautiful building designed by Stanford White.

In 1906, exactly a hundred years after his grandfather had arrived in America, Lenox organized the company under the name of Lenox, Inc., the name under which it has operated ever since.

Their china was becoming renowned, but the big fly in the ointment was the indifference accorded to it by the White House. Since 1826 Congress had been on record as requiring that, in so far as possible, all equipment for that mansion should be bought in the U.S.A. No president, apparently, had been able to find an American china good enough. Even Theodore Roosevelt, after scouring the country's potteries, felt forced to admit, "We are dependent upon foreign factories for the very dishes from which the Chief Executive of the United States must eat." He was delighted, however, with a Toby jug made at Lenox with him as prototype.

James Kerney, Sr., editor of the *Trenton Times,* stepped into the breach and urged his friend, Woodrow Wilson, who had served in Trenton as Governor of New Jersey, to create a precedent. Wilson complied. He and Mrs. Wilson chose a service of 1700 pieces designed by the late Frank G. Holmes, whose son shared with Stephen Neale the task of showing me around. Each piece had a center of creamy white, an outer and inner border of encrusted dull 24-carat gold on the ivory rim bearing the seal of the President of the United States. Only the 11-inch dinner plates were given color. These had a wide border of etched gold in an urn-and-scroll design, a band of deep rich blue, and an inner gold border in a Stars and Stripes design. In the center of each plate was the Presidential seal.

"The proud day has arrived," said the *New York Sun,* "when the United States is the possessor of a White House dining service designed by an American artist, made at an American pottery, fired in American kilns, and decorated by American workmen."

This set was used continuously until 1934 when Franklin Delano Roosevelt ordered a new service from Lenox, Inc. In 1952 Truman replaced it by the one now in use, though he had the eagle in the seal facing the other way, its back on war and its eyes on peace.

In this manner American prejudice against native china was eliminated and its prestige established. As a current quip expressed it, "If it's good enough for the White House, it's good enough for us."

In spite of this they were not done with the years of intense struggle, of high expenses and low income, of obligations which held Lenox in a vise, of debts hemming him in on all sides. But like him after whom he had been named, the Sir Walter Scott who killed himself writing and writing and writing to pay off his publishing firm's debts, so Walter Scott Lenox persisted in spite of his handicaps. Friends begged him to give up. This was sheer suicide.

"Give up now? After our wares have found acceptance! After the sacrifice of myself and my friends!"

"At least give up this mad search for quality. The men who are making cheap china are also making enormous profits."

"I shall never allow any compromise with my conscience. Lenox, Inc., has only one standard—quality."

Quality eventually paid dividends. One epic day in 1919, to "Dominie" came the supreme joy of announcing that the last note had been paid, the factory cleared of all encumbrances, the entire property freed of debt. That afternoon Lenox summoned Brown's son Leslie who had started there as kilnsman at $8 a week, and asked him if he could make a miniature clay kiln and have it fired. A few days later Leslie brought the small kiln to the office to which all the company executives and department heads had been invited. Brown got the mortgages out of the safe and Lenox burned them in the clay kiln. Tears glistened in other eyes besides those of the blind founder. That dramatic act spelled the end of a long hard fight.

It was almost the end of Lenox's physical fight, too, gallantly though he strove to carry on. At last it ceased to be a matter of courage. No longer could he be carried into his office. On January 11, 1920, he died. He was buried in historic River Cemetery overlooking the falls of the Delaware. Near him are other famous New Jersey figures. General William B. McClellan, commanding officer of the United States armies, and one-time governor of New Jersey. John A. Roebling, the great pioneer in bridge-building whose dream, the Brooklyn Bridge, began a new era. Washington Roebling II who heroically went down with the *Titanic*. . . .

Inevitably once Lenox china had become quality ware, special orders poured in. Outstanding among them was one from the Roebling Wire Works, for a service plate in triplicate to commemorate their recent bridge. Eventually there were eighteen, each decorated with a bridge ably portrayed by the late William Morley, perhaps the most famous of American china painters. Morley's skill with pigments was extraordinary. He knew exactly what color the ware would be when it came from the kiln. (Lenox kilns are circular, doughnut-shaped tables which revolve for 30 hours through a 130-foot tunnel with temperatures often at 2200 F.) In one instance he was the only member of the staff who thought he could do it—decorate a service to be a perfect match for Cardinal Spellman's hat. For a service plate of a wealthy Pennsylvania-Dutch farmer whose hogs had won a prize, he used photographs. The farmer's wife grew tired of the series of black porkers facing her and her guests from the table. When the number of plates reached thirty, she called a halt.

For Mme. Nellie Melba the Victor Company paid $1000 for a plate with musical motifs on blue with encrusted gold. $18,000 was the price for a dozen made for an exhibit at the Metropolitan Museum—it took two years to make them. Another exihibit in which they take obvious pride is one sent to the Sèvres Museum in 1918. Lenox is the only American firm represented there with a permanent exhibit.

Two plates in the showroom really intrigued me. One, two feet in diameter, had been made in 1925 for Mrs. John F. Erdmann of New York City, although the design itself had been created in 1913. The cobalt blue border has a wide etched gold edge and a well with a gold paste design of fruit, flying horses, and the family crest. In the center of the plate is the coat of arms of the Sturtevant family to which Mrs. Erdmann belonged, and the motto of her husband, a famous New York surgeon—*Ut Sariem Vulnero*—"That I may heal I would."

The other, an ordinary plain plate, was begrimed except for a small patch of smoky green at one side. It was found in a San Francisco basement after the earthquake and fire of 1905.

"Doubtless it could be cleaned," Stephen Neale said, "but we prefer it this way, evidence of Lenox durability."

He flicked a finger against it. The note it gave out was silver clear.

In the 1930's Lenox, Inc., was still doing less than a million dollars' worth of business annually. Five years later, under the presidency of Harry A. Brown, with Frank G. Holmes designing china of clean and simple lines in contrast to the elaborate and often rococo styles they had been imitating, and with William Morley head of the decorating department, it had grown to be a multimillion dollar operation.

A spurt, given by import shortages during World War II, threatened to be counteracted by the invasion of a dozen new American potters into the field. By 1943 the market had gone domestic with a bang.

But competition, the life of trade, suddenly opened their eyes to seeing that their system of having a few salesmen with packed trunks touring the country to visit important customers once a year belonged to horse-and-buggy days. This was the era of powerful automobiles—more, the dawn of the jet age. Their publicity must somehow be stepped up. Lenox launched into one of the greatest advertising programs ever undertaken.

Now, realizing that to a widespread selling campaign the small dealers were of the utmost importance, they staged exhibits in towns everywhere. Attractive displays were introduced. China was coordinated with glass and silver to make harmonious table settings. A program of educating women and girls was inaugurated. Copies of a motion picture in full color demonstrating the making of Lenox china were circulated in schools and clubs from the Atlantic to the Pacific, and from the 42nd parallel to the Rio Grande. Sales forces were intensively trained. Every step which could be taken to make America Lenox-conscious was taken by the personnel of their highly efficient publicity staff. Whenever another town was added to their customer list, a small flag was pinned on a wall map. Soon it resembled the picture of a vessel dressed for review by the Commander of the Navy.

"The Lenox trademark," they claim, "is now on perhaps one of every four pieces of chinaware purchased in the United States."

The claim was more or less substantiated in the chinaware department of Macy's where you will see a whole section of Lenox ware beautifully displayed, which would be expected, as Lenox is their best seller.

Most of the visitors to the Trenton showrooms the afternoon I was there were not interested in the special displays. They concentrated on dinnerware, of which there are ninety patterns in all. Do not go there looking for marked-down rejects, let me warn you. They sell none of them. Instead, they are sent to the cafeteria of the new streamlined plant at Pomona just west of Atlantic City.

Lenox plates come in four shapes: the contemporary rimless coupe, the familiar standard or plain Temple with a fluted rim, and Sculpture, fluted and swirled.

Among their most popular current patterns is *Kingsley,* standard shape with a solid gray-blue rim outlined in platinum and patterned with small flowers centered by jewel-like raised enamel. On the Temple shape are *Lafayette* showing a tracery of gold leaves and delicate blue flowers, and the arresting *Rutledge* with six groups of raised orange, yellow, siena, and blue flowers and deep green leaves on the classic fluted rim. Two attractive patterns employing their Sculpture shape are *Musette,* its graceful festoons of soft gray flowers centered by raised maroon enamel, and *Orleans* with a charming leaf-and-scroll pattern and a rippled edge of gold.

One of the most popular of Lenox patterns, incidentally one of their most expensive, is *Westport.* It features a solid border of Kingsley blue and dainty blossoms, bordered on both sides with encaustic 24-karat gold. Another in a high price bracket is only now being put on the market, *Meredith,* a standard shape of warm ivory with subtle green scalloping, each scallop enclosing a delicate raised gold shell. Unless I am greatly mistaken, *Meredith* will give the best-selling *Westport* a run for its money.

A delicate raised gold shell . . . shell patterns of the Old Country Belleek. . . .

Did I say the Irish strain was persistent?

Chapter 21

Coordinates

IF IT had been anywhere but at a reception for a visiting cellist, a chance remark of the hostess would have launched me on a subject long dear to my heart—coordinates or synchronized sets.

"We are serving tea and cake because I wanted to use these plates and cups and saucers my husband brought me from the Philippines."

Japanese—Noritake. Handsome! Fine white porcelain, the rim patterned in black and gold.

"We'd love to use them for dessert when we entertain formally," she went on, "if only we could complete the set."

Instantly my mind meshed into high gear. Wedgwood's new *Asia*.

"Why not a coordinate?"

Unless in exceptional circumstances, gone are the days of presenting a bride with an enormous dinner service, or of her going downtown and, after more or less deliberation, ordering a ponderous set of anywhere from 96 to 132 pieces, many of the larger ones doomed to hibernate and gather dust on a top shelf for 360 days out of the 365, perhaps in some cases 364, Christmas coming but once a year.

Even in my early teens, this did not make sense. Certainly not from an economic viewpoint. Suppose the expensive service was discontinued! Suppose a few cups, several dinner plates, and the cover of a vegetable dish were broken! Unless it was open stock, one had to buy a whole new set. My mother had that happen with her second-best dishes twice.

Besides, to a questing adolescent, there was the matter of monotony. Must every course appear on dishes of the same pattern? Why could not the different courses be served on dishes of different shapes, colors and decors? Would that not heighten a sense of anticipation, pique the curiosity, stimulate the digestive glands? Using dime store glass bread-and-butter plates and goblets, I experimented, and fancied myself an innovator. Years later, I found that the Scandinavians had long been innovators on a grand scale.

Swedish Modern, a phrase applicable in many fields, has influenced our daily lives to an unbelievable extent, but in no respect more than in table settings. Their slogan, "Functionalism with beauty," ensures that their dishes achieve the closest harmony with home life. For formal dinners, naturally, they use porcelain from their own six manufactories as well as—and not to my surprise after visiting their great department stores—English bone china. The breakfast and lunch table may be set with flintware made at Uppsala, Egernsund, or one of the small specialized ateliers. For al fresco affairs, pottery and stone-ware—you cannot visualize the intrinsic Scandinavian good taste permitting the most glamorous hostess in pedal pushers or Slim Jims setting her barbecue table with *blanc de chine*.

Kaj Franck, head of the Arabia art department, had long declared against matched sets for any meal. At Rörstrand, Carl-Harry Stålhane keeps three small tables lined up in his studio to demonstrate how, without violating the harmony, totally dissimilar dishes may be used for successive courses. Obviously the place mats, woven to his order, are the same in each case. Even Royal Copenhagen, the Danish firm where the stress is on the "royal," unbent suffi-ciently to allow the youthful Gert Botelund to design dishes of the same pattern and decor but in different colors which can be blended—she calls it synchronized.

When bread-and-butter plates are necessary, as at lunch, they match the drinking glasses of Orrefors or Kosta crystal. Casseroles of the new ovenproof, flame-proof ware created by Stålhane and Lindberg, to name only two, come in a wide range of colors, including the eye-arresting black. Black, by the way, is often the accent of the versatile centerpiece which is not necessarily placed in the center. In the case of an odd number at the table, it may stand at one end or side.

For the main course of formal meals, platters and vegetable dishes may match the plates. Usually they are of silver—Georg Jensen, David-Andersen, and recently Sigurd Persson, although his renown owes less to his silverware, magnificent in its rich simplicity, than to the vitality of his stainless steel. Persson's double casseroles, which do duty also as serving dishes, would alone have made his name.

With regard to the artist's palette, the Scandinavians have a penchant for blue. (Cobalt, the old reliable, still turns out best in the kiln.) For it there is the widest possible range. Arabia's *Decor Polaris*. Gustavsberg's *Blue Elite* and *Amulet*. Royal Copenhagen's recurringly popular *Blue Fluted* designed by Frantz Henrich Müller in 1780 when the company was under the direct supervision of the Queen Dowager, Julianne Marie, and added to a hundred years later by the artist with the spiritual face, Arnold Krog, a name revered in ceramics the world over.

Scandinavians go in strongly for white, that "combination of all colors." If throughout it is their choice, four favorites of local manufacture are *Le Select* and *Rosmarin* of Rörstrand's Sylvia Leuchovius and Hertha Bengtsson respectively, the delicate *blanc de chine* of Royal Copenhagen, and the incomparable if high-priced rice china of Friedl Kjellberg at Arabia.

The English potters, basically conservative, witnessed the trend and realized that they would have to get aboard the bandwagon if they were to stay in the parade. As a matter of fact, catering to the lucrative American market, in 1927 they began manufacturing open stock patterns of which a housewife could buy just what she wanted at the moment, or could afford. (It was because of the "afford" that they put five-piece place settings in the stores in 1945.) If later she decided that a complete service was needed, she could add to it. Open stock meant also that she could assemble her dishes in the up-to-date Swedish Modern manner, and still adhere to English bone china, traditional with many families on our side of the Atlantic, both north and south of the line.

It was traditional, indeed, with an attractive and alert young Minneapolis bride-to-be of English extraction whom I met at bridge when returning on the *Gripsholm* from my latest porcelain expedition. Her future husband was a young Swedish engineer. Appointed to a new post, he found that it would be impossible for him to get away for their planned Scandinavian honeymoon, so she had spent a month with his family to get acquainted and incidentally get their "O.K."

One morning I ran into her in the gift shop. She was practically fondling a small casserole from Hertha Bengtsson's *Rosmarin* service, and without preamble she began expressing herself forcibly on the subject of stuffy and conventional English bone china dinner services. With irresistible dinnerware such as the piece in her hand, why must one have Minton or Spode? She wished that she could assemble her dishes the way they did in Sweden. But a wealthy aunt in Toronto was giving her a dinner service as a wedding gift. English bone china, a tradition in the family! When one had a service costing that much, one had to stick with it—be stuck with it, she amended, making a face.

Almost without my volition, the "coordinates" record went over the spindle, the needle into the groove. If variety was the spice of her life, as she said, why not a synchronized set of English bone china? Granted it was conventional, but never stuffy. Once she saw some of their patterns, especially the newer ones, she would apply "irresistible" to English bone china, too. At that, I began reeling off a list.

The idea of coordinates appealed strongly to her. Her aunt would never consider the idea, though. When she found that I was returning to Winnipeg via Toronto, she begged me to stop off an extra day and use my powers of persuasion on that lady, not an easy person to persuade.

"You might even come with us to the showrooms."

Her new dining room would be finished in off-white, not quite eggshell, with crimson draperies and Carl Malmsten furniture in limed fruitwood, the chair seats a warm blue. This had to be kept in the front of our minds in making our selections.

It was the first time I had been able to let myself go with no need to consider money. A heyday! Playing no favorites, we decided to visit the showrooms in the order in which I had visited the bone china potteries. This meant the soup plates would be Wedgwood.

"First impressions," the bride-to-be said, "are of vital importance. A hostess must create an atmosphere as a singer does. When our guests enter our dining room, they must be electrified."

They will be whenever her first course is soup, for—two minds with but a single thought—she unhesitatingly selected my pattern, *Halford,* bone white and celadon, the latter sufficiently bland to go with any decor, and a platinum trim to companion her silver, *Midnight Sun,* from David-Andersen's in Oslo.

For the fish course we went to Spode-Copeland. We were shown real fish plates, hand-painted, but as she would not often serve fish—mostly *vol au vents,* soft-shelled crabs in their shells, or shrimp cocktails—she gave an order for eight *Colonel in Grey,* featuring the motif favored by the monks of the Renaissance for illustrating manuscripts. Seeing that the plates could double for high teas and dessert bridges, her aunt insisted upon cups and saucers to match.

At Minton's where we went next for dinner plates, encrusted gold was out—one day she would inherit her grandmother's set. *Blue Symphony?* Not quite right with her chairs. *Cameo in Grey?* Brides loved it and it appealed to her, but she had chosen gray at Spode's. Her aunt and I thought she had settled on the richly elegant *French Green* when she spied *Ancestral.* Her eyes sparkled as they went over the tiny blossoms in rose and blue, and the gold foliage on the rim.

"This," she said jubilantly, "was made for our dining room."

For salad plates I had suggested the lustrous ebony of Crown Staffordshire but she felt that they might smack of funeral baked meats. Instead she chose *Black Texture,* designed by the Marquess of Queensberry, each coarse black thread hand-painted on white bone china.

"Perfect for single course luncheons, and they'll harmonize with the black-and-Chinese-red casseroles my future sister-in-law chose at Gustavsberg."

While in the Crown Staffordshire showrooms she ordered enough florals, including the tiny Maybaskets, to make dozens of centerpiece arrangements. For the same purpose, at Royal Doulton she ordered two figurines to be combined with squat candlesticks, though her primary quest was for dessert plates. With so many seductive patterns it was not an easy choice, but her aunt signed on the dotted line for *Coronet,* the same as *French Provincial* except that platinum had taken the place of gold.

"You know," that lady said thoughtfully, "I've a good mind to get a coordinate set for four, for my bridge quartette."

Only the after-dinner coffee cups remained. At all times, coffee would be served in their living room, which gave her plenty of latitude in the matter of color—gray walls with turquoise drapes and fireside wing chairs of the same material, the other pieces upholstered in ivory except for one in a deep cherry red.

Red coffee cups, she had decided even before we reached the Royal Crown Derby showrooms. She considered *Heraldic* with its border of ruby-red simulated shields, and *Paradise* with the same border but a ruby ground with stately peacocks. From the way her eyes lit up over *Bali,* we knew that the brilliant tomato-red lotus of the stylized Imari pattern edged in gold had solved the problem.

"You can introduce Marco Polo as a topic of conversation," the aunt said drily, "if ever one of those twenty-minute silences should occur."

"One won't," her niece replied. "This synchronized service will always provide a conversation piece itself."

The English tradition may be maintained with something less elaborate—we do not all have that kind of money—and with fewer courses. Neither does one have to spread one's self over several manufacturers to achieve variety. A successful set may be coordinated from one. Wedgwood, for example. In their two and a half centuries since the reign of the "Prince of Potters" they have produced thousands upon thousands of patterns. In the forty years between 1879 and 1919, remember, the number was already 9,999.

Nor need one be confined to bone china. Some or all of the courses might be served on earthenware, although Minton's would be left out as they no longer manufacture it. With Spode's heirloom patterns, it might be fun to choose by the alluring names alone: *Wicker Lane, Geisha, Blue Camilla, Jacinth.* . . .

Names would serve at Haviland's too—*Bagatelle, Bergère, Ladore, Floreal.* (At the Limoges plant, they make 51-piece sets for six persons, with replacements in New York.) Unquestionably you would add one of the round, oval or oblong china casseroles made by the American Haviland's and guaranteed for a year.

Imagine a young modern given *carte blanche* in a Rosenthal showroom—say, Munich, Toronto, or New York. She would begin with the centerpiece. The old German style centerpiece, called *Schauessen*—show-eating—was generally a scene taken from an opera. It featured the principal characters about whom were grouped the lesser ones. At first they were made of sugar or wax, but later of porcelain, the minor figures often given as favors to the guests. Today's German centerpieces might consist of two or three of *Les Petits Peynets.* Or flowers floating in a flat square bowl companioned by smaller ones in the *Quatre Couleurs* of the whimsical Wiindblad. Or a single rosebud in each of a cluster of *Gala Blau* vases. Let your ingenuity be your guide.

Philip Rosenthal contends that a woman's dishes are her outer garment, an integral part of her personality, and should be selected with even more deliberation than she accords her wardrobe. His half dozen potteries provide ample scope in this respect.

In the Berlin shape one finds the large soup plate men like. Salad would be interesting served on *Goldschwann*—golden swans flying across a lustrous black background. Dinner plates in *Mimosa* or *Grasses,* each with the delicate clean look of Kakiemon. Coffee cups *Steglitz* patterned with lines, or *Wannsee* named for the lovely lake, solid blue cups on blue-and-white saucers. Sheer lavishness, and excited comments, are to be had with Fortuna-shaped coffee cups in *Persian Red,* a groundlay of that opulent shade setting off a golden nightingale carolling from a branch with "roses bedight."

Outside of the territory we have covered together, you can roam at will and on your own find unlimited treasures, such as the bird and flower plates from Barittoni of Vincenza. The little "home" potters of Norway show charming ceramics at the FORUM in Oslo—Princess Astrid often exhibits there. If you find a pattern you like, the potter will reproduce it for you in any quantity you wish. When Walter Chrysler visited the FORUM a few years ago, he was struck by the design of a woman ceramist. A meeting was arranged. The Detroit manufacturer commissioned her to make him a 48-person set of dishes, on each piece a Chrysler car. The artist insisted upon her own design, a different car for each piece. He finally gave in. When the set arrived in Detroit, he and his family were thrilled.

In the Grand Bazaar in Istanbul, one of the largest covered bazaars in the world—there are over three thousand shops, a hundred streets each with its own brand of merchandise—the friend with me bargained for several exotic briony-arabesqued plates. Made in Isnik, the merchant said.

Spain is *the* tourist spot these days, with as many drinking coffee in the street cafés of Madrid as in those of Paris. One popular day's jaunt is to Talavera de la Reina and its historic pottery. (Near the main square is the theater decorated with typical Talavera tiles.) I did not buy anything there, but reserved my purchasing for FESTIVAL, the permanent exhibition in Madrid, opened for the Spanish Government by an American, Edward Kreisler of Akron, Ohio, who remained as managing director. There I bought a copy of a seventeenth century Talavera plate for two dollars. The original would probably run into four figures. Mine, by the way, hangs on the wall.

My favorite dress-up table is synchronized "Black and White." Center piece, five Bjørn Wiinblad *Black Tulipa* candlesticks of various heights. Matching glasses also from the Rosenthal Glass Works in Frankfurt. Place mats of linen called *marcasual,* the corners molded and embroidered in black. (Made in Madeira especially for Georg Jensen.) Stainless steel flatware, Focus de Luxe, with black nylon handles. Before each place a small Rosenthal *Füllhorn* —cornucopia—which in spring holds lilies of the valley. If an autumn mood demands a high-lighting touch in addition to the tapers' tongues of orange flame, the enchanting berries of that season in rich crimson and rust are ideal. For the rest of the year there are such diminutive blossoms as forget-me-nots, Star of Bethlehem, and *Kalanchos Viking*—Burning Love—used with spectacular effect in their flower arrangements by the flower-loving Danes.

Service plates are black, fluted rim, from Rörstrand. Soup coupe and saucer in Spode's *Apollo.* Salad, Crown Staffordshire's *Ebony Matt*—with crisp green lettuce, ruby tomatoes, transparently thin cucumber slices, avocado segments, golden mayonnaise, *ad lib,* it is poles apart from any similarity to funeral baked meats. At present I am using old Belleek dinner plates, but I hope one day to have either Wedgwood's *Asia,* black Greek key flanked by gold on the rim, or Minton's *Athena.* For dessert, Royal Copenhagen's *blanc de chine* matching a lovely flat fluted bowl of that ware bought years ago.

The coffee cups violate the color scheme as I am sentimentally attached to half a dozen given to me by my son when he was in his teens. Made by Jackson & Gosling, Stoke-on-Trent, they are still kept in the black leatherette box in which they came. It is lined with white satin against which the graceful flair shape, Don, of an agreeable size and splendid in Chinese red and gold, *Grosvenor* design, is enhanced. Recently I tried to get two more, but because of the high cost of production the shape, first made more than a century ago, was dropped in 1939 at the outbreak of war, and has never been resumed.

If ever I crave a change and decide on black coffee cups, I shall get them from the Vista Alegre plant in Aveiro, Portugal. Their black, both plain and decorated, is unrivaled. In either the process is fascinating to watch. The pattern of the decorated ware is laid on in collodion, the black enamel sprayed on, the collodion torn off and the pattern hand-painted. The plain black has an edge of gold, polished first with sand, then with a woman's thumb—a bit painful, I should think, until the digit became inured.

If ever I were to switch to white coffee cups for my "Black and White"— well, you who have read this far will be able to suggest patterns to me!

And "suggest" it must always be. As they put it at Gustavsberg, *Taste should never be dictated,* advice which I reduce to capsule form—*Be yourself!*

Chapter 22

The Care of China

From the number of letters and telephone calls—editors term it "reader reaction"—which I have received since the first article on this subject appeared in print, it would seem that there are few women who are not interested in china. Yet the best of us can become so sick of the everlasting washing-up that at times we feel like throwing the whole stack into the trash can, or switching to paper plates. Even an electric dishwasher, though it may reduce thrice-a-day to once-a-day, does not eliminate all the work.

"Washing up the pots," our "daily" in Edinburgh called the process. "Pots" they were in the sixteenth and seventeenth centuries and well into the eighteenth. It must have been drudgery indeed. With today's beautiful dishes it ought to be a pleasure. We should be able to look at them in the sink with the fascination we felt when as children we watched Chinese water flowers unfold.

Unfortunately my imagination does not reach to such heights if a well-meaning guest insists that we dash out to the kitchen and tackle the job while I am practically still chewing my last bite of dessert, or dawdling over coffee in an easy chair in the living room, too delightful a ritual to forego.

Still, no one realizes better than I that dishes should not be left standing. They should at least be wiped off with a paper towel or rinsed under the tap, for food which has dried or hardened on is not only difficult to wash off but may harm the china. As a matter of fact, when I have guests and am serving the dinner myself, between courses I invariably do this. It takes no time at all, the sound is muffled by the conversation at the table, and with the dishes stacked in the sink my limited counter space is uncluttered.

Fruit acids and vinegar must *never* be allowed to remain on good china after a meal. Acids as well as alkalis attack the glaze, and, in the case of on-glaze enamels, the colors.

Tea and coffee cups should be rinsed at once. If, as sometimes happens in the best-regulated household, they become stained from standing, borax applied on a soft cloth will do the trick. Never use steel wool or a gritty type of cleanser. Abrasives scratch. Even salt, temptingly convenient, must be used sparingly.

To get around handles, in fluting, or between the elaborate ornamentation of decorative pieces such as vases, a soft brush is a necessity. Two other vital items of equipment are a rubber mat for the bottom of the sink and a plastic or rubber-coated drain rack to insure against chipping.

Dishwater should never reach a temperature above 120 F.—only as hot as your hands can comfortably bear. Hot water expands the *outside* of the ware, and results in cracks or crazing. That is one reason a porcelain or pottery teapot should be warmed before the boiling water is poured on the tea. (It also makes a better brew.) This principle applies to pre-meal care as well. Never warm dishes over an open flame or in a hot oven. Your dishes are dinnerware, not cooking utensils. Warm them gently in a warming oven, a plate warmer, or a pan of hot water. Again, not too hot.

Naturally, soft water is best. If you live in a locality where the water is hard, you will probably use a water softener. Being alkaline, it is injurious if used to excess. Use only the smallest amount required to soften the water.

Rinse in water of the same temperature. It is the washing, needless to say, and not the rinsing, which gets dishes clean. Rinsing merely removes excess soap or detergent which would otherwise leave spots or streaks.

Any mild detergent in the quantities recommended by the manufacturer may be employed with confidence. As they have been chemically researched to a high degree, they should not be used in sufficient quantity to produce suds. In fact, they do a better job before the suds stage is reached, a doctrine the manufacturer of a well-known brand preached from coast to coast. It did not go over. Women demanded suds. They did not think dishes could be clean unless treated to a bubble bath.

"Not that we mind," he added with a grin. "It means a greater sale of detergents. And of hand lotion, too."

Care of dishes includes the storing of them. They must be easily accessible. You are not likely to use the dishes most suited to a particular item on your menu if they are difficult to get at—for instance, if you have to move a pile of fruit nappies to get at special dessert plates. One solution is more shelves, closer together.

Stacking cups is apt to put a strain on handles, and chip the rims. Many potters advocate a narrow cup shelf at the back above the plates. Personally, I find cup-hooks the most convenient device, curved hooks and large enough to free the cup without resort to sleight-of-hand.

The Care of China

The foot of a bone china plate is not glazed. In time, unless some sort of protection is provided, the unglazed foot will scratch the face of the plate beneath. (This holds true for all flat pieces.) A paper napkin folded to size will do the trick.

You know how difficult it is to find a gift for someone who has everything? A wealthy woman who fitted into that category said that the most thoughtful present she ever received was a set of "separators" for her new Minton service in *French Green*. They were made of soft flannel, in pastel shades, cut in rounds, the edges pinked, two dozen of each to fit all the flat dishes from saucers to dinner plates.

They may be even more elaborate. Once I shared a seat on a plane with a woman of vivid personality. In no time we were discussing china, for she had just been in Chicago studying porcelain patterns with her soon-to-be-married daughter in mind. I mentioned separators. She laughed. She mass-produced them. For shower gifts, church bazaars, Junior League sales. Sometimes a set comprised six dozen pieces of various sizes in pink, blue, or maize. Sometimes she combined half a dozen pastel shades. Upon each separator for a bride-to-be, she embroidered the girl's initial. On the others, a single flower.

"Goodness!" she laughed away my protests. "A lazy daisy does not take me two minutes flat."

With such attractive accessories, getting one's dishes out and putting them away would be a joy.

There may be porcelain of distinction and quality which comes complete with separators, but not to my knowledge. Watch out when they are provided by a dealer. It may be a device to give a spurious value to a set he wishes to unload. Here again the old saying holds: Good wine needs no bush.

Moving can present a real hazard. If you are going to a new home, especially one at a distance, and have had no experience in packing dishes, a professional packing job may pay in the long run. Yet, except in the case of my wedding gifts, when a long slender spout had its nose broken, I have always packed my own, and without a single casualty. Into the bargain, I have moved so often that my friends say my dishes should march up on word of command to their own crates or barrels.

The only time I was tempted to hire a professional was when my mother gave me her mother's very old Bavarian service to bring home, a thousand-mile trip I was making by bus. I brought it in large cartons. Not a single piece was damaged. I saved enough on the packing alone to add Rosenthal's exquisite *Woman Drinking* to my collection. If I can do it, so can you.

How? . . . First, line the carton with blankets or quilts which have to be moved anyway. Place a couple of pillows on the bottom. Wrap figurines and valuable vases in tissue paper, then in excelsior or paper cuttings, and pack in individual cardboard boxes. Set these on the pillows.

For the dinnerware, supply yourself with plenty of newspapers, torn into squares slightly larger than the pieces to be packed. *China must not touch china.* Put a square on each dinner plate, say. Take up a pile of six and wrap in paper, then wrap the bundle in a towel. Do not lay plates flat. Stand them on edge. Cups are best stacked in threes, with an extra twist of paper on the handles. This bundle may be placed in a hollow dish, and wrapped again.

Before closing the carton, bring up the ends of the blankets and fold them over the top. Add a couple of small cushions, your final assurance.

One last injunction, from both me and the potters: Use your dishes, all of them, all the time. Love them and live with them. Every piece may be an heirloom, but don't regard it as a museum piece. You know how it is with sweet peas. The more you pick them, the more they bloom. Dishes are that way, too. The more you use them, the more their beauty blooms for you.

We have all heard of the mythical Englishman who dresses for dinner even in the African jungle. When I dine by myself, which is about half the time, I certainly do not put on an evening gown, but I do dress the section of the table where I sit, or the small table drawn up before the fireplace. I feel that I am entitled to graciousness, if not actual elegance, for companionship, to say nothing of what is owed to my self-respect. Besides, a sandwich on the corner of the kitchen table would plummet my spirits to the nadir of desolation.

Perhaps I am luckier than many in having accumulated a fair assortment of porcelain treasures, but even with fewer, one can ring innumerable changes. The permutations and combinations of a dozen pieces taken two at a time is near infinity.

One does not need treasures to achieve graciousness. I get it with my every-day dishes, Royal Doulton earthenware, pattern *Cavendish,* gay with flowers, actually brilliant against a turquoise cloth. . . . Sometimes, gratifying my aesthetic sense as well as a demand for a sort of pictorial excitement, I use my *Blue Mikado* on Chinese lace mats. There may be no truth in the story of the lovers separated by a bridge throughout life, but one's fancy may roam. . . . If my mood is poignant, what more conducive to it than *Billingsley Rose?* My morale is unconsciously lifted by my pity for the artist who made such a tragedy of his own life, yet left the world a heritage of enduring beauty. . . . And if I crave elegance, it is inevitable with good silver, fine Swedish crystal from Kosta or Orrefors, and *blanc de chine.* A single rose, Japanese style, in a

Gala Blau vase of the "2000" shape makes it a gala occasion, a dinner party of one.

How much dishes contribute to mood, or vice versa, I did not realize until recently when I spent a week in New Jersey as guest of a Norwegian woman of fine sensibilities. She did not own a conventional dinner service but her assorted chinaware was an unending delight. Her table was set with dishes chosen less with an eye for food than for mood.

"I feel Wedgwoody," she said the first afternoon at tea and produced cups and saucers in blue and white, of an old pattern without a name, merely a number.

During the week she felt Wedgwoody so often that when I got home I sent her two cups and saucers in the *Coronation* pattern, with a note explaining that they had been designed by Star Wedgwood for the coronation of George VI and his queen.

"When your gift arrived," her letter read, "I was in bed with flu. None of the antibiotics my physician prescribed did half so much to raise my spirits as those regal plumes on the rich crimson rim. I lay back on my pillows and watched the pageant of the coronation as I had witnessed it back in 1937. . . . At the present moment I am having tea in one of the cups. The other sits across the table from me, making believe that you are about to drop in. Bless you, and Star Wedgwood too."

Don't be afraid of your fine china. Enjoy it. That is what it is for. Porcelain—this cannot be reiterated too often—is practically indestructible. Not that it responds kindly to being dropped on a tile floor, though I watched a Tapio Wirkkala *Rusticana* bowl do that, then skid all the way across the kitchen without suffering chip or scratch. My nerves did the suffering.

But it was nothing to the time the handle was broken off a valuable old Wedgwood cup years ago. That struck me with the force of a global catastrophe. I tried everywhere to get it repaired. No luck. Discard it? I could not bear that. It was an extremely handsome cup, and fairly large. With nubbins of handle filed off, it could be used for mayonnaise. Only a carborundum file would have done the trick, and that I did not have. The cup and saucer were put at the back of the top shelf of the cupboard, and the handle was tossed into the trash.

Too soon . . . for shortly afterwards a magic bonding cement was perfected by an ardent china lover, called Madame Mary Fix-it by her staff, Dorien Gough by her clients, and Mary Stanley-Clark Gough by her friends. One day while Mary Gough was convalescing from a mild case of polio, a maid broke the handle off a Bow cup which had been in the family for generations. It had been included in the list of china to go to her daughter. She decided to repair it, not only so that it would look right, but so that it could be used. She experimented with commercial cements of all sorts, applying them to handles deliberately broken off cheap cups. Finally she formulated a "fixer" which would withstand boiling water. She mended the Bow cup. Her mother was inordinately pleased, on two counts—the cup was as good as ever, and her daughter had found a new interest.

"See what Mary did!" she told everyone who came to the house.

Soon a steady stream of Rolls-Royces began rolling up with prize china to be repaired. One day it occurred to Mary that what she had been doing for nothing for her mother's friends, she might as well do for others who had valued china requiring attention and would pay for it. At first, Mrs. Stanley-Clark was not exactly pleased about having her daughter turn her talent into a commercial enterprise—trade, she said scathingly—but when she saw how happy it was making her, she raised no further objections.

Mary decided to settle in Salisbury and rented a mews there not far from the cathedral with the most beautiful spire in England. She engaged two assistants whom she had to instruct in the use of the invisible cement known as Dorien Gough Bonding Cement and Dorien Gough Paste for modeling cup handles, and so on. Both, according to her modest advertisements, would withstand boiling water.

She had barely launched the project when she realized that a school was needed for teaching the mending art. Soon her class in china-mending had outgrown the mews, and she was turning away pupils, including Americans on vacation. She leased her present luxurious quarters in the Conservative Club at the Priory.* Shortly afterward, she opened another studio in Ireland with her son in charge.

The china manufacturers protest that no cement can possess all the qualities claimed for Dorien Gough Bonding Cement. However, among Mary's steady customers are many of the large china shops. Surprisingly, her clientele also includes many domestics. They will come in furtively with a piece of china they have broken. "Can you mend this right away, before the mistress finds out?" And Madame Mary does.

One middle-aged domestic dropped a hot saucepan on the vegetable dish she was filling. Casualty, one handle, from a valuable old Wedgwood piece. She met the immediate crisis by substituting silver dishes on the dinner table,

* The full address, for those who want to write or send things for repair, is Dorien Gough Studio, The Priory, Brown Street, Salisbury, Wilts., England.

and the big crisis, taking advantage of her mistress's going to the seaside for a fortnight, by herself traveling the fifty miles to Salisbury to have the handle put back. Could the Dorien Gough Studio do the job? It was terribly important. In one month she was due for an increase in wages, but it was contingent on her not having broken anything of value in the past year.

The mended dish was filled with silverware and lifted by the handles to demonstrate to her mistress how strong it was—better than new! She got her increase and wrote Madame Mary a grateful letter.

"When I get my fortnight's vacation I shall come and take the course. I was too worried about the vegetable dish to see Salisbury Cathedral proper, and Stonehenge not at all."

"Chances are," said Mary, laying down the letter, "there is an employer who is going to lose a good servant. Almost always the course embarks the student on a new career."

Closer home is another distinguished firm of china and glass repairers, A. Ludwig Klein and Son.* [No difficulties with customs back and forth, either.] Back in 1786 in Germany, Johann Ludwick Klein set up a business of repairing the costly porcelains which were often broken en route to buyers from the Meissen imperial factory. Johann's son Frederick carried on the traditions of quality of his father and was awarded the Crown Seal of Great Britain for completing a restoration for the City Museum of London. The Klein firm later moved to Vienna, and eventually, about forty years ago, to Philadelphia, where it still preserves its quality traditions. After a Klein repair it is often hard to find the spot that was broken. Many British, European, and United States museums, as well as individuals, are among its clients.

The most active member of the firm now is W. Karl Klein, who also teaches restoration and repair of china and glass at the Junto in Philadelphia, the oldest school for adult education in the country. W. Karl Klein has written an encyclopedic book, *Repairing and Restoring China and Glass* (Harper & Brothers), which tells in detail, with many pictures, how to make successful repairs on art objects and heirlooms, on favorite cups and figurines.

So if you *should* snap off a handle from your best Minton cup, or a Spode salad plate slips from your hands and you hear a sickening crash, you won't really have to despair too much these days. But save those pieces!

* 621 South 9th Street, Philadelphia 47, Penna. The Klein firm supplies the materials you need for home repairs and is happy to give advice on difficult problems. They also will make the repairs themselves if you prefer.

Chapter 23

Magic in a Cup

MANY of you will be able to visit the potteries of your choice in person, not vicariously as in these pages, for nowadays women are going abroad in greater numbers all the time. According to a successful travel agent, 65 per cent of those for whom he arranges trips are women, and of these 65 per cent are between sixty-five and seventy.

Needless to say, you do not have to fit into that age category. One sure thing, if your trip has a definite purpose, a specific objective, you will have dropped too many years to fit into it upon your return.

In his book on Spain, H. V. Morton suggests that a rewarding trip could be made through that gourmet country with a knife and fork. (He should have included a notebook for recipes.) Any woman who, on a European tour, makes the pottery district of any country her pivotal point for a fortnight will have an equally rewarding trip.

The United Kingdom draws the highest percentage of visitors from our side of the Atlantic. The English Midlands with its 181 potteries remains the center of pottery-making for the world—in most ears and on most tongues that trinity of words, *English bone china,* spells enchantment.

On one trip, naturally, you cannot visit all the potteries in the Black Country, not so black now that the old bottlenecks have been replaced by electric kilns, but you may have time to include in your itinerary the best known, and make side trips to Derby and Worcester as well.

The Crown in Stone or the North Staffordshire in Stoke-on-Trent makes a good starting-point. At either of these hospitable hotels you will be given excellent maps, addresses, directions, as well as pertinent information about what is to be seen besides the potteries. At the plants, of course, you cannot buy anything except "rejects," but their brochures list the shops selling their wares. By having your purchases sent to your ship, you save the British purchase tax, a considerable item.

206

Many of you will order a dinner service while there. If so, you will cherish it with a new love and understanding because of the art it represents. And how you will enjoy remarking at your own candlelit table one evening when you have guests, "Do you know, I saw a dinner service like this actually being made!"

Some of you may be content with souvenirs. Before you leave home it is a good idea to decide upon the form they will take. For reasons of comparison, focus upon a single artifact—native dolls, costume jewelry, candlesticks, fans. The word "souvenir," as you are probably aware, means merely "to remind you." If the souvenirs are not just an assortment of miscellaneous, haphazard, dust-catching trifles, but things of beauty which can be used frequently, you will be reminded so frequently of your trip that what began as an adventure will gradually blend its brilliance and glamour into the over-all picture of your life. More than that, well-chosen souvenirs will give significance to the words of Richard le Gallienne:

> I would make a list against the evil days
> Of lovely things to hold in memory.

For a china lover, what more practical souvenir than a cup and saucer from each pottery? It is something you can use every day.

In my china my afternoon tea is not only the cup that cheers but a potion conjuring up more pictures than my two Leicas took. Each cup is a magic carpet on which I soar blithely from place to place, from image to image, from new friend to new friend. Alone? Yes, but never lonely. . . .

Tea table tour of Staffordshire I call it when I get out one of my cups from the Six Towns, and am transported to any of a dozen beauty spots. Say, Trentham Gardens, a short bus ride from Stone, once the home of the Dukes of Sutherland but now a recreation center for the workers. Except for the conservatory and sculpture gallery, the mansion has been pulled down, but the Italian gardens are still the finest of their kind in England.

To steep yourself completely in medieval times, wander for an hour or two in Tamworth Castle, then in the terraced gardens beside the River Tam. Not far away is Lichfield, Samuel Johnson's town. The "Ladies of the Vale" there, a gem of architecture and sculpture, is one of the smallest but one of the most beautiful cathedrals in Britain. The three spires reflected in the Minster Pool will tax your camera for quantity—and be sure to take your wide-angle lens for the engrossing West Front.

Nearby, too, is Wells Cathedral and its clock with fully caparisoned knights riding out to strike the hour, plus an aura of a familiar nursery rhyme—legend says that a greedy bishop or steward was named Jack Horner. When the swans in the moat around the Bishop's Palace are hungry, they pull a rope which rings a bell. An incredibly age-worn staircase to the Vicar's Close branches off to the right halfway up, leading to the upper chapter house with its fan-vaulted central column which has the stunning effect of a palmtree frozen in stone.

Tea in a Crown Derby cup sets me picking my steps across the tetherstones of the Dove where Izaak Walton fished and wrote part of *The Compleat Angler;* or to taking a bus to Ashburton, there to be mellowed by the chimes of the Church of St. Oswald which inspired Thomas Moore's poignant poem, *Those Evening Bells,* and to be entranced by the vicar, a fount of fascinating lore. Here's a tip: If you want interesting material about a place, look up the vicar.

Before I visited the city on the Severn my grandmother's Royal Worcester cup was merely a cup. Now its genie plants me before the Guildhall, a rare specimen of Queen Anne architecture. Above the doorway, in stone, is Cromwell nailed by the ears, for thus the Faithful City showed its contempt for the Puritan enemies of the Crown. In the lower hall is a curious kind of helmet called "branks," once used for keeping female scolds in their place.

Hop-picking time is the time to visit Worcester. If you are interested in having your fortune told, the gypsies will oblige with alacrity. One buxom lass, hoping to wheedle from me the choker of cheap pearls necessary with that particular costume, strode beside me for half a mile of country lane. She made no effort to foretell my future, but she did bring to light, and in incredible detail, an unresolved problem known only to myself.

"How," I asked as nonchalantly as I could, "did you get all that without tea leaves, cards, or reading the lines of my palm?"

"Ah, Milady, I feeled it coming out of you strong."

Tea in a Haviland cup. The sunny old-world square in Limoges, the enchanting restaurant *Lion d'Or* with its handsome woven red cloths and its enormous fireplace with *three* rotisseries and a surmounting coat of arms, a stroll along the old canal, an array of antique shops, a nun with a winged hat speeding past on a motorcycle. My Quimper cup, of rich ocherous pottery embellished with crowing cocks, carries me from one to another of the delightful, quaint Breton fishing villages steeped in the traditions of King Arthur, Tristan and Isolde, and Bluebeard.

A Selb cup becomes a pair of Seven League Boots in which I traverse Germany. Bonn—drinking in the panorama of the Rhine from my picture window in the Königshof, hearing from the far bank the faint echoes of the Lorelei.

Magic in a Cup

In the less well known parts of northern Bavaria a circular church with onion domes, at Waldsassen a monastery with a library in typical Bavarian wood carving. The caryatids—can caryatids ever be male?—support the gallery and at the same time embody the history of a book, beginning with the ragpicker who collected the rags from which the paper was made, and ending with the bookseller, a sly Near East figure, bland when viewed from one angle but crafty from the other. Coffee and cakes in a baroque castle given by Frederick the Great to his sister Wilhelmine. Bayreuth which once had a carillon of porcelain bells. Wagner's shrine. Arias from his operas in close harmony as, reveling in the autumn tones of the landscape, we drive back through the Fichtelgebirge Mountains in the sunset.

No pottery is in an arid desert, certainly not those of the Scandinavian countries luring women in ever-increasing numbers.

From a Rörstrand or Gustavsberg cup, the *mise en scene* of Sweden unrolls. Sundahl, the much-photographed plush carpeted stairway of the Knaust Hotel. . . . Uppsala: Cathedral and castle encarnadined by late afternoon sun. Mead drunk from a horn in a tearoom over four centuries old. . . . Stockholm: Gorgeous tableau from the roof of NK. Skansen, outdoor theater, the magnificent effluence of Jussi Bjoerling's golden voice now forever stilled. Millesgaden more for the setting than for Milles' sculptures. Drottningholm Theatre, baroque architectural gem of its era. . . . South to Växjö, glass center of the world. . . . The children's exciting horse races on the Baltic island of Gotland, its capital the unforgettable medieval walled city of Visby with tradition in every inch.

A rice china cup from Arabia. Suomi—Finland—unfolds. Twenty thousand lakes and three hundred and fifty thousand *saunas,* the Finnish steam baths. Paavo Nurmi's statue beneath a barrage of cameras at the gate of the Olympic Stadium in Helsinki. The Big Church, a white landmark far out at sea. Fresh flowers before the impressive tomb of Field-Marshal Mannerheim. Finnish roadsigns. Fairylike birch groves. Rowan trees weighed down by crimson fruit. Thrill of your hand on the post marking the line of the Arctic Circle. The floor show in the ultramodern hotel in Rovaniemi, capital of Finnish Lapland.

Any Bing & Grøndahl or Royal Copenhagen cup contains Denmark. *Wonder-ful, won-der-ful Co-pen-ha-gen,* the famous Tivoli merely a symbol of its gayety. Northward to Elsinore, southward to Roskilde. Across the Belts to Zealand, its capital Aarhus boasting a town hall which at night seems to be constructed of phosphorescent green glass. To Fyn and Odense where Hans Christian Andersen was born in a small house, now a museum, a block or so from one of the best and most picturesque inns anywhere, Den Gamle Kro.

Instead of rhapsodizing for pages, as I could, about the Danes, let me tell you a story which more than anything else typifies their philosophy.

Beside every church is an inn. When a countryman drove his family to church on the Sabbath, he let them out there, then, having stabled his horses, slipped into the inn for a "quick one." Sometimes it and its follow-ups lasted so long that he was too late for the service.

"Ah, well!" he solaced himself. "Better to sit in the inn and think of the church than sit in the church and think of the inn."

Norway recalls another line of le Gallienne:

> There's too much beauty on this earth
> For a lonely man to bear.

It would be true about Norway except that you are never lonely. The friendly Norwegians see to that. But there is almost too much beauty. At times it seems that you must become sated with it. The country of magic landscapes, I call it. The most beautiful country of Europe.

My Porsgrund cup swooshes me with the speed of a super-jet from one panorama to another. Molde, City of Roses, my picture window in the Alexandra Hotel looking out over Romsdalsfjord and eighty-seven mountain peaks. . . . Olden—I have a highly chromatic certificate to prove that I rode a Norse pony to climb to Jostedalsbre, the largest glacier in Europe. . . . Geiranger on the fjord of the same name, unbelievably lovely, withal majestic, with its stark brooding mountains, countless thundering waterfalls, and a transcendent serenity. . . . Røros, a ski resort high in the mountains near the Swedish border, almost a ghost town until revived by the mine owner's son who founded a thriving industry by wresting wrought iron elegance from the horseshoes rusting at the entrance to the abandoned pits. . . . Lillehammer, on Lake Mjosa, royalty's favorite hunting ground, so chosen as their headquarters by the Nazis, and where, with poetic justice, they signed the capitulation. . . . Trondheim, the ancient capital, its impressive cathedral reflected in the River Nid. Monks' Street. The renowned Palm Court in the Hotel Britannia, Bergen. Old Hanseatic League houses. Fantoft stave church, one of the finest—not only a cross to keep the Devil away, but dragons as well. Edvard Grieg's home, a national shrine, exactly as his beloved Nora left it. . . . Oslo's unrivaled setting on Oslofjord. The grim castle where Quisling was executed. The Viking and the Kon Tiki Museums. Frogner Park given by a grateful nation for the controversial sculpture of Gustav Vigelund—you may love it or hate it, but you cannot be indifferent to it; Vigelund may prove to be the greatest sculptor of our age.

But these are *my* fond recollections. As you visit potteries you will acquire your own storehouse of memories evoked by a cup or a plate or a figure.

Magic in your cups. Into the bargain, if you have chosen them with care, you will have a collection of lasting value.

How does one choose? What is the criterion, the yardstick?

Young brides, often prone to be impetuous, fall for the pretty-pretty, an example of choose-in-haste-and-repent-at-leisure. This happened to an attractive and intelligent girl who married a struggling but up-and-coming young architect of exceptionally good taste. He hated their dishes, but could not afford to replace them. Too much in love to criticize her choice, he gradually began finding fault, in a sardonic way, with the food she put on their plates at dinner, the coffee she poured into their cups. An excellent cook, she was bewildered, and considered leaving him. She might have done so had not a chance remark he made one evening opened her eyes. Their hostess, a member of the crowd with which he had grown up, was giving her first postnuptial dinner party.

"Porcelain for posterity," he said, studying his plate. "A new pattern but as good twenty years from now as today. Not like—"

Not like ours. No, they were not. Looking at theirs with opened eyes, she realized that if for twenty years she lived among his friends and absorbed their culture, she would pass the pretty-pretty dinnerware without a second glance. She asked him to help her choose new dishes, in separate courses, six or eight as dictated by their budget. Now that the others are used only in the breakfast nook, he actually likes them.

So choose with an eye to twenty years from now. If you are a bride, look ahead to see yourself as mature, the wife of a prominent man entertaining prominent guests. Also buy with an eye to your grandchildren. In that way, you will assure yourself of heirlooms to be passed down the generations. If you can afford only four good plates at first, buy only four. Use paper plates and cups to fill the gaps.

In this respect I always think of the wisest young couple I have ever known. Close friends of ours were this young lawyer and his wife, the latter a member of a family with wealth. Both had impeccable taste, and a restraint imposed by his dictum that his money alone would furnish their home. We visited them a few weeks after their marriage. When the bride summoned us to dinner, their wedding present china, glass, and silver made me gasp. But we sat on orange crates and ate from a card table. The only pieces of furniture—and in them he had invested his entire cash holdings—were a handsome Empire bed, a gorgeous Kermanshahan rug, and, as his bride was a pianist of almost concert caliber, a Bechstein grand. Each time I visited them, usually at two year intervals, a number of pieces of furniture of lasting worth had been added. By the time their children were twelve and eleven, they had an outstandingly beautiful home.

Moral—but you do not need a blueprint. What you probably need, as I should, is a sufficiently strong character to exercise such restraint.

In choosing your dinnerware, stick to what Sir John Wedgwood calls "persistent" patterns. Leave the arty and modernistic, the freakish surrealist decors and grotesques to those whose taste, as the saying goes, is all in their mouths, or to those who can afford to indulge in novelties. Enter the chinaware salesroom thinking of what Josiah Wedgwood said in the eighteenth century, and what the Josiah Wedgwood who is at the head of the great firm says today: "Unless a pattern will last for two hundred years, scrap it." Choose, I repeat, with your grandchildren in mind. Best of all, choose a pattern which looks as if it has been designed in love, for love is of the stuff that endures. To quote Robert Henri, "All real works of art look as if they were done in joy."

Vaguely, I had always felt that way, but I did not realize the full force of it until a short time ago in the Metropolitan Museum. Instead of rushing through the ceramic section in the brief hour usually at my disposal, and looking at the pieces which especially appeal to me, such as Chantilly and the glowing Deruta ware, I decided to fix my feet on the floor in front of two examples attributed to Bernard Palissy for long enough to try to find out why his often crude and over-colored plates and pitchers have become the priceless treasures they are today. Consciously, perhaps, I did not find the answer. Unconsciously I did. For every dot raised in his rich glaze, every line and scallop and hue, was ebullient with a joy still virile enough to pierce the thick glass of the cabinet, and send me away treading air.

Try it and see!

Not surprisingly then, I repeated Honey's words:

The period of the Napoleonic Wars marks a definite break with the old tradition of craftsmanship. The financial and cultural impoverishment they caused left the industrializing process, already begun by Wedgwood, irrevocably complete.

Admittedly, Wedgwood began the industrializing process and ushered in the machine age of ceramics, but was the result complete cultural impoverishment? Was he not also a herald with a trumpet ushering in for women everywhere an era of gracious, dignified, even elegant living? Did not his industrializing process, by giving an impetus to pottery manufacture, manifest itself in progress?

Progress is not the exclusive perquisite of any one industry. It is vital to most. As for the potters, their survival depends upon it. Even those whose original patterns are in as great demand as ever must continually offer the public new designs.

To fit the changing times, new shapes and new decors must constantly be produced. If by the twenty-first century Raymond Loewy's "2000" shape has been superseded by that of another supreme commercialist, if another "playboy of ceramics" has stepped into Stig Lindberg's winged shoes, if another rugged individualist has fallen heir to the mantle of Tapio Wirkkala and of Carl-Harry Stålhane, another romantic has carried forward the whimsies of Raymond Peynet and Bjørn Wiinblad, then will the housewife move with the times and choose for her table the wares of tomorrow.

Nevertheless, if she chooses well now, she will display and continue to use the precious porcelain of the present. Speaking for dedicated potters everywhere, Philip Rosenthal completed a trilogy of slogans when to Wedgwood's envied "A Living Tradition," and Spode's "Every Piece an Heirloom," he added, "Today's Treasures, Tomorrow's Traditions."

Reference Books Consulted

Cox, Warren E. *Pottery and Porcelain*
Eyles, Desmond. *Good Sir Toby*
Hall, Wendy. *Green Gold and Granite*
Hayden, Arthur. *Spode and his Successors*
Honey, W. B. *Dresden China*
———. *English Pottery and Porcelain*
Hughes, G. Bernard. *Collecting Antiques*
Hughes, Bernard and Therle. *The Collector's Encyclopedia of Ceramics*
———. *English Porcelain and Bone China*
Lane, Arthur. *French Faïence*
Mankowitz, Wolf, and Haggar, R. G. *The Concise Encyclopedia of English Pottery and Porcelain*
Moore, N. Hudson. *The Old China Book*
Pickman, Dudley Leavitt. *The Golden Age of European Porcelain*
———. *Pouring Vessel Vagaries*
Rackham, Bernard. *Medieval English Pottery*
Rosenthal, Ernest. *Pottery and Ceramics*
Savage, George, *Ceramics for the Collector*
———. *18th Century English Porcelain*
———. *Porcelain Through the Ages*

Encyclopedia Britannica
Columbia Encyclopedia
Brochures from the various potters

Some Pottery Terms Defined

ACID or ENCRUSTED GOLD—a pattern etched in the glaze by hydrofluoric acid, then gilded, only the raised portion being burnished.

BARBOTINE—ornamentation made by pressing clay into fired pottery molds, extracting the figures, flowers, or leaves by a special process, and applying them to the moistened surface of the piece to be decorated.

BISQUE or BISCUIT—the porous clay after the first firing.

BOCAGE—shrubbery at base of figures of persons or birds, to serve as support. Lavishly used at Meissen, Bow, Chelsea, Worcester, etc.

BODY—composite materials of which potters' clay is made, e.g., earthenware body.

CASTING—making figurines and hollow pieces by pouring slip into molds.

CHAMOTTE—fragments of fired clay used with a mixture of fresh clay to diminish the shrinkage in firing.

CHICKEN SKIN—Chinese bubble-and-pit glaze.

COUPE SHAPED PLATE—a plate curved upward at the edge without a shoulder.

CRAQUELÉ—crackle—a method of forming cracks by having the glaze contract more than the body, then filling the cracks with pigment and reglazing.

EN CAMIEU—monochrome—painting in several tones of one color.

EN GRISAILLE—a monochrome in grays.

FETTLING—cleaning a figurine with a metal tool so that no seams are left where the parts have been joined.

FRIT—vitreous composition from which soft porcelain is made.

GADROON—edging of olive or ruffle form.

GLAZING—covering with glass or vitreous liquid to fire for a smooth surface.

GLOST FIRING—the second or glaze firing.

GRAFFIATO, GRAVIATA, or SRAFFIATO—a type of decoration in which the glaze of slipware is scratched in a design to show the basic ground color, then reglazed and refired.

215

GROUNDLAY—a colored background to contrast with a painted or printed design.

GUILLOCHE—an edging made by pressing a twisted rope into wet clay.

JOLLEY—cup-making machine.

JIGGER—machine on which plates are made.

LITHOGRAPHING—pattern reproduced by printing.

LUTING—cementing parts together.

MUFFLE KILN—one which does not expose the pottery to direct action of fire.

PASTE—composite material of which porcelain is made.

PÂTE DURE—hard paste.

PÂTE TENDRE—soft paste.

PÂTE SUR PÂTE—ornamentation made by painting paste upon paste until the desired thickness is obtained.

REPAIRING—assembling the various parts of a figurine.

REPOUSSÉ—a form of decoration done by inserting a hand in the damp clay vessel and pushing out "bosses" or bubbles.

RETICULATED—pierced, sometimes with the interstices filled with glaze.

SAGGERS—fire-resistant containers for articles to be fired in a bottleneck.

SLIP—clay mixed with water to a creamy consistency.

STEATITE—soapstone.

STENCILING—sketching a line to show the depth of the band of color in groundlay.

STONKER—the worker who affixes handles, etc.

THROWER—the platemaker who throws the clay on the plaster mold which shapes the front of the plate.

TURNER—the worker who shaves off the surplus clay on hollow pieces.

WASTERS—pieces marred in the kiln.

A Word of Thanks

In the matter of expressing appreciation, I hardly know where to begin. I am forever indebted to the factory heads who devoted their valuable time and extremely courteous attention to a rank tyro, which I undoubtedly was the forenoon Major John Wedgwood—Mr. John, as he was affectionately known in the plant—took me in tow. Further thanks are extended to their deputies who conducted me on tours-of-one and patiently answered my naïve questions. Without their forbearance I should have come out knowing little more than when I went in. Thanks are also due to the Toronto and New York representatives of potteries everywhere for providing me with extra photographs and keeping me posted on their firms' activities; to George Savage for having written his *Porcelain Through the Ages* which was for a long time my only specific work of reference, and to all the authors of the fascinating, informative, and authoritative books mentioned in these pages or in the list at the end. Nor can I fail to include a word for Dr. Erling Christophersen, chief of the cultural division of the Royal Ministry of Information, Oslo, who made it possible for me not only to see Peter Hofnagel's masterpiece in the Kunsindustrimuseum but to hold it in my hands, and another word for Miss Vivian Schiedemantel of the Chicago Art Institute who pointed out the ewer and basin of Capo di Monte, an early Toby jug of Ralph Wood, a red teapot of Böttger, the self-styled alchemist, and other treasures, after which she took me behind the scenes to show me some precious acquisitions not then released for display, and let me hold a bowl of Bernard Palissy, the celebrated sixteenth-century peasant potter of St. Onge, now Charente Inferieure, one of the old provinces of France.

Heartfelt gratitude goes, too, to friends and acquaintances who have gone to no end of trouble to bring out their old family porcelain and the stories connected with it; to the schooldays friend who at her marriage was given six

217

elegant Sèvres plates of the Louis-Philippe period and uses them when I dine with her, making me feel as as regal as if I had a tiara on my head; and to all the understanding bridge companions and telephone visitors who realized that when a writer wanted to write she wanted to write, and granted me the boon of precious working hours.

Words fail me when it comes to a New York friend of long standing. An editor, she insisted that my mind worked in book lengths, and that I should never be fulfilled until I was published between hard covers, for they alone give a sense of permanence. She prodded me, scolded me, stimulated me, gave of her warmth and love. When the bulky manuscript was finally accepted, she was, her husband said, happier about it than I was myself.

Now I come to that grand and affectionate couple, Ken and Mary Granger of vista-ed Hill Top Farm. Without them I doubt that I should ever have visited a single pottery and gradually come to recognize the part porcelain plays in the intrinsic character of women all over the world.

It is hardly necessary to mention my son who has been most patient, but if I failed to include my publishers I should be most remiss. George W. Jones and Harold E. Grove of Harper & Brothers bore patiently with me for three years and as many drafts of this book, the first being a blow-by-blow account of pottery manufacture from some time around 8000 B.C. if not actually in the late Pliocene age, the second draft updated by several millennia but still bearing little resemblance to a volume of easily accessible information about porcelain for a bride in the flurry of prenuptial festivities. Came a period of working on the third draft, turning it in, and scurrying off to Europe.

On the island of Rhodes, which Zeus considered beautiful enough to present to his son, Apollo, is a spot called Petaloudes—Valley of the Butterflies. There from July until September the air is patterned with fluttering red and gold wings. One day toward the end of August, when my mailbox produced a missive bearing Harper & Brothers on the corner of the envelope, I felt as though the whole swarm of butterflies had deserted Petaloudes and had settled in my stomach. They flew hastily back to their sun-kissed valley once I had taken in the opening paragraph of the letter accepting *Modern Porcelain*.

Alberta C. Trimble

INDEX

219

Index

Index